LIFE AFTER DEATH

LIFE AFTER DEATH

THE EVIDENCE

DINESH D'SOUZA

Since 1947
REGNERY
PUBLISHING, INC.
An Eagle Publishing Company • Washington, DC

Library of Congress Cataloging-in-Publication Data

D'Souza, Dinesh, 1961-
  Life after death : the evidence / Dinesh D'Souza.
      p. cm.
  Includes bibliographical references and index.
  ISBN 978-1-59698-099-0 (alk. paper)
  1. Future life—Christianity. 2. Immortality. 3. Near-death experiences.
I. Title.
  BT921.3.D76 2009
  236'.2—dc22

                                    2009038050

Published in the United States by

Regnery Publishing, Inc.
One Massachusetts Avenue, NW
Washington, DC 20001
www.regnery.com

Manufactured in the United States of America

10 9 8 7 6 5 4 3 2 1

Books are available in quantity for promotional or premium use. Write to
Director of Special Sales, Regnery Publishing, Inc., One Massachusetts
Avenue NW, Washington, DC 20001, for information on discounts and
terms or call (202) 216-0600.

Distributed to the trade by:
Perseus Distribution
387 Park Avenue South
New York, NY 10016

For Pete Marsh
Visionary, Mentor, and Friend

CONTENTS

FOREWORD

BY RICK WARREN

Who hasn't wondered, "What happens after death?" It would be both unreasonable and foolish to live your entire life never considering and being unprepared for an event that we all know is inevitable. The mortality rate on earth is 100 percent.

This book by my friend Dinesh D'Souza is a brilliant investigation of the fascinating and crucial issue of what happens when we die. It is an inquiry conducted on the basis of scholarship and reason, and it provides a convincing answer that is explosive in its impact.

It has often been stated that we are not ready to live until we are prepared to die. The truths in this book are not meant simply to prepare you for eternity; they are foundations on which you can build a meaningful life of purpose.

In *The Purpose Driven Life*, I pointed out that the Bible teaches that our time on earth is essentially preparation for eternity. We were made to last forever, and this life is like a warm-up act, a dress rehearsal, for the real show in eternity. Once we fully grasp this, it makes all the difference in the world, affecting our choices, values, relationships, goals, and how we use our time and resources. We reorder our priorities and start emphasizing the enduring, important things over temporary things that ultimately won't matter.

So where can we learn the truth about the afterlife? We have two choices—speculation or revelation. Throughout history philosophers have conjectured about it, but even our brightest minds are just guessing. The better alternative is to discover what God has revealed in Holy Scripture. Of course, today we've seen the rise of an atheistic secularism that denies all revelation. But the objections of the so-called "new atheists" are not really new at all, and they have been soundly discredited by scientists, philosophers, mathematicians, and theologians for centuries. Unfortunately, most people don't read the classic apologetics, so they become quite gullible in believing that the atheists' arguments are new and irrefutable.

That's why this book is so important. It clearly and boldly exposes the fallacies that are often accepted today without question. The implications of this cultural gullibility are huge. If this life is all there is, there is no basis for any meaning, hope, purpose, or significance to life. Everything in your life would simply be a random change of fate at best, or an accident at worst. Your life, and your death, would not matter at all. The logical end of such a life is despair. Moreover, we can forget about being decent or ethical, with no basis for human dignity, rights, or liberty. Even the American constitution points out that our "inalienable rights" are "endowed by our Creator," not by the government or any other human source.

My friend Dinesh D'Souza is an outstanding thinker and a first-rate scholar. For most of his career he was a secular policy maker and influential think-tank intellectual. His previous book *What's So Great About Christianity* follows in the line of other great thinkers like C. S. Lewis. In this book, he has turned his considerable talents to an even deeper issue. Even atheists like Christopher Hitchens have acknowledged that D'Souza is a world-class advocate for theism and the Christian faith.

This is also a book for *genuine* seekers of the truth, not for those who are simply looking to reinforce their bias. The word "prejudice" means to pre-judge. As you read this book, I hope you will lay aside all your prejudices, and with an open mind, consider the facts, the evidence, the logic, and the implications of life after death—not just for our culture as a whole, but for you personally too.

I'd love to hear your reaction to this book.

—Dr. Rick Warren
The Purpose Driven Life
pastorrick@saddleback.com
twitter @rickwarren

Chapter One

LET'S STOP PRETENDING

The Big Question, Considered in a New Way

But at my back I always hear
Time's winged chariot hurrying near.[1]

—Andrew Marvell, "To His Coy Mistress"

T he year before I met Dixie, the woman who was to become my wife, she was involved in a harrowing car accident. She told me about it on one of our first dates. At the age of nineteen she was driving from North Carolina to Washington, D.C., to enroll in a journalism program. Due to some unmarked construction work, the highway narrowed and her car hit a groove and spun out of control. Dixie saw her Saab Sonnett careen off the highway and plummet into a ravine. On the way she felt the bump, bump, bump of the car hitting trees. Finally the vehicle flipped over, crashed, and landed upside down.

At this point, things got a little strange. Dixie saw a man running up to the car; he was a truck driver who had apparently witnessed the accident. He rapped on the glass and called to her. Soon some other onlookers crowded around the site. Dixie could hear one say, "How is she? Is she dead?" Dixie told me that at this point she freaked out. "The weird thing," she said, "is that I was looking at the whole scene from outside my body. I was somewhere above, and I could see the crowd and the car and myself inside it. I tried to open my mouth and scream that I was still alive, but my body wasn't moving and I couldn't hear any sounds coming out of my mouth." Eventually the ambulance arrived and extracted her from the car. She sustained some broken bones and a concussion, but "I should have been dead," Dixie told me. Even now when she recalls the accident, she says, "I consider it a miracle that I survived." The incident struck me as bizarre at the time, and only many years later did I realize that my wife had had an "out of body" experience. In retrospect, however, I think it was one of the first specific things that kindled my interest in what happens at the point of death.

Two other vivid incidents have made me confront death. The first occurred in the year 2000. I was going about my normal life when suddenly I had a phone call that my dad was in the hospital and being given shock treatment to keep him alive. A few hours later he was dead. My dad was my hero, and even a decade later the shock of his death has not fully abated for me. Then, a couple of years ago, my best friend Bruce went in with a routine medical complaint and was informed that he had kidney cancer. "Man, I was not ready for that," Bruce says. "No one is ready for that. Every single thing I was doing before that, all my plans for my business and our investments and our house and everything else just became irrelevant. For two days after I heard the news, I couldn't eat or sleep. I just walked around my house in a daze."

These experiences have brought to center stage for me the issue of what, if anything, comes after death. I have thought about the question for many years. I am aware that it is a big taboo, but I think it is time to confront it. Is death the end, or is there something more? This is the ultimate question. It has been the defining issue for entire cultures from the ancient Egyptians to the present. And in truth, there is no more important question that any of us will face. It is the issue that makes every other issue trivial. If you have doubts about its significance, go to a hospital or a funeral or talk to a parent who has recently lost a child. You will discover very quickly that the apparent normalcy of everyday life is a sham. Death is the great wrecking ball that destroys everything. Everything that we have done, everything we are doing now, and all our plans for the future are completely and irrevocably destroyed when we die. At bottom, we already know this. Only teenagers live in that state of temporary insanity when they believe themselves immune from death. But as we get older, especially when we move beyond the midpoint of life, starting our way on the downhill slope, we begin to acknowledge our mortality. "Our life is a loan received from death," the philosopher Arthur Schopenhauer writes, "with sleep as the daily interest on this loan."[2]

Oddly enough, some people claim what comes after death is of no interest to them. One of my good friends, a successful San Francisco entrepreneur whom I highly respect, told me he would like to read my book, but only to "resolve an intellectual conundrum." He insists that he has never given so much as a serious thought to whether he might survive beyond the grave. "Why should I?" he says with a businessman's pragmatism. "Even if it was true, it would not affect my life in any way. Since I can't do anything about it, I may as well not worry about it." Perhaps, he continued, we should be content with more realistic forms of survival, such as living on through our children, or through the memories of friends, or through lasting works of art and enterprise.

I confess I am not very consoled by all this. Yes, I would like to live in the memory of those whose lives I influence, especially my wife and daughter. George Eliot wrote a lovely poem about her aspiration to join "the choir invisible of those immortal dead who live again in minds made better by their presence." Such a continued existence, however, can only be brief, even in the recollections of our descendants. The proof is that we know only so much about our parents, much less about our grandparents, and little or nothing about the generations that came before them. A better prospect for immortality is to write books or produce art that puts your name in the history books, or to have a college, a museum, or even a city named after you. But alas, these are bogus forms of immortality, since you wouldn't be around to enjoy any of them. My sentiments are entirely with comedian Woody Allen, who remarked, "I don't want to achieve immortality through my work. I want to achieve immortality through not dying. I don't want to live on in the hearts of my countrymen. I would rather live on in my apartment."[3]

I shared this quip with my entrepreneur pal, and we had a good chuckle about it, but what I refrained from telling him is that I find his attitude on this topic to be utterly incomprehensible. For me, this isn't a mere intellectual conundrum; it is literally a matter of life and death! How can it make no difference whether we face annihilation or not? If you found out that you had six months to live, undoubtedly you would make some big changes in the way you live now. Or say that you could double your lifespan; wouldn't that knowledge alter your retirement plans and many other priorities? Of course it would. So we cannot be indifferent to the question of whether there is life beyond the grave. If there is life after death, we have grounds for hope; if not, we must be reconciled to our plight of hopelessness and despair. Despair seems unavoidable, because when we reflect on our life in this world, we are in the position of a man in a burning building. We know that the fire is going to consume us, and the only way to avoid being annihilated is to jump out of the open window. So then the question arises: is there a fireman's safety net below? How odd it would be if someone in this situation were to say, "I really don't care one way or the other."

At first glance such obstinacy seems simply obtuse, but more likely it is the product of deep denial. So traumatic is the idea of jumping out of the window that it is easier to pretend the fire will never reach us. It is the same with death: we know it's approaching, but we act as if it is never going to come. Notwithstanding my friend's pragmatic pose, denial is the least practical approach in this situation. Still, he is not alone; the vast majority of us, especially here in the West, construct our lives based on a denial of death. We live each day as if we are not going to die tomorrow, and then one day we are struck with dismaying force by the recognition, "I am going to die tomorrow." This unnerving prospect causes us to suspend the thought and continue life with the motto: "let's pretend." Even some religious believers avoid the topic. There is the story of the English vicar who was asked whether he expected to go to heaven and what he thought he would find there. "Well, I suppose I believe in eternal bliss if it comes to that," he replied, "but I wish you wouldn't bring up such depressing subjects."[4]

Even our cultural institutions operate in a mode of full denial. In his study *The Hour of Our Death*, historian Philippe Aries notes that death used to be considered part of life. Even the young were fully acquainted with it. People typically died at home, and a common sight in communities was the funeral procession, a dramatic scene with the body on display and a good deal of conspicuous wailing and shrieking. It's still that way in other cultures, including that of my native country, India. But now, Aries writes, the West has developed an elaborate procedure for "hushing up" death. In America and Europe, people no longer die at home, in full view of the family; they die in hospitals, cut off from the world around them. Even family members just visit; they don't experience death up close. In the final scene of this arid drama, the doctor comes in and solemnly informs you, "He's passed away," or "He's gone." Euphemisms abound; they don't even have the courage to say, "He is dead."

When you hear the news, you are permitted to grieve, but the grief must be private. No screaming or hysterics are allowed at the funeral, even for the wife or the children. Aries calls this "the indecency of mourning." People in the West go to funerals out of a sense of obligation, but no one wants to go. It is discomforting to see a dead body in a casket. We don't like to be put through this, and we can't wait to get out of there and back to our normal life.[5] I notice that even in conversation people avoid bringing up the names of dead people. It's almost as if they have played their part and are now expected to permanently exit the stage. In the West, people don't die; they just disappear. And as for the question of what death means and whether there is something beyond death, these topics are never, ever publicly discussed. For all the morbid curiosity of our tabloids and television shows, this particular issue never seems to come up. Life after death is the elephant in the living room, the one that we are not supposed to notice. Our culture, which prides itself on its open-mindedness and candor, shows an intense antipathy to facing the greatest of all human questions.

Interestingly, for most of history this great question was not even regarded as an open one. Rather, it was held to have an obvious answer. Across the cultures of the world, both East and West, and right through the long march of history, people have affirmed that this life is one chapter in a larger story of existence, and that there is life after death. We think of this attitude as religious, fostered by the clergy, and for the most part it was. Many of the world's greatest scientists and philosophers, however, from Socrates to Cicero to Galileo to John Locke to Isaac Newton, also affirmed their belief in the afterlife. Even skeptical Enlightenment figures such as Thomas Paine, Thomas Jefferson, and Benjamin Franklin professed similar views. Europe is the only continent where a bare majority of people believe in the afterlife. By contrast, nearly 80 percent of Americans today affirm life after death, and the percentage is even higher, in fact close to 100 percent, in non-Western cultures.[6]

Some people are baffled by the persistently high numbers of people who believe in the afterlife. How could people who never saw anyone come back from the dead continue to uphold the idea of survival beyond the grave? Where did they get such a crazy notion? I will answer these questions, but for now I note that our attitude of bemused incomprehension is something that itself requires explanation. We have become alienated from our own past, so that our forbears have become complete strangers to us. We are also inhibited from comprehending cultures outside the West which, even today, have the same core belief in life after death that was once universal in our society.

How did we get to this strange pass? How did such a chasm of understanding open up between us on the one side, and our ancestors and the rest of the world on the other? The reason is the emergence in America and Europe of a new way of thinking. This outlook has been adopted by many intelligent people in society and by our most influential institutions. Philosopher Charles Taylor calls this the secular ethos, but it could just as accurately be termed the Enlightened People's Outlook. It dominates what is taught in high schools and universities, what is exhibited in our museums, what is said by our technical experts and political leaders, and what is affirmed as true in our most reputable magazines, newspapers, and in the electronic media. It forms the dominant ideology of public discourse in the West today, and it shapes the minds of our children.

According to the Enlightened People's Outlook, there is no life after death, and it is silly to suggest otherwise. We have this life, and that's it. We know this because science has shown us our true nature—and our true nature, like that of other animals, is mortal. Moreover, we are material creatures in the world—creatures with material bodies—and when these bodies disintegrate there is nothing left to live on. "Once we die," writes philosopher Owen Flanagan, "we are gone."[7] As for the soul, well, science has looked and looked and found nothing like a soul inside of us. Nor do we have free will, although we labor under the illusion that we do. "Free will," writes biologist Peter Atkins, "is nothing more than the organized interplay of shifts of atoms... as chance first endows them with energy to explore and then traps them in new arrangements as their energy leaps naturally and randomly away."[8] Sure, we may want to resist these facts on religious or moral grounds, but reason and evidence compel us to accept them.

The Enlightened People's Outlook derives its confidence from the findings of modern science. According to this view, science is the best, if not the only, means of getting reliable knowledge. Religious claims are based on faith, but scientific claims are based on reason. While the religions of the world make competing and contradictory claims, the Enlightened People's Outlook reminds us that there is no Chinese science or Middle Eastern science or Indian science; science is universal. Even religious people seem to recognize that science works. "Those who would deny science this role," writes physicist Victor Stenger, "had better do so on stone tablets rather than the printed page, and via smoke signals rather than the Internet."[9] The Enlightened People's Outlook is acutely aware that we trust our lives to science every time we get on an airplane. Consequently it holds that we should accept the conclusions of science because they are the closest to real knowledge that we are going to get.

Religion, according to the Enlightened People's Outlook, is a big public nuisance. Enlightened People condemn religion not only for making false claims like life after death, but also for invoking those claims to endanger world peace. They blame religion not only for fostering ignorance, but also for promoting intolerance, social divisions, and conflict. Consider, for example, the nutty followers of Jim Jones, who followed his instructions to commit suicide by drinking poisoned Kool Aid, all in the hopes of an immediate entry into paradise. More recent, although equally insane, is the conduct of the September 11 terrorists and that of other Islamic radicals. In these cases, the violence was both suicidal and homicidal, but again the motivation seems to have been one of heavenly reward. As Richard Dawkins wrote a few days after September 11, "Religion teaches the dangerous nonsense that death is not the end."[10] It's time, we're told, to stop allowing the hope of the next world to ruin our lives in this one. Instead of focusing on the afterlife, the Enlightened People's Outlook urges us to focus our sights on problems facing us in the world today.

By now we are accustomed to hearing such statements from people who are usually called "atheists" or "radical secularists." In recent years a crop of new atheists has aggressively promulgated the Enlightened People's Outlook to a mass audience. I am thinking of such figures as biologist Richard Dawkins, social critic Christopher Hitchens, neuroscientist Sam Harris, philosopher Daniel Dennett, physicist Steven Weinberg, chemist Peter Atkins, and cognitive psychologist Steven Pinker. These men have proven adept at surfing the wave of contemporary events, and they have found receptive supporters in education and in the media. The new atheists, however, stand in the shadow of the great atheists and agnostics of the nineteenth and early twentieth centuries. This group includes some of the most prominent philosophers, scientists, and social critics of the era, men such as Charles Darwin, Thomas Huxley, Friedrich Nietzsche, Karl Marx, Bertrand Russell, Sigmund Freud, Martin Heidegger, and Jean-Paul Sartre. Today's new atheists can be understood as updating and elaborating on the ideas of their distinguished predecessors. Together, both groups have shaped our public culture of unbelief.

In a negative sense, this culture can be understood as a denial of God and the afterlife. In a positive sense, it is committed to a powerful philosophy that has gathered force over the past couple centuries—the philosophy of reductive materialism. I am not using the term "materialism" to refer to the propensity of people to go on shopping sprees. Rather, materialism here refers to the philosophical position that material reality is the only reality. Materialists hold that there is only one kind of stuff that exists—material stuff. We know this because material objects are objective; their existence can be verified by the techniques of science. Even human beings and other living creatures are ultimately collections of atoms and molecules, or if we break these down further, of quarks and electrons. Quarks and electrons are all that exist in the universe; there is nothing else.

Reductive materialists don't deny that there are subjective or immaterial experiences and entities. They insist, however, that upon examination those are caused by and are expressions of purely material forces. Love, for example, feels immaterial but it is nothing more than the electrochemical impulses that evolution has implanted in your brain and nervous system. Your soul, too, is just another word for some of the operations of the neurons in your prefrontal cortex. So everything ultimately "reduces" to material reality and that is why the term "reductive materialism" is apt. It is easy to see why such a philosophy leaves no room for claims that there is a reality that lies outside sense perception and outside the reach of modern science. If reductive materialism is true, then belief in an immaterial God is a fiction and life after death is impossible.

Reductive materialism not only provides atheists with their arguments; it gives them an underlying philosophical framework to understand reality. Many atheists consider reductive materialism to be synonymous with reason and science, and indeed there are many philosophers and scientists who agree with them. Moreover, this form of materialism gives today's atheists the confidence to laugh off what the vast majority of the world believes. Such beliefs, they say, have no scientific basis and therefore must be the product of wishful thinking. As Sam Harris writes, "Clearly the fact of death is intolerable . . . and faith is little more than the shadow cast by the hope for a better life beyond the grave."[11] Reductive materialism empowers atheists like Harris to believe that they are right and everyone else is wrong. Indeed atheists are convinced that in reductive materialism they have the weapon they need to wipe out religion and expose beliefs in God and the afterlife as illusions.

Even though reductive materialism is so thoroughly hostile to religious belief, it goes largely uncontested in the public arena. This is not so surprising in secular Europe, but it is very surprising in the United States. Life after death is a classic case of this. It is a belief upheld by all religions and one that is especially central to Christianity. Christ's resurrection, after all, is the event on which Christianity is based and without which Christianity would not exist. Yet do you regularly hear Christians—even Christian pastors and leaders—defend the resurrection or life after death in the public sphere? Me neither.

In fact, Christians rarely respond to any atheistic claims that are made on the basis of science and reason. When the atheists attack them, they say nothing. Certainly some Christian groups react when their religious beliefs are directly assaulted, as in the case of atheist attempts to teach evolution as a refutation of divine creation. But even here there is a tendency to dismiss reason and science, which makes the Christians seem parochial and anti-intellectual. As an atheist friend of mine quips, "How can these Christians be against logic and inventions?" Actually, Christians aren't opposed to either. Rather, they recognize that, to a large degree, science and reason have become enemy-occupied territory. Science and reason have been hijacked by the bad guys. And with the collaboration of many scholars, the bad guys are using science and reason in order to narrow the scope of reality, to say that "science proves this" and "reason forces us to accept that." Christians believe that reality is much bigger, and that there are ways of apprehending reality that go beyond rational syllogisms and scientific experiments. What looks like anti-intellectualism on the part of Christians is actually a protest against reductive materialism's truncated view of reality.

The danger of abandoning the ground of science and reason, however, is that it compels Christians to live in the land of two truths. There is one truth that we hear in church and there is another truth that we hear about in the general culture. Revelation—the language of religious faith—becomes divorced from reason, which is the language of education, work, and secular society. This produces a kind of schizophrenia, especially among Christian students and Christians who work in science and technology. Your work is based on science and your faith is based on ignoring science; the two approaches seem contradictory. Or you have the awkward dilemma of trusting either your pastor or your professors; one tells you about Scripture and the other tells you about scholarship, and there is no way to believe both.

This is a frustrating way to live, and it's an even more frustrating way to try to communicate Christian beliefs to others. After all, we live today in a secular culture where Christian assumptions are no longer taken for granted. There are many people who practice other religions, and some who practice no religion at all. The Bible is an excellent source of authority when you are talking to Christians, but it is not likely to persuade non-Christians, lapsed Christians, or atheists. In a secular culture the only arguments that are likely to work are secular arguments, and these can only be made on the basis of science and reason. Moreover, science and reason are very powerful forces in education and the media, and these institutions have a huge impact on the development of our children. To relinquish science and reason is to concede precious cultural real estate to the atheists, and to risk losing our children to atheism and radical secularism. Indeed, as pollster George Barna shows, many young Christians do give up their childhood faith and become skeptics and unbelievers.[12] In sum, a rejectionist strategy is fatal not only because it puts Christians on the defensive, but also because it plays into the hands of the atheists.

To reclaim the hijacked territory, Christians must take a fresh look at reason and science. When they do, they will see that it stunningly confirms the beliefs that they held in the first place. What was presumed on the basis of faith is now corroborated on the basis of evidence, and this is especially true of the issue of life after death. Remarkably, it is reason and science that supply new and persuasive evidence for the afterlife—evidence that wasn't there before. The supreme irony is that the strategy designed to destroy the religious point of view ends up confirming the religious point of view. Poised as he is to kick the Christian's rear end, the atheist ends up kicking himself in the butt!

This is what this book is all about. I write it as a Christian, although in truth I have not always been a committed Christian.

I was born Catholic in Mumbai, India. My family comes from a part of India called Goa, which was a Portuguese colony until 1961. My ancestors were converted to Catholicism by Portuguese missionaries several centuries ago. The reason, given to me by my grandfather, is that we used to be Brahmins or high-class Hindus who engaged in lofty interactions with the Portuguese top brass. This D'Souza family lore is almost certainly wrong. History shows that it was the low-class Hindus who were the most eager to convert to Christianity. So what seems to have distinguished our family was its lack of distinction.

Moreover, Portuguese conversion was not typically accomplished by lofty discussions. This was the era of the Portuguese Inquisition, in which an approved technique for changing minds was to round people up and hit them over the head. At this point the dazed converts would promptly take the Christian names of their assailants. (Now you know how I got the Portuguese name D'Souza.) Despite the blow to family pride, however, there is a poignancy to this story. Not all the conversions were the result of coercion. Indeed, many Indians rushed into the arms of the missionaries, demanding to be baptized. That's because in the Hindu caste system, there is no way to move up from the bottom rungs of the ladder, no matter what your merits. Many untouchables and other low-rung Hindus hurried to adopt a faith that promised them equality in the eyes of God and a universal idea of brotherhood. So Christianity brought something new to India. This, by the way, was also true of Islam, which is why many low-class Hindus headed in that direction, too. In any event, recognizing the dignity that Christianity conferred on our family, I have always been grateful to those heavy-handed Portuguese missionaries.

While I recognized the cultural benefits of Christianity, however, I was little more than a social Christian. That's the Christianity I brought to America in 1978 as a high school exchange student. That's the Christianity I took to Dartmouth College, where I studied, and then to Princeton, where I studied and worked. I met my wife Dixie, a committed evangelical Christian, in the Reagan White House, but even after we got married I remained lukewarm in my religious beliefs, and this carried over into my writing career. I have been a secular scholar and writer for two decades.

Only seven years ago, following my dad's death and our family's move to California, my wife and I started attending a Calvary Chapel church in San Diego. Here I found Christians who didn't go to church for social reasons; they wanted to go, and they went more than once a week. Indeed, their Christianity wasn't primarily a matter of attending services but one that passionately engaged their whole life. I found my own faith deepening. Then with the emergence of the new atheism, I saw an opportunity to bring my religious beliefs and my scholarly work together. The result was my book *What's So Great About Christianity*, which became the basis for more than a dozen debates I have now had around the world with leading atheists such as journalist Christopher Hitchens, *Skeptic* magazine editor Michael Schermer, bible scholar Bart Ehrman, bioethicist Peter Singer, and philosopher Daniel Dennett. I love the idea of confronting the atheists in their own arena, taking them down with their own strength, and forcing them to tap out. This book is a continuation of my attempt to demonstrate Christian martial arts.

For the Christian cage fighter, it's fun to take on your opponent with one hand tied behind your back. I do this here by giving up all claims to biblical truth or revelation. This is not because I reject such forms of truth; far from it. Rather, I want to engage atheism and reductive materialism on their own terms, and to beat them at their own game. The philosopher Immanuel Kant once wrote a book called *Religion within the Limits of Reason Alone*. That defines very nicely my approach, which is to demonstrate life after death exclusively on the basis of reason. I am not going to appeal to divine intervention or miracles, because I am making a secular argument in a secular culture. To see what I am getting at, think of life after death as a great transition, akin to a caterpillar who becomes a butterfly. Imagine asking the caterpillar, do you know that you will one day be a butterfly? The answer would be, of course not, it's impossible, it's ridiculous, how can a caterpillar become a butterfly. But of course one doesn't need to invoke divine intervention or miracles to show how a caterpillar becomes a butterfly; one can demonstrate this through the workings of nature and scientific laws. I am going to demonstrate the existence of life after death in precisely the same way. Later in the book, when I discuss heaven and hell, I will show God's central role in the entire transcendental scheme.

Although this secular, "just the facts" approach may seem unusual, it is an essential part of what may be called Christian bilingualism. We speak one kind of language in church, and must learn to speak another while making our case in secular culture. This secular vocabulary is especially effective in reaching two groups that are often ignored in this debate: "seekers" and "fence-sitters." The seekers are the ones who genuinely want to know the truth but haven't found it. The fence-sitters are those who are alienated from traditional religion, especially traditional Christianity, but cannot bring themselves to embrace outright atheism either. Both groups have grown very large in our society, and together they are an influential "swing vote" in the culture. The atheists are convinced that reason and science will bring the seekers and fence-sitters over to their camp, and they are right that many of these people don't respond favorably to the usual arsenal of Bible quotations. They don't want to hear about the Garden of Eden, or about fire and brimstone. They are suspicious of what is called the "God of the gaps"; in other words, they reject an approach popular with some Christians, which is to make routine appeals to the supernatural to account for unexplained natural phenomena. But these folks wonder if there is something more beyond death, and they are eager to hear an argument that meets them where they are, uses facts they can verify, and doesn't already presume the conclusion it seeks to establish.

Even some atheists may be open to an argument that proceeds in this way. When I debate atheists, and especially my friends Michael Shermer and Christopher Hitchens, I always keep in mind that despite their confident assertions that there is no life after death, this is a subject on which they cannot be sure. The honest and thoughtful atheist has to consider the possibility of being wrong, and this may open his mind to persuasion by rational argument. In this book I also address atheists who are ready to turn skepticism on itself and examine their own assumptions.

Finally, a word about how I make my case for life after death. The argument proceeds as a gathering storm, moving from the significance of the issue to its possibility, then its probability, and then its practical benefits, and finally why we should go for it. I explore the main rival conceptions of life after death, including those of Eastern thought. I cover a number of fields—brain science, physics, biology, psychology, history, and philosophy—and the interdisciplinary nature of my subject ensures that no one is an expert. I attempt to proceed like a district attorney in a case where there are no eyewitnesses. The D.A. is not himself an authority on ballistics, handwriting analysis, or DNA. He summons expert testimony when necessary. The job of the D.A. is to put the pieces of the puzzle together and to communicate the argument in a coherent and understandable form to the jury. That's what I do, and you are one of the jurors. I address you as a juror who is intelligent but knows nothing about the matter at hand. I realize this is an unprecedented inquiry; I am taking you down an untrodden path. I also recognize this is a complex subject that will occasionally stretch your mind. To make the task easier and more enjoyable, I write in a colloquial and sometimes light-hearted tone that belies the weight and *gravitas* of our inquiry. One clarification up front: there is no spooky stuff in this book—no ghosts, no levitations, no exorcisms, no mediums, no conversations with the dead. I do not dismiss the paranormal out of hand, but I am dubious about it, and have chosen to exclude it altogether. My case is entirely based on reasoned argument and mainstream scholarship.

The core of the book consists of three independent arguments for life after death: one from neuroscience, one from philosophy, and one from morality. Any one of these arguments is decisive; collectively, they offer a highly persuasive legal brief for the afterlife. Still, it is in the nature of the subject that we cannot be sure. If we think of this as a courtroom trial, I do not claim to have met the criminal standard; I will not prove life after death beyond a reasonable doubt. I do, however, claim to have met the civil standard, and proven my case by a preponderance of the evidence. I also show why it is good for us to believe even in the absence of complete certainty, and which version of the afterlife is the most plausible. Finally, in the last chapter, a surprise! I provide a case study—the only one in history—that shows how life after death isn't just a future prospect; it has already happened for a single individual. This event opens up a stunning new possibility: not just life after death, but eternal life right now.

Chapter Two

VENDORS OF UNBELIEF

Atheist False Advertising

Death, the undiscovered country
From whose bourn no traveler returns[1]

—Shakespeare, *Hamlet*

O n July 7, 1776, the writer James Boswell visited philosopher David Hume as Hume lay close to death. Boswell is the author of the best biography in the English language, his life of Samuel Johnson. By his own account, Boswell went to see Hume to assuage a perverse curiosity. Boswell had often heard that no one is an atheist in the trenches—in other words, the prospect of imminent death makes believers of us all—and he wanted to see if Hume, the great skeptic, would convert on his deathbed. Hume didn't. Not only that, but Boswell found him "placid and even cheerful." In another account of his death, given by the economist Adam Smith, Hume mused about his quarrel with Death, in which he asked Death to give him some extra time to revise a manuscript. Death cunningly told him that manuscripts are always in need of further revision, called him a "loitering rogue," and demanded that he get in the boat. Conversing with Boswell, Hume said that since he was a child he had never taken the idea of immortality seriously. As a Christian, Boswell was unnerved and at the same time strangely impressed to see Hume calmly and confidently face his end.[2]

Hume seems to have inspired some of our own atheist contemporaries. Recently I saw Richard Dawkins being interviewed on Bill Maher's television show, and Dawkins declared that he wanted to have his own death videotaped. Asked why he might do such a strange thing, Dawkins replied that religious believers would probably spread rumors that he had converted on his deathbed, and he wanted to make sure there was a record to show he did not. Equally insistent about maintaining his unbelief in the face of death is philosopher Daniel Dennett. A few years ago, Dennett went in for a nine-hour heart operation that could well have been fatal. It was, Dennett admits, a "harrowing experience" that tested his atheism. In an essay "Thank goodness!" published after his recovery, Dennett said his atheism emerged quite intact and in some ways strengthened. Dennett reported that it was the medical community, not God, who deserved credit for his survival. Consequently Dennett conveyed all his gratitude to them. Nor did he appreciate efforts on the part of his relatives and friends to bring God into the picture. Informed by others that they were praying for him, Dennett informed them he had "gladly forgiven them" for such foolishness. Dennett says he resisted the retort that they might as well have sacrificed a goat or paid a voodoo doctor to cast spells for his recovery.[3]

Reviewing these episodes, I find myself mildly revolted by the arrogance of Dawkins and Dennett and, at the same time, charmed by Hume's affability. What I want to focus on, however, is what these incidents have in common. All three atheists seem willing to go to their deaths without taking seriously the possibility of life after death. In other words, they act as if they know that there is no such life. And this is the "knowledge" that Dawkins and Dennett are disseminating in the culture and in the classroom. So what do they know that we don't, and how did they come to know it?

The atheist confidence that there is no afterlife is, of course, matched by the religious believer's confidence that there is. Ask a Christian if there is survival beyond the grave and he or she will answer, "Of course there is." Pretty soon you are getting the full details about what such a life will be like in the good place and the bad place. When you demand sources for such a thorough account, you find that they are the familiar ones: the Old Testament, the Gospels, the Book of Revelation. When I raised this issue with a member of my church, he pointed to a sticker in the parking lot, "The Bible says it. I believe it. That settles it."

Evidence of this sort makes atheists apoplectic. In *The End of Faith*, Sam Harris writes, "Tell a devout Christian that his wife is cheating on him or that frozen yogurt can make a man invisible, and he is likely to require as much evidence as anyone else, and to be persuaded only to the extent that you give it. Tell him that the book he keeps by his bed was written by an invisible deity who will punish him with fire for eternity if he fails to accept its every incredible claim about the universe, and he seems to require no evidence whatsoever." Harris insists that "it is difficult to imagine a set of beliefs more suggestive of mental illness" than religious claims, and "while religious people are not generally mad, their core beliefs absolutely are."[4]

It is important to see that, notwithstanding his petulant tone, Harris is to some degree speaking common sense. Harris's point is that the Christian is using a kind of in-house logic. How do we know that there is an afterlife? Because the Bible says so. How do we know that the Bible is correct? Because God wrote it. How do we know that God wrote it? Because it says so in the Bible. Yes, we have to admit that this is circular reasoning, and those outside the circle are unlikely to accept it. The atheist Michael Shermer, editor of *Skeptic* magazine, presses the point even further. No one, he writes, has ever met a dead guy who came back to report on the afterlife. Lots of people have died, and none have filed reports or presented themselves for television interviews to give us the riveting details about what we can expect on the other side.[5] Shermer's point is that the believer has no good arguments for asserting that there is life after death. The believer's view is held in the complete absence of evidence. It is an assertion not of reason but of faith.

Shermer has a point, but it can easily be turned around. What does the atheist know that the religious believer doesn't? Nothing at all. Atheists haven't interviewed dead people any more than believers have. Nor have any atheists themselves crossed the river in death's boat to discover what lies on the other side. Death remains, as Hamlet tell us, the undiscovered country, and we don't even have the ghost of Hamlet's father to provide any clues. Indeed the ghost informs Hamlet that while he could tell quite a story, "I am forbid to tell the secrets of my prison house." So mum's the word from behind the curtain, and atheists as well as believers have got to acknowledge this. The atheist has no better proof that there isn't life after death than the believer has that there is. Both groups are claiming knowledge that neither group actually possesses. For the atheist, no less than for the believer, it is entirely a matter of faith.

This equivalence between atheism and belief might seem equally damaging to both positions, but in fact it poses a much bigger problem for atheism. First, the faith of the believer at least has a plausible source. That source is divine revelation as expressed in a sacred text. So the believer is trusting in what is held to be an unimpeachable source, namely God. From where, by contrast, does the atheist get his faith? Who or what is the atheist's authority? To this, the atheist typically replies that he is trusting in reason. Sam Harris writes that the truly rational person makes "the same evidentiary demands in religious matters that we make in all others."[6] Richard Dawkins writes, "I believe not because of reading a holy book but because I have studied the evidence."[7] In this case, however, Harris and Dawkins have rejected the afterlife on the basis of no evidence whatsoever. So here we find a second difference between the religious believer and the atheist. The believer is usually honest and self-aware enough to recognize that his view is based on faith; the atheist, meanwhile, deludes himself that his position is based on reason and evidence.

How, then, do atheists convince themselves that they know things when they actually don't? The answer, surprisingly enough, has to do with a profound misunderstanding of science. In a famous incident a few decades ago, a group of Soviet cosmonauts returned from a space mission with the triumphant announcement that they had searched and searched but not found God. On this basis the cosmonauts affirmed the Communist doctrine that there is no God. I suppose by the same evidence the cosmonauts could have declared that there is no heaven. When I mentioned this incident, over drinks, to the atheist writer Christopher Hitchens, he laughed and said, "It's hard to believe those guys were really that naïve." Hitchens understood right away that the Soviets were looking for God in all the wrong places. They were still captive to the medieval picture of heaven "up there" and hell "way down below" and earth somewhere in the middle. But for many centuries now, religious believers have asserted that God and heaven can only be found in realms that transcend the universe. Imagine poor Hamlet running around the castle saying, "I've looked everywhere, and I can't find Shakespeare. I'm forced to conclude that Shakespeare does not exist."

In his book *God: The Failed Hypothesis*, physicist Victor Stenger insists that the issue of life after death is a scientific question. The problem, however, is that "no claimed connection with a hereafter has ever been verified . . . in controlled scientific experiments."[8] Biologist Francis Crick writes that if religious believers "really believe in a life after death, why do they not conduct sound experiments to establish it?"[9] The answer to Crick's question is that most religious believers don't believe in the afterlife on the basis of scientific tests. So they are unlikely to devise any such experiment. One might have expected that scientists such as Crick and Stenger would suggest some tests that could help decide the issue. If the claim that "there is life after death" is a scientific hypothesis, then it seems reckless to reject it without even attempting an empirical refutation. Even so Crick and Stenger do reject it, causing me to wonder if these gentlemen routinely adopt positions in the absence of facts.

Such a criticism is a bit unfair, however, because as many atheists realize, there are no controlled empirical experiments that can resolve the issue one way or the other. Consequently atheists seek to affirm the rationality of their position by taking a different route. They appeal to an argument offered in the late nineteenth century by William Clifford. In a famous essay, "The Ethics of Belief," Clifford argued that "it is wrong, always, everywhere, and for anyone, to believe anything upon insufficient evidence." Clifford offered the example of a ship-owner putting a ship to sea without performing the necessary safety checks; he wished the passengers well, but when the vessel sank, he calmly collected the insurance money. The ship owner had no regrets, since he didn't know the ship was unsafe. Clifford's point is that the man was a scoundrel. He should have known! He had no right to declare the ship seaworthy without collecting all the evidence. Clifford's conclusion is that we should believe as true only propositions that come with sufficient proof; we should reject as false those that don't. This position can be summed up in the popular atheist slogan, "The absence of evidence is evidence of absence."[10]

While admiring Clifford's heroic attachment to truth, for a long time I have distrusted his principle without being able to say what is wrong with it. Now I think I know: it confuses "what is known by a given person under the circumstances" with "what is or is not the case." Imagine a fellow living in ancient Greece in the fifth century B.C. As far as he can determine, using all the experience and evidence at his disposal, there are only three continents on the planet, no other planets in the galaxy, and only a handful of stars in the universe. What does this tell us about the actual number of continents, planets, or stars in existence? Absolutely nothing. It only tells us that ancient Greeks had very limited information at their disposal. Or consider efforts on the part of contemporary scientists to find life on other planets. So far scientists have found nothing. Should we, therefore, refuse to believe that there is life on other planets on the grounds that the absence of evidence is evidence of absence? Clearly this is premature. The absence of evidence may indicate only that we haven't figured out how to locate what we are looking for. "Not found" is not the same thing as "found not to exist."

These examples show the limitations of the "absence of evidence" principle, but the issue of life after death poses an even deeper problem. To see this, let me offer an analogy between life after death and having a large sum of money in a Swiss bank account. Imagine if I asked you whether or not I have such an account. You declare your firm belief that I do not. As evidence, you cite the fact that you have never seen me go to the bank. Moreover, you have observed me shopping and notice that as I spend money my wallet gets thinner. You infer that at some point my wallet will be empty and I will be broke. So clearly I don't have a bank account. Then I ask you, do you have access to the bank's internal records? You do not. Have you ever been to the bank? You have not; in fact, you have never been to Switzerland. Have you organized 24-hour surveillance of the bank in question so that if I did go there, you would be notified? Of course not. Obviously we can conclude that you have arrived at a most unreasonable conclusion. You have far too little information to decide one way or another. And this is precisely the situation facing the atheist with regard to the afterlife. On the basis of the available facts, not only does the atheist not know what happens after death, he cannot possibly know. The absence of evidence is evidence of nothing.

How do atheists respond? Basically, they say that to give up reason and evidence, even in situations that seem outside the bounds of reason and evidence, is to open the door to all kinds of craziness. Should we start believing in unicorns and centaurs on the grounds that there is no way to disprove them? The philosopher Bertrand Russell gave the example of a celestial teapot that is said to rove the solar system but is undetectable by all scientific instruments. Should we believe in such an absurdity simply because it cannot be refuted? With some glee, Richard Dawkins invokes the example of an invisible Flying Spaghetti Monster that controls the operations of the universe. These way-out examples can't be disproved, Dawkins writes, "yet nobody thinks the hypothesis of their existence is on an even footing with the hypothesis of their non-existence."[11] In other words, the odds in favor aren't the same as the odds against.

A little scrutiny of these examples will quickly show that the craziness here is entirely on the part of the atheists. We have combed the earth without locating a single unicorn, so we seem justified in rejecting unicorns. Centaurs are believed by scientists to be biologically impossible. In these two cases, the odds are clearly against. Celestial teapots are also very unlikely, as are Flying Spaghetti Monsters, but our derision is prejudicially solicited by the particular examples chosen. Teapots do not fly, and pasta is an unlikely ingredient to produce flying monsters. On the other hand, if we modify the examples slightly to involve matter and energy that is undetectable by scientific instruments and yet is presumed to exist in order to account for the motions of the galaxies, we have just described "dark matter" and "dark energy," widely accepted by scientists today. Here the odds are heavily in favor, even if the phenomena in question are strange and not well understood.

I agree with Russell and Dawkins that even when propositions seem outside the bounds of verifiability, there is no cause to give up reason; I am merely arguing that we should be constantly aware of what reason does, and doesn't, tell us in a given situation. Moreover, there may be things outside our experience that have features different from what is within our experience, and we should be open to such possibilities and not dismissive of them in advance. Consider the possibility of aliens that exist in some galaxy far away. Is there anything we can say about them that would automatically count as absurd? For instance, can we reject out of hand the possibility that the aliens each have ten eyes? No. Can we dismiss the suggestion that they weigh less than a speck of dust, or more than a skyscraper? No. Can we laugh out of court the idea that they don't have hearts, or that they communicate by telepathy, or that they sustain themselves by consuming metal? In each case, no. So the bottom line is that there is nothing about the possibility of aliens that is prospectively out of bounds; we simply have no idea about what aliens, if they exist, might be like. Perhaps there is even one that looks like a Flying Spaghetti Monster! If atheists wrote about life on other planets in the way that they write about religious claims, their derision would be immediately seen for the ignorant prejudice that it is.

Still, the atheists have one further argument to salvage their reputation for adopting positions based only on reason. This argument was recently hurled at me when I was debating Daniel Dennett on his home campus of Tufts University. Dennett is a burly fellow who looks like Santa Claus, and he is the intellectual inspiration for an atheist society at Tufts. I wanted to challenge him in front of his own admiring students. His influence on them could be seen in the fact that strewn throughout the audience sat several little Santa Clauses. During the question and answer session, one of them stood up and argued as follows: Let me acquaint you, he said, with the Principle of Parsimony. According to this principle, there are two ways for a claim to be true. The first is for it to be true by definition. If you say "all bachelors are single," we know that's true because being single is part of the definition of the word "bachelor." A second way for claims to be true is by empirical verification. If you say "Walter is a bachelor," this amounts to saying that Walter is not married, and we can establish that only by checking the marriage records. The student insisted that a given assertion can only be true in one of these two ways; if a claim does not meet either criterion, it is not even untrue, it is meaningless. Now, the student said, let's apply this two-part test to God and immortality. Are those claims true by definition? No. Well, can we check them out empirically? No. Therefore, the student triumphantly concluded, these concepts are not only false; they are meaningless.

Now this is a very clever argument, and I recognized its source in the writings of the skeptical philosopher Hume. The student called it the Principle of Parsimony, but the argument is known as Hume's Verification Principle. Hume used it to argue that all metaphysical claims are empty. He wrote, "If we take in our hand any volume; of divinity or school metaphysics, for instance; let us ask, does it contain any abstract reasoning concerning quality or number? No. Does it contain any experimental reasoning concerning matter of fact and existence? No. Commit it then to the flames: For it can contain nothing but sophistry and illusion!"[12] Hume's Verification Principle became the basis for the twentieth-century philosophical movement called "logical positivism," which sought to credit verifiable scientific laws as knowledge while dismissing unverifiable metaphysical propositions as nonsense. I trace this intellectual history not for its own sake, but because these movements provide the underpinning of what many educated people in the West have believed over the past couple of centuries.

When I heard the student's question, the first thought that occurred to me was that his so-called principle of parsimony not only wiped out religious claims; it also wiped out atheism. Consider the statements "God does not exist" and "there is no afterlife." Are these statements inherently true? No. Nor can they be shown by external verification. Consequently they, too, are incoherent by this standard. I did not, however, answer the student in this way. Rather, I took aim at the very principle he invoked. If there are only two ways to tell if something is true, let's apply the two-part test to the Principle of Parsimony. So is the principle true by definition? No. Well, then, can it be confirmed empirically? Again, no. Well then, I said, by your own criteria the principle is meaningless. We can toss it out and not bother with it any further.

This was a good moment for me, having shown that Hume's verification principle could not itself be verified. But in fact I had not made the strongest argument that can be made against Logical Positivism. In reality, Hume's principle not only wipes out all metaphysical claims; it also wipes out the whole of science. No scientific law can meet Hume's test. Consider one of the most basic scientific laws: light travels at the speed of 186,000 miles per second in a vacuum. Now ask yourself, how do we know this? Yes, we can repeatedly measure the speed of light. But as Hume himself pointed out, from no amount of empirical observations, however large, can we derive a general conclusion that is true as a matter of logic. How do we know that, in a galaxy far away, light travels at 186,000 miles per second? In fact, we do not know. We presume that because light travels at a given speed over here, it must also travel at that speed over there. In fact, we presume that for the billions of years that the universe has been in existence, light has always and everywhere traveled at the same speed. But of course there is no way to verify whether this is so. As philosopher Karl Popper noted, all scientific laws are like this. Scientific claims are general statements that cannot be definitively proven.[13] The best we can say is, "This is something we believe to be true based on previous tries."

Many people who recognize the validity of Popper's statement nevertheless believe that scientific claims are highly probable. We may not know for certain that light always and everywhere travels at a given speed, but we can be 99.9 percent sure that it does. This claim, however, is false. Even if you have measured the speed of light a million times on earth, you cannot be even 1 percent certain that light travels at that same speed on a planet where you haven't measured it. Again, it is Hume who tells us why. "Probability," Hume writes, "is founded on the presumption of a resemblance betwixt those objects of which we have had experience and those of which we have had none."[14] Hume noted that when we presume a resemblance between what we know and what we don't, the equivalence is derived from custom or habit; there is nothing in reason to uphold it.

The point has special force when we consider life after death. How can the atheist invoke the experiences of this life to make reliable or even probabilistic claims about existence beyond this life? We are faced here with a horizon problem. A horizon is a kind of knowledge boundary. In physics, the horizon refers to the "observable universe," which is the part of the universe that we can know about. Since the universe is approximately 13.5 billion years old, and no information travels faster than light, there is no way to study any part of the universe that is more than 13.5 billion light years away from us. Our knowledge operates within a large circle with us at the center and a radius of 13.5 billion light years. What lies beyond the horizon is out of our reach. We can make guesses, based on what we do know, but these are only conjectures.[15] In the same manner, we can think of the afterlife as something beyond life's horizon. We can speculate about it given our knowledge within the circle, but at the same time let's recognize that the rules inside the circle may not be the ones that operate outside the circle.

At this point we need to consider a final desperate attempt on the part of atheists to establish their intellectual superiority on the issue of life after death. Atheists often argue that the whole subject is not worth discussing, because belief in the afterlife is obviously a case of wish fulfillment. Philosopher Richard Rorty attributes such belief to "the infantile need for security, the childish hope of escaping from time and chance." Richard Dawkins writes that "the idea of immortality... survives and spreads because it caters to wishful thinking."[16]

Here the classic analysis is by Sigmund Freud in his book *The Future of an Illusion*. Freud distinguishes between an error and an illusion. An error is false, while an illusion reflects wishful thinking.

For a servant girl to think a prince is going to marry her is not an error, because however unlikely, this could happen. Such a belief, however, is an illusion because it is the product of hope rather than reality. Freud argued that since the belief in life after death is obviously an illusion, "we disregard its relationship to reality." Why, then, do such illusions arise? According to Freud, we have a child-like feeling of helplessness in the face of nature's harshness and death's inevitability. So we project our wish for a protective father figure onto an imaginary God. And we invest Him with supernatural powers to confer on us what nature denies, namely a continuing, secure, happy existence after death. Freud concluded that the hope for an afterlife shows "the obsessive neurosis of humanity" that only science can diagnose and cure.[17]

What can we make of Freud's famous analysis? First, just because I have a wish for something says nothing about whether that something is true or false. I wish to have some good friends; does this make having good friends an illusion? The prisoner wishes to escape from the surveillance of the guard; this hardly implies there is no way to do this. A farmer wishes for rain, and he may or may not get his wish, but either way there is nothing irrational about such a desire. Freud seems to have delivered his medical diagnosis without first establishing that the patient has a problem. Far from showing that there is no life after death, Freud seems merely to have presumed it.

Second, the whole idea of wish fulfillment is based on the premise that religion promises you a more wonderful life than the one you have now. But anthropologist Pascal Boyer notes that for tribes he has studied, "a religious world is often every bit as terrifying as a world without a supernatural presence." The Fang people of Cameroon, for example, believe in an afterlife dominated by witches and evil spirits who take relish in eating people. In the same vein, the classical scholar Mary Lefkowitz writes in *Greek*

Gods, Human Lives that the pagan religions of classical antiquity did not promise heavenly bliss; on the contrary, they provided "a world full of evil forces, unpredictable change, difficult conditions, and inevitable defeat and death." So the belief in Greek religion cannot be put down to wish fulfillment.[18]

When we consider Judaism, Islam, and Christianity, I can understand how the concept of heaven meets the criterion of wish fulfillment. Heaven is believed to be the place where there is no suffering and no death. An atheist I debated called heaven "adult Disneyland," and I can see how he got the idea. But what about hell? Hell is also part of the Jewish, Christian, and Islamic scheme. And hell is portrayed as vastly worse than anything we endure in life. Hell is even worse than death, because while death is merely the end, hell is identified with eternal damnation and irrevocable separation from God. Hell is a big problem for the wishful thinking analysis.

Finally, wish fulfillment raises a difficulty that has been pointed out by biologists. "From an evolutionary point of view," Lewis Wolpert writes in *Six Impossible Things before Breakfast*, "beliefs should help the individual survive."[19] Evolution is a doctrine of survival of the fittest. The way to survive is to have an accurate picture of what's going on in the world, especially when it comes to finding food and avoiding predators. By this logic, a creature that routinely develops false beliefs and acts on them is not likely to make it. Imagine a deer who wishes that wolves were friendly and begins to approach them in a friendly manner. That's one less deer in the forest. Cognitive psychologist Steven Pinker writes that wish fulfillment theories cannot explain why minds would evolve to take solace in false beliefs. "A freezing person finds no comfort in believing he is warm. A person face to face with a lion is not put at ease by the conviction that he is a rabbit."[20] Pinker suggests the same reasoning applies to belief in another world. If humans invest their time and energy in an imaginary world to come, they have fewer resources to devote to survival and success in this world. That makes no evolutionary sense. Pinker and others conclude that wish fulfillment cannot be squared with natural selection, and while many Christians may not see this as a problem, it is a big problem for atheists who swear their fidelity to evolution.

My objective in this chapter is to show the pretensions of the atheist claim to knowledge. The atheists say they have reason to believe there is no afterlife; now we can see that there is no reason at all. Sure, many Christians may also be unable to provide a rational basis for their position, but then these Christians understand that their position is rooted in faith. So the playing field in one sense is level between the atheist and the believer: neither can really justify his position rationally. In another sense, however, the Christian's position is an honest one, while the atheist is engaged in false advertising. Atheists in the classroom and in the culture pose as apostles of science and rationality, but in truth they sell their product on the basis of smoke and mirrors. At this point it is best for all of us to admit the limits of our knowledge and to be open to learning something new. Let's keep an open mind.

Chapter Three

A UNIVERSAL LONGING

Two Types of Immortality

The religious impulse, the quest for meaning that transcends
the restricted space of empirical existence in this world,
has been a perennial feature of humanity.[1]

—Peter Berger, *The Desecularization of the World*

Atheists regard life after death as a religious claim, one that does not have to be taken seriously. The reason is that there are many religions in the world, and they seem to offer competing visions of the afterlife. In the atheist view, clearly all of them can't be right; at most one can be; and most likely all of them are wrong. For atheists, life after death is part of a religious picture of the world, a picture that has been largely discredited by science. Religion, in short, is bad science, and atheists say it is time that it gave way to good science. In this chapter I test these arguments and show they are dead wrong. Life after death is not exclusively a religious belief but is also one that is

35

shared by Western philosophy going back to Plato. Moreover, there is complete agreement among the world's religions that there is life after death. In other words, the afterlife is a universally held belief. When we see how such beliefs developed in early civilization, we can dismiss the hypothesis that they amount to primitive science; this is not their source at all. Finally, when we examine what the major religions say about the afterlife, we discover that their differences on this issue are much smaller than atheists suppose. In fact, there are just two main versions of life after death: the Eastern version and the Western one. The Eastern view is that of the soul reuniting after death with some transcendent and ultimate reality; the Western view is one of bodily resurrection. These are the two main forms of immortality that people actually believe in, and these are the ones we will be concerned with in this book.

Let's begin with the atheist objection, and then we will spend the rest of the chapter testing it to see if it is true. In our age of aggressive atheism, unbelievers like to ambush religious believers and ask: how do you know that your religion is right and all the other religions are wrong? Here is the atheist writer Kai Nielsen, "Why the Bible rather than the Quran...the canonical Buddhist texts...the Hindu texts? There is no more reason to rely on the Christian revelation than any of those others."[2] The atheist has a point. There are many religions in the world, and most believers have not carried out a comparative study to determine which of these sets of beliefs is correct. In fact, most Christians became Christians because they were born in Tulsa, Oklahoma, or San Diego, California. Had they been born in Kabul, Afghanistan, they would most likely have been Muslim. "With very few exceptions," philosopher Bertrand Russell wrote, "the religion which a man accepts is that of the community in which he lives, which makes it obvious that the influence of environment is what led him to accept the religion in question."[3] So on what rational basis does the believer assert the exclusive truth of his own particular religion and consequently its particular conception of the afterlife?

In one of my debates, my opponent even accused me of being an atheist. He noted that there have been many gods that have been put forward through the grand sweep of history as worthy objects of human veneration and worship. He asked, you don't believe in Krishna, do you? No. What about Buddha? No. What about Baal or Thor or Poseidon or Ahura Mazda? No. Well then, you're an atheist! After all, you reject 99 percent of all the gods. The only difference between you and me, my atheist opponent concluded, is that I add your god to this long list. Some Christians go along, at least most of the way, with this line of reasoning. I was listening to a taped debate from the 1960s between a Christian apologist and an atheist. The atheist launched vituperative attacks on Islam, Hinduism, and Buddhism. They were senseless; they were vicious; they were intolerant. The Christian cheered him on, saying, in effect: go ahead and slam those religions. I'm with you. I'm only going to defend my own religion, namely Christianity. The atheist thought it comical that each man is appalled by the idea that his own religion is foolish or vicious, but readily agrees that the world's other religions have a lot to answer for. So we are back to the atheist's question: if there are so many religions, what makes yours true and the rest false?

This question has a direct bearing on the issue of the afterlife. It seems that each religion, at least each of the Western religions, has a different conception of life after death. Moreover, it appears that each view is entirely created in its geographical milieu. We can see this by comparing various notions of heaven. For Muslims in the Arabian desert, heaven is depicted as an oasis with palm trees and dates. American Indian tribes envisioned Happy Hunting Grounds full of deer and buffalo. The Vikings hoped to gain

Valhalla after death, where they would do battle in the day and enjoy victory feasts and revels at night. These ideas seem to be the obvious product of cultural hopes and expectations. As for the Eastern religions, they are pretty much ignored in this debate. When atheists mention them, they typically stress how remote their beliefs are from those of Western religions.

Most atheists spend little time investigating religious claims because they consider the whole enterprise misguided from the outset. For many atheists, religion is a kind of bungled science. Each particular conception of eternity is embedded in a larger religious narrative about the world, and from the atheist point of view, these narratives arose as primitive attempts to explain phenomena that seemed frightening or mysterious. In a November 2008 debate I had against philosopher Daniel Dennett in Puebla, Mexico, Dennett patronizingly said that religion was a kind of helper plant, a precursor to the rise of scientific knowledge. Dennett argued that religions offered their subjective and largely fanciful pictures of reality until scientific objectivity came along. Now, he insisted, the crude speculations of religion need to be replaced by the rational explanations of science. Similar arguments have been advanced by astronomer Carl Sagan, physicist Steven Weinberg, and others. In the view of these atheists, religious views of the afterlife can now be dismissed as part of that primitive package.

The atheist critique deserves an answer, but one aspect of it we can reject at the outset. The atheist is simply wrong to assume that religious diversity undermines the truth of religious claims. When it comes to differing views of life after death or any other doctrine, the presence of disagreement in no way implies the absence of truth. Nor does the fact that you learned your Christianity because you grew up in the Bible Belt imply anything about whether those beliefs are true or false. The atheist is guilty here of what in logic is called the "genetic fallacy." The term does not refer to genes; it refers to origins. Think of it this way. If you are raised in New York, you are more likely to believe in Einstein's theory of relativity than if you are raised in New Guinea. Some-one from Oxford, England, is more likely to be an atheist than someone from Oxford, Mississippi. What does this say about whether such beliefs are true? Nothing. The geographical roots of your beliefs have no bearing on the validity of your beliefs.

But what about the larger atheist claim that religions are a kind of ersatz science, not only lacking scientific objectivity, but also making competing claims that cancel each other out? Let's test this by taking a short excursion through history and examining what different cultures believe about the afterlife. We are not doing comparative religion, an idea that many Christians despise for a reason given by the priest and author Ronald Knox. "The study of comparative religions," Knox wrote, "is the best way to become comparatively religious."[4] Here, however, we are doing something quite different. We are not trying to affirm religious diversity or to proclaim all religions equally valid; rather, we are testing a set of atheist claims about the religions of the world against the empirical reality of what the religions of the world actually believe.

One of the most striking things about the afterlife is that belief in it is absolutely universal. This point is clearly established in Alan Segal's magisterial study *Life after Death*. Segal shows that every culture, from the dawn of mankind, has espoused some con-cept of continued existence. Early civilizations in Egypt, Mesopotamia, China, India, and the Americas all held the belief that there is some sort of life beyond the grave.[5] Segal recognizes, of course, that not every individual in those cultures expected to have life after death. In fact, most early cultures made provision only for the future life of the ruling aristocracy. The peasants and

ordinary people were not considered important enough to warrant consideration for the afterlife.

In Egypt, for example, it took the labor of thousands to build
the three pyramids at Giza. The Egyptians sought to preserve the
bodies of their pharaohs, wrapping them in bandages and sometimes burying them in several coffins, one inside the other. Masks
were usually attached to the head to preserve the identity of the
person. Excavations in Sumer have shown that members of the
ruling class were buried in tombs containing an extraordinary
selection of objects, including jewelry, crowns, games, weapons,
and eating utensils. Servants were occasionally buried with their
masters to serve in the next life. These facts refute the idea that
ancient religion was merely a tool for elites to reconcile the common people to their lot by promising them a wonderful existence
in the next life. In reality, ancient cultures only attended to the
postmortem prospects of their pharaohs and rulers. "The inequal-
ities of this life," theologian John Hick writes, "were assumed to
continue in the next."[6]

The universality of belief in an afterlife is astonishing, because
life after death is not one of those empirically obvious beliefs that
one would expect every society from the dawn of mankind to
share. No one is surprised at the universal belief in mountains or
rainstorms or animals, because such things are undeniably present to our senses. But it is an entirely different matter when all cultures in history right down to the present jointly proclaim a
proposition that seems impossible to confirm through experience.
This is a striking convergence of views that demands explanation.
Of course it is easy to downplay the universality of belief in life
after death by saying that it merely reflects primitive explanations
of nature. But anthropologists insist that it does not make sense
to understand the religious beliefs of prehistoric and preliterate
societies in this way. Consider the belief of many ancient peoples

that the skies are patrolled by a multitude of gods. Today it seems irresistible to view this as a poor attempt to answer the questions, "Why does the sun rise?" or "why does it rain?" But it is not obvious that these questions stimulated the curiosity of ancient man. In fact, it takes a particularly sophisticated type of mind to consider the rising of the sun and the falling of the rain to require some sort of convincing explanation. Only when you presume that nature is rationally intelligible and governed without exception by lawful processes do such questions even make sense. There is no reason to think that any of those cultures made such assumptions. The atheist is anachronistically projecting the modern inquiring mindset onto ancient peoples.

I am not saying that ancient peoples were stupid or that they did not seek to explain natural phenomena. They did. But as we find from anthropological literature, they sought explanations at a different level than the ones that satisfy us today. Consider the belief of an African tribal chieftain that the gods must be angry when a famine or illness ravages the community, so that shamans are required to perform rites of propitiation. From the atheist point of view, what could be a more obvious case of bad science! Perhaps we need to bring in biologist Richard Dawkins to explain to the chief that the illness is caused by a particularly venomous type of insect. But the African chief would not likely be impressed. His argument would be something like, "Of course I know that the insects are doing this, but my question is why this is happening now to my people. Why is my tribe being weakened while other tribes have not been ravaged?" The chief would not be denying a natural explanation; rather, he would be denying that a natural explanation is complete or adequate. The scientist is telling him "how," but what the chief really wants to know is "why."

Anthropologist Pascal Boyer writes that "when people find supernatural causes, it is not because they have ignored the work of mechanical and biological causes but because they are asking questions that go beyond these causes."[7] In other words, the roots of humanity's religious impulse are not in scientific ignorance but in what Rudolf Otto called the "sense of the numinous." This is a sense that there is something terrible and awe-inspiring and sublime about existence that seems to derive from another kind of reality.[8] Death, in this view, links together two dimensions of life. Ancestors are revered for their wisdom, in part because they are now part of this other dimension and have, as it were, the full perspective on things. So life after death is part of an emerging intuition on the part of human beings that there are two kinds of reality: the world that we live in, and another, more permanent, "world behind the world." Our world is dependent and somehow less real than that other world, and religious feelings and rituals are a human way of trying to connect with that deeper reality.

Now let's examine what the three Abrahamic religions—Judaism, Christianity, and Islam—have to say about the afterlife. We find that in all three cases there is an official teaching and an unofficial teaching. Both are widely held and therefore both deserve to be traced and examined. The official teaching is bodily resurrection. The Muslims are famous for portraying the afterlife in terms of the pleasures (and pains) of the body; heaven, for instance, is characterized by hearty meals, restful sleep, and lots of sex. The alternative, unofficial, view—held in all three religions by more contemplative types—is the immortality of the soul. In this view the body perishes but the soul lives on. Oddly enough, this idea is first articulated not in biblical or Quranic sources, but rather in Greek philosophy.

Atheists who insist that life after death is a religious concept may be surprised to discover that it is also a philosophical idea that was widely discussed in the fifth century BC. In fact, the emphasis on this topic in the thought of classical antiquity inspired philosopher Leo Strauss to remark that "transcendence is not a preserve of revealed religion."[9] In ancient Greece and Rome, the most interesting ideas about the afterlife came not from the temples but from the philosophers. They were based on reason, not revelation. Greek religion had a very weak, diluted concept of the afterlife. In the society portrayed in Homer's *Iliad* and *Odyssey,* only the gods are immortal, while mortality is part of what it means to be human. The best that humans can hope for is enduring fame through exploits in war or victory in the Olympic festivals. Not that there is no future for humans beyond death, people were held to descend to a shadowy, insubstantial underworld called Hades. In this view, only a fortunate few made it to the Isles of the Blessed, usually heroes who were the offspring of the liaisons of the gods.

While Greek religion, like most other systems, made assertions about the afterlife without any accompanying attempt to justify them, it is Socrates, in Plato's *Phaedo*, who offers the first known argument for life after death. Socrates argues that our bodies are mortal because they are made of perishable materials, but our souls are not subject to those constraints. Socrates contends that since philosophers seek the liberation of the soul from the body, a release of the mind from physical desires and preoccupations, life after death is the realization of what philosophers have always wanted. In fact, to the degree that one can attain this kind of intellectual mastery in this life, one gets a preview of what to expect in the next one. No wonder Socrates was unperturbed as he drank the hemlock.

Socrates lived around the time of a great flourishing of religion throughout the world, a period that scholars have called the Axial Age. This period, around the fifth century BC, witnessed the spread of Zoroastrianism in Persia, Confucianism and Taoism in China, and Buddhism in India. Hinduism and Judaism also entered a new phase of their development. It may seem odd for me to speak of religions as "developing." But there is nothing peculiar in the notion that religious ideas evolve or that our understanding of heaven has a history. Most religious believers have no problem with this. Atheists sometimes imply that religion is merely updating itself to bring its teachings in line with reality. But isn't that what science does also? We don't judge science by the works of Thales or Ptolemy; we routinely speak of scientific progress. As we see in the Axial Age, religion, too, can progress. No one is saying that truth itself changes—remember that the principle of relativity operated for billions of years before Einstein discovered it—but our human understanding of truth can and does.

A classic case of religious progress is the development in Judaism from unbelief to belief in the afterlife. The ancient Jewish denial of life after death is ironic. Jews, after all, were the founders of monotheism. Yet the people who came first to the idea of one God were latecomers to the idea of life after death. The Torah—the first five books of the Old Testament—makes no explicit mention of the afterlife. In the books of Job, Ecclesiastes, and others, several passages seem to suggest that we live and we die, and that's the end of the story. For the Jews, however, the idea of the afterlife strangely emerged out of a frustrated idea of justice. The ancient Israelites held that obedience to God's laws would bring rewards, and these rewards were expected in this life. Long life, large herds, lots of concubines: what more can a man want? Even Zion, God's promised restoration of Israel, was expected on earth.

But when the Jews suffered devastating losses and conquests, such as the Babylonian captivity in the sixth century BC, they began to doubt both the prospects of this earthly restoration as well as the terrestrial equation of virtue and reward. During this period, the Jews never questioned their own status as a chosen people. Nor did they, despite a good deal of doubt and backsliding, give up on their fidelity to God. Rather, the Jews came to believe that there is a postmortem existence in which the New Jerusalem will be established and all human accounts will be settled. This view is reflected in later books of the Old Testament, such as Isaiah and Daniel. We read in Daniel 12:2, "Many of those who sleep in the dust of the earth to the end shall awake, some to everlasting life and some to shame and everlasting contempt." In this view, the coming of the messiah will signal the end of the world and the time of judgment. On judgment day, God will determine the nature of our postmortem existence. Some will go to their heavenly reward, and others will be scorched by the flames of hell, an image that the Jews may have derived from the centrality of fire in the Zoroastrian religion.

The Jewish consensus about what happens after death emerged as a consequence of a debate between the Sadducees and the Pharisees. The Sadducees were the biblical literalists who based their rejection of immortality on what is said, and not said, in the Torah. The Pharisees were the intellectuals who made arguments that went beyond the literal text. They insisted, for example, that since we are created in the image of God, we share in God's immortality. The debate lasted for two centuries and was only settled in favor of the Pharisees around the first century BC. Now, according to historian Jacob Neusner, the belief in life after death is "authoritative" in Judaism. The reason for this status, perhaps, is that it enabled the Jews to see how, in the face of their sufferings as a people, God's justice could still be vindicated. "The idea of immortality in Judaism," writes Abraham Neuman, "arose not to appease man but to vindicate God."[10]

While the Jews were slow to accept the idea of life after death, when they did they gave it a radical new thrust. We can see this by contrasting the Jewish idea of immortality with that of Socrates. While Socrates held that the soul escapes the body at the point of death and lives on in an empyrean of ideas, the Jews affirmed the resurrection of the body. The Jews held that at the time of judgment, God reconnects body and soul so that the whole person survives beyond the grave.

The Jewish idea of bodily resurrection was officially adopted by the Christians. This is hardly surprising, because Christianity is the only religion in history to consider another religion, Judaism, to be wholly true. Yet as theologian N. T. Wright points out, resurrection for the Jews was a relatively peripheral teaching; Christians made it absolutely central. Jews expected resurrection at the end of time; Christians asserted that the messiah had already come, and three days after he was crucified he rose from the dead. While Jews generally held that we are resurrected in our earthly bodies, Christians declared that after death we will have new supernatural bodies akin to the one that Christ had when he appeared to the disciples. According to the New Testament accounts, Christ had a normal-looking body and could eat fish and touch his followers, yet it was also an unusual body that could, for example, go through walls. Taking a cue from Christ, Christians affirmed that after death God will unite our souls to new bodies that are incorruptible and indestructible. In this form, we live forever as embodied souls in the presence of God.

If Jews affirmed bodily resurrection, and this idea was taken up by Christianity, why do some Christians today believe that only our souls live on after death? Part of the reason was the enormous influence of Platonic philosophy on early Christianity. An even bigger reason was the challenge to medieval Christian cosmology posed by the Newtonian scientific worldview. The Middle Ages had a three-story view of the universe, with heaven up in the sky, earth in the middle, and hell down below. With the collapse of the

Ptolemaic universe and the rise of Newtonian astronomy, it became increasingly difficult to specify the physical location of heaven and hell. Newtonian physics also included laws of matter that seemed difficult to square with the notion that bodies can somehow survive past death or be permanently restored. Many Christians began to rethink their ideas of the soul, heaven, and hell. The Platonic idea of the immortality of the soul became newly attractive because it avoided the cosmological difficulty. If what survives us is only the immaterial soul, then there is no need to explain how our bodies survive our deaths. Moreover, there is no problem any longer in having to specify where heaven and hell are located. They are not anywhere because only material objects have a spatial location. Rather, heaven and hell are immaterial states inhabited by immaterial souls. In recent years, theologian N. T. Wright and others have forcefully argued against this Platonic view, and in favor of the original Christian idea of the resurrection of the whole person.

In any event, the Christian understanding of immortality was historically influenced both by Judaism and Greek philosophy. Christians, however, formulated their own distinctive teaching about time. For the Jews, as for the Greeks, the concept of eternity meant forever. In the Old Testament, heaven and hell seem to project time extending indefinitely into the future. And God is believed to be eternal in the sense that He has lived forever in the past and will continue forever in the future. In the Jewish understanding, human souls are immortal but not eternal. They are not eternal because they haven't always existed; God created them, as he created the world, out of nothing. The Church father Augustine, however, offered a startling modification of these ancient ideas. Augustine argued that time itself is not eternal. In his view, God made the universe not in time, but with time. God created time along with the universe! "Prior to" the universe, there was no time. The medieval Christians drew on these Augustinian ideas to formulate a new vision of life after death, one that is lived in an eternal realm disconnected from space and time. Since eternity is conceived not as a continuation of time but as a suspension of time, Christianity since Augustine does not espouse life "after" death, but rather life "beyond" death.

Now it is time to go east and examine the Eastern religions, notably Hinduism and Buddhism. Here we encounter a very different perspective on life after death, one that bears a slight resemblance to Platonic philosophy but is nevertheless quite distinct from it. Before we explore this issue, however, I want to dispel the claim that Eastern systems such as Confucianism, Buddhism, and Taoism are atheistic and reject the notion of life after death. Thomas Huxley, for instance, wrote of Buddhism as "a system which . . . counts the belief in immortality a blunder and the hope of it a sin."[11] Others have written in a similar manner about Confucianism and Taoism.

This view of Eastern thought is wrong, but it contains a small element of truth that keeps it going. Confucianism is probably better described as an ethical code rather than a religion. "You do not know about life," Confucius once told a disciple, "so how can you understand death?"[12] Here Confucius' position resembles that of Socrates, who said that his object of study was not nature, but rather human nature. Even Confucius' ethical code, however, is based on an allegiance to what he calls the Way of Heaven. Confucius is quoted in the *Analects* as saying that "heaven is the author of the virtue that is within me." The Confucian scholar Tu Wei-Ming writes that "heaven . . . features prominently throughout the Confucian tradition."[13]

We find the same result in Buddhism, at least in the way it is commonly practiced throughout the world. One species of Buddhism, called Hinayana or Lesser Vehicle Buddhism, mostly found in Sri Lanka, Thailand, and Cambodia, is indeed godless. But this cannot be said of Mahayana or Greater Vehicle Buddhism, which is by far the most widespread form, predominant in China, Korea, and Japan. Mahayana texts such as the Lotus Sutra feature a pantheon of celestial beings that leave their heavenly realms to become active in the world, helping people achieve nirvana or enlightenment. In *Discovering God*, sociologist Rodney Stark points out that most Buddhists worship the Buddha himself as a God, and "most Buddhist temples are chock-full of lesser Gods."[14]

Moreover, despite their differences about the gods, Hinayana and Mahayana monks both accept life after death because they both endorse the Buddhist doctrine of continuing rebirth. This doctrine holds that humans go through a cycle of births and deaths. Not that Buddhists are happy about the prospect of this endless ride; rather, Buddhism holds that it is a sad, sorry journey, and our best bet is to disembark! This exit can only be achieved through nirvana. One popular Chinese version of Buddhism, so-called Pure Land Buddhism, even identifies nirvana with a literal, physical place of perfect bliss that awaits the enlightened and the virtuous.[15] The centrality of this doctrine can be verified by entering Buddhist temples across Asia where rebirths and future lives feature prominently in the artistic depictions and the monastic devotions. As for Taoism, the Taoist scholar Liu Xiaogan writes that "Taoist religion regards the possibility and importance of immortality as its cardinal principle."[16]

The oldest and most influential Eastern doctrine of life after death can be found in Hinduism. In fact, Buddhism adapted its notion of the afterlife from the Hindus; after all, Gautama Siddhartha, the founder of Buddhism, was born in India and raised as a Hindu. The Hindu doctrine of reincarnation—a continuing cycle of birth and death—has been affirmed for three thousand years and influenced the whole Eastern conception of the afterlife.

According to Hinduism, not only is there life after death, there is also life before birth. Indeed the life you are living now is an intermediate stage in a long procession of lives. In each case your body deteriorates when you die, but your soul lives on, each time reinstalled in a new body. Reincarnation thus solves the geographical problem of where exactly we live all these lives: the answer is, right here on earth! Moreover, Hindus believe that each life in the succession is connected to the next not only by possession of a single soul, but also by a cosmic law.

This is karma, the universal moral law of cause and effect. Karma means that "you get what you pay for" or "what goes around comes around." Your destiny in one life is the effect of your actions in the previous life. So people who are miserable now must have done something horrible in a previous existence. By living well this time around, however, they can improve their future prospects. Some critics of Hinduism have alleged that karma implies fatalism or inaction; if I see a man who is hungry or drowning, I should not help him because this is his deserved fate. This objection is answered by the sages in their commentaries on the Vedas, the ancient Hindu text. The sages' answer is that of course I should help him; it was part of his karma that I should come along in his time of need.

In the Axial Age, this ancient Hindu doctrine of reincarnation was transformed by a philosophical work called the Upanishads. The Upanishads inaugurated a new understanding of Hinduism, sometimes called Vedanta or "post-Vedic" Hinduism. According to the Upanishads, we live in an unreal world that we mistake for the real one. In other words, we wrongly assume that the world as we perceive it is the world as it really is. But this is the trick of "maya," or illusion, and it is a trick that uses the mirrors of space and of time. Actually, reality is entirely different from what our senses perceive. We experience objects in the world as differentiated, and we think of ourselves as individual souls separate from the world. But if we could see behind the mirrors of experience, if we could somehow lift the veil, we would realize that reality preserves none of these distinctions. In reality, everything is one. The Upanishads insist that there is only one way to break the tedious cycle of reincarnation, and that is to realize that our individual souls are identical with the oneness of ultimate reality.

As I mentioned earlier, the Hindu idea of reincarnation was adopted and is now shared by Buddhism. But Buddhists modified the idea of reincarnation into an idea of rebirth. In Buddhism, people are born into a succession of lives, but these may not all occur on this earth or even in this universe; Buddhism posits a multitude of worlds. While Buddhism holds to a causal connection between these lives produced by karma, one is not the same person from one life to the next. In the Buddhist understanding, the actions of my previous life help to explain my current circumstances, but those earlier actions weren't done by the same person who is now "Dinesh." Moreover, Buddhists reject the idea that we are individuals or that we have souls. Of course Buddhists recognize that we experience the world as individuals, but their point is that this experience is misleading. Part of our enlightenment is to recognize that the very concept of "I" is illusory; in reality, there is no man behind the curtain. The term nirvana literally means "blowing out," and in case you're wondering, you are the one who must be blown out, like a candle.

What have we learned from this survey of competing conceptions of life after death? Contrary to what atheists say, the belief in the afterlife is not merely a Western idea; it is a universal idea. Moreover, it is not an exclusively religious idea, but also one that has roots in Western philosophy. We see that beliefs in life after death, far from being deviant or parochial, are actually the normal way of thinking both globally and historically. Basically there are two rival perspectives on life after death. The first is survival without the body, and the second is survival of the whole person, body and soul together. But now there is a third position unique to our culture and our age. Today, for the first time, a constituency exists that not only denies life after death, but considers this denial to be the only reasonable way to think. Since we recognize the choices before us, we are ready to consider empirical evidence to find out which position is correct.

Chapter Four

VIEW FROM THE EDGE

Exploring Near-Death Experiences

I was confronted by a red light, exceedingly bright...I was aware that this light was responsible for the government of the universe.[1]

—A. J. Ayer, "What I Saw When I Was Dead"

It would be wonderful if we could confirm life after death by meeting dead people and carrying on conversations with them. Unfortunately, this seems to happen only in fiction. In Shakespeare's *Julius Caesar*, Brutus receives a warning from the apparition of the dead Caesar, and in Charles Dickens's *A Christmas Carol*, Scrooge is taught a lesson by the ghost of Christmases past. Films like *Ghost* and *The Sixth Sense* provide glimpses both appealing and terrifying about what it might be like to communicate with those who have died. In nineteenth-century England and America, people sometimes consulted "mediums" to receive messages from dead relatives. There are parapsychologists, even today, who credit such accounts, but I cannot take them seriously. If the dead could communicate with us, one would expect that they would do so more regularly. How likely is it that, given the millions upon millions who have died, a mere handful would return, through the kind facilitation of some somber intermediary, not to give us any important information but rather to speak mostly gibberish?

If we cannot have dialogues with the dead, however, there seems to be another way that we can pursue our empirical inquiry into life after death. This is to carefully examine the reports of persons very near death, who might have caught some glimpse of what lies on the other side. In other words, we need to consider the veracity of "near death experiences." And to keep our inquiry fair and comprehensive, let's also consider the empirical evidence for reincarnation. Even if there is no way to prospectively confirm life after death, we may be able to retrospectively confirm life before birth. This result would at least tell us there is something beyond the normal life span. Nor do such inquiries need to be regarded as supernatural quests in any sense. Advocates of reincarnation, after all, insist that the process is entirely natural—this is just the way the universe operates. Reincarnation, Hindus coolly affirm, is simply an undiscovered law of nature.

While reincarnation seems pretty far out to many of us in the West, let's remember that some of our own beliefs about religion, science, and society probably sound bizarre to people in other cultures. Probably just as many people in the world today believe in reincarnation as believe in Jewish or Christian concepts of life after death. Between 20 and 25 percent of Americans and Europeans believe in reincarnation today.[2] And historically, reincarnation is an important idea not only in the East but also in the West. Pythagoras and Plato endorsed versions of it; the Gnostics embraced it; even atheist philosophers such as David Hume and

Arthur Schopenhauer took it seriously, with Hume declaring that it was the version of immortality most congenial to philosophy.[3]

For a long time, advocates of reincarnation conceded that the idea could not be shown directly, but they argued that it helps to make sense of otherwise puzzling facts about the world. For instance, we sometimes visit a place for the first time, and yet we have the *déjà vu* sense that we've been there before. Well, say advocates of reincarnation, maybe in a previous life, we have. Love at first sight seems mysterious until you consider the possibility that the two people in question were actually acquainted in an earlier existence. Sometimes children seem so strikingly different from their parents that people around them begin to wonder how they got that way; reincarnation provides an explanation for such notable dissimilarities. And consider child geniuses such as Mozart who were composing symphonies and even operas at an absurdly young age. Could Mozart really have learned those skills through training or cultural environment? Believers in reincarnation say it's more reasonable to suppose that he developed them in a past life.

These arguments are unconvincing because the phenomena in question can be accounted for without recourse to reincarnation. My *déjà vu* feeling can be explained by a similar past experience that I might not currently recall. Besides, if strange places sometimes seem oddly familiar, it is equally the case that familiar places sometimes seem strange. None of these feelings require for their comprehension so extravagant a premise as reincarnation. Love at first sight has shown itself unreliable if it is not confirmed by second sight. Why call upon reincarnation to explain it when human impulsiveness and myopia will do? And the findings of biology and heredity show that children can acquire traits from their ancestors that make them markedly different from their parents.

The case of young geniuses who display prodigious musical or mathematical talents is trickier. The skeptic Paul Edwards notes that the facts of biology combined with those of modern neuroscience provide an adequate explanation. He contends that the configuration of Mozart's brain, specifically his auditory cortex, provides an "entirely plausible" explanation for the man's inventive genius.[4] But this is mere supposition. What is so unique about Mozart's brain that makes it capable of generating those exquisite symphonies and operas? Edwards has no idea, and neither does anyone else. Even the richness of musical talent in Mozart's gene pool still leaves a considerable residue of his ability unexplained, since Mozart was so obviously in a class of his own. The problem for reincarnation is that it hardly solves the problem. Where did Mozart get his genius? He got it from another guy. And where did that fellow get it? He got it from still someone else. Well, where is their musical corpus? Moreover, at some point this chain of inheritance requires a first link. So how did that first person get such genius? To say that he was "born that way" provides no answer, because then we could simplify all our detective work by simply saying that Mozart himself was born that way.

But if arguments for reincarnation seem unpersuasive, so do the usual arguments against it. The poet Lucretius and the church father Tertullian both disputed reincarnation on the grounds that if we have lived previous lives, we should be able to remember them. But as philosopher C. J. Ducasse pointed out, this objection proves little because most of us have no memory of the first few years of our present lives. "Indeed the case is really worse than that, for we have also no memories of the great majority of the days of our life."[5] Do you know what you wore or what you had for dinner three weeks ago? Even if you don't, it hardly leads to the conclusion that you did not then exist.

Another criticism, also made by Tertullian, is that reincarnation seems to presuppose that the population of the world is stable, because each person is born again and again. Since the population is always growing, however, how do all the new souls get added to the world? In a book devoted to refuting reincarnation, the skeptic Paul Edwards lists this as his "favorite argument."[6] But if the Hindu version of reincarnation is true, then it is not so formidable. After all, in Hinduism souls can migrate from humans to animals and from animals to humans. Moreover, souls are regarded as emanations from a single reality in the same way that light beams on earth are emanations from a single sun. So the Hindu answer is that new souls can arise in the same way that souls come to exist in the first place.

The reincarnation debate has been taken to a new level by psychiatrist Ian Stevenson, a longtime professor at the University of Virginia. Stevenson has published multivolume case studies of children who specifically recall their previous lives. Altogether he has more than 2,500 cases, and more are regularly being added. Stevenson concedes that some of his cases may involve misidentification or even deception, but taken as a whole, he argues that he has assembled a body of data that demands to be taken seriously. The popular holistic guru Deepak Chopra agrees in a recent book, citing Stevenson's work as strong empirical evidence for reincarnation.[7]

In one case, Stevenson tells of a young Indian boy named Prakash who informed his family that his real name was Nirmal and that he lived in another village. He gave details about this "real" family, including the operations of the family business, and the names of relatives and friends. He made several attempts to run away to this other home until his parents beat him for this behavior. A few years later, Prakash was able to visit his "real" father and immediately recognized him. The man actually had a son named Nirmal, who had died before Prakash was born. Prakash also recognized a number of those he said were former relatives and friends and provided precise details about them and about his former home. Stevenson, who investigated the case a few weeks after the reunion, listed thirty-four separate items that Prakash remembered. In checking with the relevant people, he found every item to be correct. Prakash had detailed knowledge of the life circumstances of this other family, even though members of both families testified they had no prior knowledge of each other.

Stevenson presents such cases in a rigorous and balanced way. In some cases he shows that children have birthmarks or diseases that are eerily similar to those of the alleged previous incarnation. More than one case involves a child whose phobia about water seems partly explained by the fact that the identified previous incarnation died by drowning. Some of his most interesting cases involve xenoglossy, where children speak in a language that they do not know. Since children with a gift for language can absorb foreign words and phrases from all kinds of places—movie scenes, billboards, a book read by a fellow passenger on a train— xenoglossy by itself proves little. Far more significant are Stevenson's cases where the child can converse and answer questions in the other language. Undoubtedly Stevenson's most sensational cases involve children who bear the physical marks of wounds that they claim to have sustained in previous lives. Stevenson's data include more than a dozen such cases, in which children not only name their previous incarnations, but also give accounts of how they were killed in stabbings or shootings. Stevenson and his colleagues began by confirming the existence of those named individuals. Then in each case they verified that the violence in question occurred. Most remarkably, they were also able to find scars on the bodies of the children in precisely the same spots. Stevenson's papers provide photographs of the scars. He offers alternative ways to read the evidence and argues that a reincarnation hypothesis makes the most sense.[8]

Stevenson's data have certain weaknesses that he is ready to acknowledge. Some of his case studies are quite old. Many involve sources who recall previous existences that were lived out in the next village, or a short distance away. This proximity makes it possible that the child is not reporting information recalled from a previous life but rather information that could have been obtained in some other way. Significantly, Stevenson has no good cases in which a child reports detailed information about a previous personality born in a different country. Nothing in the doctrine of reincarnation says that all the incarnations have to occur in the same geographical area. A review in *Skeptic* magazine of one of Stevenson's books contends that Stevenson's data seem vague and even a little fudged in precisely matching the wounds of the dead with the scars on the bodies of their alleged subsequent incarnations. Still, I found the matches to be close enough. Stevenson's work is sufficiently impressive that atheist John Beloff credits him with raising a "formidable puzzle," adding, "I do not doubt that something paranormal is going on."[9]

I do. In order for me to accept reincarnation as something that happens to all humans, I would at the least like to see evidence for it from around the world. While Stevenson and his colleagues do have cases from Sri Lanka, Brazil, Turkey, Lebanon, Nigeria, and even America, the vast majority of his cases are from India. Stevenson argues that this is because the Hindu culture encourages children to speak about these experiences; elsewhere, he writes, children who raise such subjects meet such shock and disbelief that they keep their stories to themselves. Yes, but if reincarnation is a global phenomenon we would expect that there would be a large number of bold children who would overcome their cultural inhibitions and speak their mind, as they have been known to do on other matters. Another serious problem is that Stevenson does not speak the native languages, so he has to rely on translators. This in my opinion greatly increases the chance of setups that go undetected. I grew up in India, and I know how children who claim to be religiously anointed become celebrities, sometimes attracting a large following and also donations of money. It is easy for me to see how families might conspire to produce the appropriate "evidence." Certainly this cannot be happening in most or all of Stevenson's cases, but since we don't know which ones are authentic it is hard to know how to evaluate them. My conclusion is that reincarnation is possible but unlikely.

When we move from reincarnation to Near Death Experiences (NDEs), we immediately see that our field has widened, both in terms of the number of scholars who are involved, and in the range and quality of the data collected from different countries. Yet here, too, the field was initiated by a single man, physician Raymond Moody, in his 1975 book *Life after Life*. Moody reported on 150 cases of people, from a wide range of religious and social backgrounds, who had been declared dead or were very close to death, and who had a set of astonishing experiences. What made the reports even more incredible was that most of these people had similar, and in some cases virtually identical, experiences. While emphasizing that individual cases showed some variation, Moody nevertheless provided a composite account distilled from these reports.

In this ideal or composite account, a person shows the clinical signs of death or is pronounced dead by his doctor. Yet far from losing all awareness, he hears a loud noise and finds himself moving swiftly through a dark tunnel. He is now outside his physical body and can see it from a distance. (This is the out-of-body experience my wife had following her accident.) Even so, he is not a disembodied soul but has some kind of a new and different body. He encounters the spirits of relatives and friends who died. In some cases he reports seeing Jesus or other celestial beings. He is also dazzled by a bright light that envelopes him with warmth and love. The subject now finds his whole life before him, so that he can panoramically review or evaluate it. Oddly enough, time feels compressed, as if he is living out his past and his future in a single unending present. At this point he approaches a barrier, signaling a point of no return. He wants to cross over but realizes that his time is not yet and he must return to earth. Somehow he is reunited with his body. He tells other people about the experience but cannot express it fully. He also finds that others laugh and scoff at him. Even so, his life is profoundly affected, and he loses his fear of death and becomes a gentler, more loving person.[10]

Moody recognized that his reports might sound fantastic to many, so he cited numerous examples from history to show that near death experiences were not uncommon. Plato reports in his *Republic* the story of a soldier who had been mortally wounded in battle. As the man's body was tossed on a funeral pyre, waiting to be buried, he somehow revived and felt his soul leaving his body. The soul went through a passage where it joined other spirits. The souls were met and judged by divine beings that brought before them everything they had done in their earthly lives. The soldier, however, was told he would not be judged but should return to the physical world. He awoke to find himself back on the funeral pyre. The eighth-century monk Bede reports a similar case in his history of the English people. The *Tibetan Book of the Dead*, also compiled around the same time, instructs dying people to prepare to give an account of their lives as they go through the darkness into the radiant light of pure reality.[11]

Ernest Hemingway, wounded by shrapnel in World War I and lying in a hospital bed in Italy, wrote to a friend that on a fateful night in 1918, a huge bomb exploded in the darkness. "I died then. I felt my soul or something coming right out of my body, like you'd pull a silk handkerchief out of a pocket by one corner. It flew around and then came back and went in again and I wasn't dead anymore." Hemingway said he was transformed by the experience, which he used as the basis for a scene in *A Farewell to Arms*. Following a heart attack, psychologist Carl Jung also had a near death experience in which he felt himself come out of his body. "Life and the whole world struck me as a prison," he wrote. Somehow "everything that happens in time had been brought together.... One is interwoven into an indescribable whole and yet observes it with complete objectivity." When it was over, "three weeks were still to pass before I could truly make up my mind to live again." Even the atheist A. J. Ayer, whose heart stopped in an intensive care unit, wrote of a near death experience that confounded his previous assumptions. Ayer suddenly found himself in a realm where "the laws of nature had ceased to function as they should." He felt that "it was up to me to put things right." He was "confronted by a red light, exceedingly bright" that he somehow recognized was "responsible for the government of the universe." Then he returned to consciousness. While Ayer remained an atheist, he confessed that experiences like his provide "rather strong evidence that death does not put an end to consciousness."[12]

While Moody's book stirred up immediate controversy, it also attracted a multitude of new researchers seeking to confirm or discredit his claims. Prominent among them was psychologist Kenneth Ring, who carried out the first systematic study of near death experiences. Pediatrician Melvin Morse focused on such experiences in children. Cardiologist Michael Sabom, who at first "truly believed Raymond Moody was pulling a fast one," compared the experiences of cardiac patients who reported NDEs with a control group of patients who didn't. The work of these researchers confirmed, extended, and systematized Moody's original claims. Shortly after Moody's book, the International Association for Near Death Studies was founded to study the NDE phenomenon, and its publication, the *Journal of Near Death Studies*, has featured a wide body of data from around the world. Near death research now involves separate tracks of inquiry into the various categories of the near death experience—the out of body phenomenon, the tunnel of darkness, the bright light, the sensation of love and warmth, the life review, and the subsequent life transformation. What emerges from this work is how vivid and real these experiences are to the people who have them. Moreover, several people reported seeing things when they were clinically dead that seem impossible for them to have been aware of. One 11-year-old boy who suffered cardiac arrest and had no heartbeat told of an out-of-body experience in which he could see the doctors and nurses working on his body. After his recovery he accurately summarized the resuscitation procedures used on him, the colors and whereabouts of the instruments in the room, and even what the medical staff said to each other.[13]

Another remarkable case involved a Seattle woman who reported a near death experience following a heart attack. She told social worker Kimberly Clark that she had separated from her body and not only risen to the ceiling but floated outside the hospital altogether. Clark did not believe her, but a small detail the woman mentioned caught her attention. The woman said that she had been distracted by the presence of a shoe on the third floor ledge at the north end of the emergency room building. It was a tennis shoe with a worn patch and a lace stuck under the heel. The woman asked Clark to go find the shoe. Clark found this ridiculous because she knew the woman had been brought into the emergency room at night, when she could not possibly see what was outside the building, let alone on a third-floor ledge. Somewhat reluctantly, Clark agreed to check, and it was only after trying several different rooms, looking out several windows, and finally climbing out onto the ledge that she was able to find and retrieve the shoe.[14]

Some of the most sensational claims in NDE research involve blind people reporting out of body experiences in which they were able to see. These were first mentioned by Elisabeth Kübler-Ross, a pioneer in research on the stages of death. In her book *On Death and Dying*, Kübler-Ross told of patients who had been blind for at least ten years recounting near death experiences in which they could give detailed descriptions of their medical procedures and even identify the jewelry and colors of the clothing of people around them. Unfortunately Kübler-Ross offered no case studies, but in their book *Mindsight*, Kenneth Ring and Sharon Cooper cite more than twenty cases of blind patients who reported detailed near death perceptions "indistinguishable from those of sighted persons."[15]

In 1982 the Gallup organization published *Adventures in Immortality*, revealing that more than 15 percent of Americans reported having an "unusual experience" when they were on the "verge of death" or had a "close call" with death. Since these terms were somewhat ill-defined in the survey, this may be an exaggerated figure as it pertains to near death experiences. Even so, replies to Gallup's specific questions show that millions of Americans report having undergone at least some aspects of the classic NDE. One might expect that as resuscitation technology and procedures continue to improve, more people will revive from the edge of death and report near death experiences. NDEs have now been studied in Europe and Asia and are acknowledged to be a global phenomenon. On the face of it, they provide strong support for life after death. Indeed, a 2005 survey of American doctors showed that 59 percent now believe in some form of afterlife, a much higher percentage than is found in other scientific professions. Possibly their encounter with patients who have had near death experiences is partly responsible for this. I doubt they learned it in medical school.[16]

Not surprisingly, near death research has faced derision and even ferocious attack from various quarters. Oddly enough, some of that derision has come from religious believers who might be expected to welcome this empirical support for one of the central tenets of their faith. The liberal theologian Hans Küng and the evangelical magazine *Christianity Today* both criticized near death experiences. To an extent, we can understand why liberal theologians might be hostile. Some of them regard religion as mainly about sharing and social justice and consider the whole subject of the afterlife to be an embarrassment. It's less obvious why traditional Christians might protest. The reason could possibly be summed up in Billy Graham's objection that "seldom in these experiences does death appear to have any negative consequences." In a 1992 monograph, John Ankerberg and John Weldon write that near death research seems to promote "a universal religion" in which "God seems to be indifferent to evil" and just about everyone ends up living happily ever after. This, they argue, is not Christianity.[17] These objections might sound vindictive to some, but I think they reflect a legitimate concern with justice that is not specifically religious. Which of us would be comfortable, for instance, in contemplating Hitler enjoying eternal bliss without having to pay for his monstrous crimes?

Even so, the Christian objection seems overdrawn. Certainly the overwhelming majority of near death experiences seem to be about love, forgiveness, and bliss. These themes resonate in the work of Moody, Ring, and Sabom. But physician Maurice Rawlings in *Beyond Death's Door* reports a number of frightening and hellish near death encounters, sometimes experienced as retribution for bad things that the person has done. Rawlings suggests that only about half of NDEs are positive, but that people with negative experiences either repress them or are embarrassed to report them, a phenomenon commonly observed in victims of rape and abuse. Rawlings is an evangelical Christian who has been faulted for producing work that tracks his religious beliefs. But Dr. Bruce Greyson and Nancy Evans Bush have issued their own report on "Distressing Near-Death Experiences," and the British researcher Margot Grey in her study *Return from Death* also reports a number of dark, gruesome NDEs that are very similar to those in Rawlings's work. So Christians need not worry that NDEs somehow undermine mainstream religious beliefs. Most significant for Christians and other believers, Sabom and other researchers consistently report that "NDEs seem to produce a stronger faith and a higher level of commitment to traditional religious practice."[18]

Most of the critics of NDEs are atheists who recognize the potency and persuasive power of this research and have raised a multitude of objections. The first, and most obvious, is that these people are not really dead. Strictly speaking, this is true. No corpses have risen out of coffins to deliver surprise orations at their funerals. If death is defined as the irreversible breakdown of human functions, then obviously there can be no real "death experience." Indeed, the philosopher Ludwig Wittgenstein pointed out almost a century ago that we never truly experience death, just as we never truly experience falling asleep. One moment we are awake and the next we are asleep; our consciousness does not experience any in-between stage. So, too, death itself is not an experience; it is the termination of experience.

Even so, the criticism seems to be based on a quibble. We are trying to elicit information about what comes after death, and if we cannot get such information from those who are actually dead, then our best bet is to get it from those who are nearest to the edge. So "near death" isn't "dead," but it is as close as we are likely to get. After all, many people who report NDEs show no heart functions or respiration. They are "clinically dead." Today, death is understood more in terms of a cessation of brain functions rather than heart functions. Significantly, in a recent Dutch study of nearly 350 patients, published in the British medical journal *The Lancet*, physician Pim van Lommel reported several near death experiences that took place even after the patient's brain activity had completely ceased.[19]

A second attempted refutation is that near death experiences are memories that derive from not from the process of dying but from the process of being born. The suggestion here is that, at the end of life, we in a sense return to the womb and once again experience the original birth process. Carl Sagan embraced this view in his book *Broca's Brain*. At first glance, this explanation would help to account for several features of the NDE: the tunnel, the sensation of floating, the movement from darkness into light. But Sagan's hypothesis has been largely discredited by the work of philosopher Carl Becker, who draws on research in the field of infant perception to show that newborns cannot see anything as they emerge from the womb. Even if they could, newborns don't have developed mental faculties and cannot be expected to have any recollections of the birth process. In any case, the birth canal is not like a tunnel through which a child gracefully floats; it is a tight, compressed passage from which a newborn emerges, typically head first and sometimes chafed or bruised. Finally, there are near death reports by people who were born by Caesarian section and never went through the normal birth process.[20]

A more sophisticated alternative is that reported NDEs are unreliable because they are culturally conditioned. Carol Zaleski's

Otherworld Journeys details how in such experiences Christians tend to see Jesus, Hindus the head of an elephant, and Jews an angel or merely the bright light. Because of this, Zaleski prefers to read such experiences as "literary motifs" conveying psychological and moral truth. But this doesn't follow. Obviously we interpret our experiences through a cultural lens. A Christian may see a radiant being and say it's Jesus, while a Muslim might say it's Muhammad. Since no one knows what either Jesus or Muhammad looked like—and let's assume the radiant being isn't wearing a name tag—clearly the identification shows an element of cultural projection. But one cannot conclude from this that there was no radiant being, or that this was simply metaphor. The whole literary metaphor idea, which is especially popular with literary types like Zaleski, is rendered even more suspect when we see that, notwithstanding the variation across cultures, there are common elements in the near death experience that occur globally. This is the conclusion reached by sociologist Allan Kellehear, following a cross-cultural comparison of near death experiences. Even Susan Blackmore, a strong critic of NDEs, finds that they have "similar features appearing in different forms across times and cultures."[21]

Undoubtedly, the favored explanation among atheist critics is that NDEs say nothing about life after death because they reflect distorted brain states. One possibility, raised by psychologist Ron Siegel, is that NDEs are dreamlike experiences of a kind that people have when they take hallucinogenic or mind-altering drugs. Many people who take recreational drugs do experience a range of perceptions and emotions, from wild colors to soaring sensations to drowsiness to disorientation to decreased vision. During this time, however, most of them know they are on drugs. Also, they don't have anything like the coherence or content of the near death experience. And people who do have such experiences aren't typically on recreational drugs. In fact, many of them aren't even on anesthetic agents, narcotics, or painkillers. Researcher Melvin Morse compared a control group of heavily medicated children with children who reported near death experiences. He found that none of the control group had such an experience. Morse's conclusion is that "a person does need to be near death to experience an NDE."[22]

While some atheist critics concede that the familiar types of drugs won't cause NDEs, they suggest a more exotic cocktail of drugs and treatments that can. Neuroscientist Michael Persinger claims that he can simulate the NDE by placing a helmet on subjects and electrically stimulating parts of their brains. Psychiatrist Karl Jansen has proposed that the anesthetic drug ketamine can reproduce the characteristics of NDEs.[23] But many patients with NDEs haven't undergone any of these treatments or taken any of these drugs. Persinger's helmet is a hit-or-miss device; atheist Richard Dawkins tried it, and it had no effect on him. Ketamine is no longer in general medical use because its side effects include disorientation and paranoia. These reactions are radically different from what patients experience with NDEs. Even if ketamine had no such side effects and reproduced all the features of the NDE, the fact remains that ketamine is now out of circulation, and people continue to report near death experiences.

Moreover, there is a bigger problem here, which is that these are artificially induced states. Sure, you can give laboratory patients ketamine or electric shock treatment and record their subsequent experiences, but what does this prove? If I tell you that I am being blinded by the sun, you cannot prove that this is a mental illusion by showing me that you can also blind me with a flashlight. The situation with near death experiences is even stronger than this analogy suggests. NDEs do not merely occur without external inducement; they also happen to people whose hearts and in some cases brains have stopped functioning altogether.

Well, say the critics, perhaps the brain releases these drugs naturally. And a number of different neurotransmitters and receptors have been proposed, such as serotonin, endorphins, and the amino acid glutamate. Michael Shermer argues that under traumatic conditions, these brain chemicals can generate experiences similar to those in the NDE.[24] An outstanding cyclist himself, Shermer knows that athletes sometimes have out of body experiences, activated by sensory deprivation or the low levels of oxygen found at high altitudes. Critics also have an evolutionary argument to make in this connection. They say that when life is threatened we may, as a last ditch defense mechanism, mentally leave our bodies and watch what is happening in a kind of third-person way. This helps to reduce pain and might even reflect the feigned death strategies used in the distant past by our primitive ancestors, and even today by some animals, to survive predators.

The evolutionary argument is interesting but irrelevant. The problem is that people who have virtually no brain function and whose hearts have stopped beating are not in a position to feign anything. Try coming up with shrewd survival strategies when you are in a comatose state; you couldn't even devise them while you are sleeping. And while athletes may experience runner's highs and even out of body experiences, they typically don't go through tunnels, see bright lights, or report meetings with deceased relatives. As far as I know, the only time they report interactions with Jesus is when they have scored a winning touchdown. As psychologist Susan Blackmore says, any explanation of near death experiences cannot merely account for one or another feature of the NDE; it must account for all the features simultaneously. It must also explain why this cluster of experiences seems consistent across cultures. Finally, it's not enough to say that "these are all just mental states"; you have to give a reason for why these particular mental states. In other words, why are there tunnels and bright lights, and where do all the love and warmth come from?

Blackmore's own explanation has been termed the "dying brain hypothesis." She suggests that when the brain breaks down, its mechanisms of pattern recognition continue to generate images. In other words, the brain attempts to reconstruct a memory model of reality that seems perfectly real, even though it does not reflect anything outside the brain itself. How, then, does Blackmore meet her own criteria for a good explanation? In her dying brain hypothesis, the tunnel is the result of constriction in the visual pathways. The joy and peace come from endorphins and natural opiates released by stress. The tunnel and lights are a kind of special effects generated by a brain cortex that is derived of oxygen. A breakdown in body image and the brain's model of reality can account for the out of body experience. The life review is a consequence of the brain's memory systems trying to organize themselves as they fail and falter. The same memory systems conjure up images of deceased friends and relatives. And finally the impression of timelessness or eternity is fostered by a self that is disintegrating and relinquishing all experiential notions of time and place.

The strength of Blackmore's argument is that she does explain the similarity of NDEs around the world by suggesting that "everyone has a similar brain, hormones and nervous system, and that is why they have similar experiences when those systems fail."[25] Critics, however, point out that dying brains typically don't generate such experiences. If they did, then virtually everyone who is dying would have an NDE! Moreover, as those who have watched a loved one die can easily testify, dying brains tend to produce faded recollections, incoherence, and disorientation. These symptoms are radically different from the perceptual clarity and bliss of the typical NDE. If NDEs are the result of a dying brain, then a breakdown of mental faculties has already taken place; but in fact most people who report near death experiences are living normal lives. So how have their brains reversed the dissolution and gotten all their normal perceptual faculties back? Blackmore has very little to say about any of this. And finally, as I think Blackmore would concede, nothing in the dying brain hypothesis accounts for how clinically dead people seem to know things that are apparently out of the range of their perceptual capacities.

I conclude that there is much stronger evidence for the veracity of near death experiences than there is for reincarnation. While the critics of NDEs have raised some interesting possibilities—it might be this and it might be that—on balance, near death experiences do suggest that consciousness can and sometimes does survive death. By itself this is a very damaging conclusion for those who deny the afterlife. From their point of view, near death experiences that point to an afterlife should not only be very rare; they should be impossible. So a single authentic case would be sufficient to refute the premise that "nothing comes after death," and to show that there is something more. But we should not overstate what we have learned here. Since only some people have NDEs, it is possible that only some people's consciousness survives their death. Also, the fact of some sort of out-of-body survival in these cases tells us very little about what the afterlife is really like. By definition no one has reported a near death experience that fully crossed that barrier from this life to the next. Finally, "survival" is not the same thing as "immortality," because theoretically we could survive our deaths and still lose our consciousness shortly thereafter. Let us forge ahead, therefore, and ask whether the laws of science permit and even imply more lasting possibilities for the afterlife.

Chapter Five

THE PHYSICS OF IMMORTALITY

Multiple Universes and Unseen Realms

The overarching lesson that has emerged from scientific inquiry
over the last century is that human experience is often
a misleading guide to the true nature of reality.[1]

—Brian Greene, *The Fabric of the Cosmos*

Near death experiences don't prove life after death, but they do suggest it is possible. In this chapter we examine the relevant findings of modern physics. Atheists invoke physics to allege that we are purely physical creatures made up entirely of atoms and molecules. The behavior of matter is lawful, and the laws are known to scientists today. Given the recognized qualities of matter, our chances for life after death are nil, since human bodies break down and disintegrate. Moreover, atheists say, the religious concept of eternity presumes the existence of exotic locales like heaven and hell. The problem is that we live in a physical universe, and these alternative realms seem to exist nowhere, or perhaps only in the imagination of the devout. Consequently it is simply ridiculous to think that humans can continue their lives beyond their deaths. The materialist view, atheists say, is supported by hard evidence in physics. I will show in this chapter that the atheist argument is false. Far from undermining the chances for life after death, modern physics undermines the premises of materialism. Moreover, new discoveries in physics provide scenarios under which matter can survive with different properties in realms other than our universe. Fantastic though it sounds, modern physics has legitimated the possibility of the afterlife.

Let's begin by asking what has to be true for life after death to occur. The afterlife, to count for something, requires some sort of enduring postmortem existence. As we have seen, there are two main conceptions of immortality: survival of the soul, or survival of the restored whole person. Right away we can see a formidable set of conditions that would have to be obtained for these conceptions to be viable. All these conditions go far beyond the reach of human experience. The Buddhist idea of rebirth in other worlds requires the existence of those worlds. In Christianity, heaven and hell are eternal realms not only beyond the universe, but also beyond space and time. So this conception needs realms or universes without space or time. The Abrahamic religions also affirm that after a final judgment we will all possess reconstituted bodies that are material in some sense and yet imperishable. For this to happen, matter must be capable of qualities that are radically different from any matter that we have ever experienced. What does modern physics say about all this? Are such things even possible, and does it make sense to believe in them?

Philosopher Bertrand Russell contemplated these questions and emphatically answered, "No." Russell argued that all our experience is bound up with space, time, and matter. We have tested laws that show us what matter is like and how it behaves. Since this is how we define "experience," it makes no sense to talk of experiences following death that are not like this. "All experience," Russell contended, "is likely to resemble the experience we know." And if we cannot even imagine our kind of experience continuing after death, well, then we have to say that there is no life after death.[2] Even in the mid-twentieth century, when Russell wrote these words, this was a very dubious argument. As Russell should surely have known, the preceding few decades had witnessed a revolution in science no less epochal than the Copernican revolution. This revolution, which represents the transition from classical to modern physics, involved a complete reformulation of the laws of space, time, and matter as they had previously been understood and as they still seem to us in everyday experience. I speak, of course, of Einstein's theories of special and general relativity, and of the laws of quantum mechanics. So surprising, unexpected, and even counterintuitive are these laws that the physicists who discovered them spent countless hours debating whether nature could actually behave this way. One of the leading figures in quantum physics, Niels Bohr, would sometimes tell his students, "The problem with your idea is not that it is crazy, but that it is not crazy enough." Bohr's point was that reality has shown itself stranger than science fiction; indeed it is sometimes more bizarre than anything we can imagine. This strange new world offers possibilities that weren't thought of before.

Let's begin our examination of modern physics with Einstein's revolutionary discoveries about space and time. Einstein developed his theory of special relativity by contemplating an intriguing question: Let's say you are riding alongside a light beam, traveling in your spaceship at half the speed of light. If you used a light meter to measure the speed of light from the spaceship, what would your light meter say? Actually there is no spaceship that can go that fast, but we can give an answer to the question based on experience. If I am in a train going at 60 miles per hour, and I travel alongside a train going at 120 miles an hour, obviously I would measure the speed of the other train at 60 miles an hour. Now since light travels at a known speed of 186,000 miles per second, we might expect that a spaceship going in the same direction at half that speed, 93,000 miles per second, would measure the speed of light at 93,000 miles per second. This is what experience would lead us to expect, but experience is wrong. The laws of physics, as stated in a famous set of equations by James Clerk Maxwell, require that light always and everywhere travels at the same speed. So you standing still on the ground, and I in my spaceship going at half the speed of light, would both measure light traveling at the same constant speed of 186,000 miles per second.

Now how can this be? Einstein's genius was to recognize that when things speed up so much, the rules of space and time must be different. This does not mean that light goes weird on us under certain conditions, but that the universal laws of space and time must be different from those understood since Newton. Einstein advanced the radical idea that space and time are not absolutes but are relative to each observer. Depending on how each of us is moving, you have your space and time, and I have mine. It is tempting to speculate that this must be the result of faulty measurement: our clocks must not be not properly synchronized, or maybe they don't work right when we are going really fast. But this is not the case at all. There is nothing wrong with the clocks. Relativity means that in different situations our clocks, working perfectly well and accurately measuring time, will nevertheless measure different times for you and for me. In fact, if you could travel at the speed of light, your clock would stop ticking, again not because clocks break down at high speeds, but because time itself would have stopped for you. Hard to believe, but we just have to get used to it.

Building on these counter intuitive ideas of special relativity, Einstein broadened them with his discovery of general relativity. Some people, mainly in the humanities and social sciences, have taken all this scientific talk about relativity to imply cultural and moral relativism: everything is somehow relative. But this is non-sense. For Einstein, everything is not relative. The speed of light is not relative but fixed. And while space and time are not absolute, something else is. Einstein called this spacetime. This concept has radical implications. Gravity, for instance, is the "curvature" of spacetime and can be measured using a non-Euclidean geometry, the new geometry of spacetime. We experience space in three dimensions and time in one dimension; Einstein brought them both together into the new four-dimensional entity of spacetime. The point of all this is that space and time are in reality very different from how we experience them; our normal experience is not a reliable guide to these phenomena under all conditions.

If Einstein's conclusions about relativity, spacetime, and curved gravity seem bizarre, the discoveries of quantum mechanics show that we ain't seen nothing yet. Einstein had examined the extremes of the macroscopic world—things that are very large or move very fast—while quantum physics deals with the world that is very, very small. And here, Dorothy, we find that we are not in Kansas anymore. Is light a wave or a particle? Actually, it's both. One might regard this as some peculiar characteristic of electromagnetic radiation that doesn't apply to solid stuff like matter. But as the French physicist Louis de Broglie showed in the early twenti-eth century, matter also has a dual nature. He asked, is matter a particle or a wave? Experiments have shown that matter, too, is both. And things get even stranger when we send two very tiny particles to opposite ends of the universe. We want to know whether the behavior of one particle over here can somehow affect the behavior of the other particle over there without anything being sent or communicated between the two particles. Astonishingly, experiments have shown that it can.[3] Moreover, the rules of quantum mechanics don't just apply to subatomic particles. They are measured at that level, but they apply to all matter and all energy, from stones to chairs to trees to your body to the entire planet Earth. The startling implication of quantum mechanics is that the behavior of matter is not completely governed by fixed laws and predictable outcomes.

Now it is time to see why even our four-dimensional world of space and time may be part of a larger multidimensional world, several of whose dimensions are hidden from us. This idea of multiple dimensions is part of a powerful new approach to physics called string theory. Many scientists regard string theory as the best prospect for unifying Einsteinian relativity with quantum mechanics. In its most famous form, so-called M theory, scientists tell us that reality is divided not into four but rather eleven dimensions, ten of space and one of time.[4] So where are the other dimensions? Well, string theorists say they are hidden dimensions, somehow positioned so that they are invisible and inaccessible to us. While we can't see them, they help to account for the things that we do see. As physicist Lisa Randall puts it, "We are in this three-dimensional flatland.... Our world is stuck in this three-dimensional universe, although extra dimensions exist. So we live on a three-dimensional slice of a higher-dimensional world."[5] H'm, multiple dimensions! I wonder what Bertrand Russell would have said about that.

I suspect Russell would be just as flabbergasted by recent discoveries in physics that show matter and energy to be radically different from the way that we ordinarily conceive them. Most of what we call "matter" is actually empty space. Press down on the table; you will feel it as solid and pushing back, but in fact there is virtually nothing there. How do physicists know this? By probing the structure of the atom. The nucleus of the atom contains almost its entire mass, and yet the nucleus is only a tiny fraction of the size of the atom. You can envision the nucleus as a baseball in the center of Wrigley Field, and that would give you some idea of the proportions we are talking about. Beyond the nucleus there is mostly nothing except for a few electrons. Probe the nucleus further and you'll find that it is made up of quarks. So the atom is a lot of empty space with a few quarks and electrons. But no one has seen a quark or an electron; their properties are inferred from complex experiments. Quarks and electrons are often pictured as tiny objects, but they are better understood as mathematical concepts or probability distributions. Bottom line: we think of matter as solid, massy stuff, but for the most part there's nothing there. How awkward it must be for materialists who assert that everything is made up of matter to admit this.

Even more remarkable than matter behaving weirdly is the existence of matter that we can't detect at all. Yes, this is spooky invisible matter, and I warn you that you may end up whistling the theme from the *Twilight Zone*. Most physicists today accept that most of the matter and energy in the universe are made up of so-called "dark matter" and "dark energy." Dark matter is inferred to exist because the galaxies hold together in clusters, yet the gravitational force of ordinary matter is not strong enough to make this happen. Therefore, scientists say, there has to be some other kind of matter that we don't see. Dark energy was "discovered" in a similar way. The universe is expanding at an accelerating pace. The primordial explosion called the Big Bang can account for the expansion, but it cannot account for the acceleration. To see why, imagine a big blast that sends a stone flying into the air.

However fast it goes, it can be expected over time to slow down. But what if it goes faster and faster? Well, some other force must be pushing it. Scientists say that "dark energy" is the force that is required to explain the increasing pace of the universe's expansion. So how much of all the matter and energy in the universe is dark matter and dark energy? The figure is an astounding 95 percent! Ordinary matter and energy make up a mere 5 percent of all the matter and energy in the universe. The vast majority of matter and energy in existence cannot be observed or detected with any instruments. Dark matter and energy have qualities that are radically different from any matter or energy that we can see and measure.[6]

These recent discoveries show us why the kind of experiential objections raised by Russell against life after death carry no weight at all. They are based on a kind of common sense which is itself based on the physics of earlier generations, and which has now been shown to be a completely unreliable guide to reality as a whole. Moreover, dark matter and dark energy pretty much render all generalizations about matter irrelevant. How can you make statements about something when you can only claim to understand 5 percent of it?

Now let's focus on two of the most important discoveries about the universe: that it had a specific beginning, and that it is fine-tuned for the existence of life. Religious thinkers have pointed to them as proof of God's existence. I explore these arguments in my book *What's So Great About Christianity*. But here I want to show how some of modern science's most fascinating conclusions arise from a desire to avoid the theological and supernatural implications of these discoveries. We will consider why scientists are so allergic to the idea of the supernatural. My focus here, however, will be on the proffered alternatives to divine creation. They have important implications for our investigation into life after death.

The real significance of the Big Bang is not the idea that the universe had a beginning. Yes, it does confirm what the writers of the Hebrew Bible asserted more than three thousand years ago. These writers stood against the claims of ancient religion, and also Hinduism and Buddhism, that the universe has been around forever. The Book of Genesis says no: God made the universe out of nothing. Initially there was nothing and then there was a universe. The writers of the Bible didn't make this claim on the basis of any scientific experiments. They basically said, "God told us." And in essence they were right. We have to score one for these prescient Jews.

An even more remarkable implication of the Big Bang, however, is that space and time had a beginning. This is not some controversial conjecture; it is the direct consequence of the Big Bang and is routinely taught in introductory physics courses in college. From the Big Bang we learn that the universe didn't begin *in* space and time; it began *with* space and time. "Before" our universe, there was no time. "Beyond" our universe, there is no space. The universe began with what scientists term an initial "singularity," a point in which all the mass in the universe was compressed into a state of infinite density.[7] Then—in perhaps the biggest ever case of Poof!—we got the universe, space, and time all together.

It's worth pausing to consider how counterintuitive this is. Imagine if someone tells you that space stops at that wall over there. Obviously that would be ridiculous; there is also space on the other side of the wall. Or imagine someone who says that time began a million years ago. That makes no sense either, since before that was 1.1 million years ago. Neither space nor time by itself suggests a beginning. In Newtonian physics, space is presumed to stretch without restriction in all directions, and time is presumed to stretch infinitely into the past and the future. The evidence of modern science is that these presumptions are wrong.

Space and time, it turns out, are properties of our universe. So, by the way, are the laws of physics. It's best to think of those laws as a kind of grammar of the universe. Just as grammar describes the operations of language, the laws of physics describe the operations of the objects in our universe. Can we have grammar without language? Of course not. Similarly we cannot have laws of physics without the universe whose operations those laws of physics describe.

But if space, time, and the laws of physics are local to our universe, any realms beyond our universe—if such realms exist—could operate independently of our conceptions of space and time, or without space and time altogether. Now suddenly we see the coherence of the Christian concept of eternity, a realm beyond space and time and the known laws of science. For centuries this idea remained the province of papal encyclicals and Sunday sermons, but it was entirely unsupported by anything in experience or in science. In the last few decades, as the Big Bang has become widely accepted in the scientific community, eternity has become a coherent concept. This is not to say that these other realms beyond space, time, and the laws of science exist, but it is to say that, within the understanding of modern physics, they are possible.

Atheists find the Big Bang troubling for a reason given by physicist Steven Weinberg: "The weight of scientific evidence has been in favor of an origin, giving some comfort to those who believe in supernatural creation."[8] Remarkably, however, it is not only atheists who are distressed; so are modern physicists. The scientists are working hard to come up with an explanation for the Big Bang that avoids having to posit a creator. Unlike the atheists, the scientists are not necessarily motivated by anti-religious prejudice. Rather, many of them are doing what science requires, which is to search for natural explanations for natural phenomena. This is the job description of science, just as it is the job description of base-ball umpires not to make the rules but to apply the rules in given situations. Taking up this challenge, Stephen Hawking has pro-posed a scenario in which the universe could have come into exis-tence without an original singularity. Hawking's proposal involves something called "imaginary time," a mathematical concept refer-ring to the square root of a negative number. Nothing in the world is known to operate in imaginary time. "In real time," Hawking concedes, "the universe has a beginning." Nor does Hawking have any empirical evidence for his alternative; he allows that it is, well, purely imaginary. Another more plausible idea is that the universe simply sprang into existence as the result of a quantum fluctuation. The only problem is that even quantum fluctuations occur in time and space. There was neither time nor space "prior" to the Big Bang. In fact, as we have seen, "before" the Big Bang there were no operating laws of physics, and this means that the laws of quantum fluctuations weren't operating either. In any case, even if Hawking's proposal or the quantum fluctuation proposal turns out to be right, it takes more than laws to make a universe. If you have the blueprint for a car, that doesn't by itself produce a car. As Hawking concedes, we still don't know what or who put the fire into the equations.[9]

Oh no, science may be forced to confront the G-word. And here's a bigger problem, created by the second spectacular finding of modern science that I mentioned earlier. This is the discovery of the fine-tuned universe, otherwise known as the Anthropic Principle. As John Barrow and Frank Tipler point out in their authoritative book *The Anthropic Cosmological Principle*, our universe operates according to a whole set of specific numeric val-ues, and our existence in the universe depends on those values being precisely what they are. This idea, surprising when it was first proposed, has now become conventional wisdom in physics.

"Life as we know it," writes physicist Steven Weinberg, "would be impossible if any one of several physical quantities had slightly different values." Weinberg points to a number called the cosmological constant, which represents the energy density of empty space. In order for life to exist, Weinberg writes, this number requires "incredible fine-tuning ... accurate to about 120 decimal places." Hawking gives another example in *A Brief History of Time*: "If the rate of expansion one second after the Big Bang had been smaller by even one part in a hundred thousand million million, the universe would have recollapsed before it ever reached its present size." Astronomer Martin Rees sums up the situation in *Just Six Numbers*: "The nature of our universe is remarkably sensitive to these numbers. If you imagine setting up a universe by adjusting six dials, then the tuning must be precise in order to yield a universe that could harbor life."[10]

The significance of the Anthropic Principle has not been lost on leading atheists who are desperate to avoid the obvious inference to a creator. Richard Dawkins, for example, concedes fine-tuning but argues that "it doesn't have to mean that the universe was deliberately made in order that we should exist. It need mean only that we are here, and we could not be in a universe that lacked the capacity of producing us." This in science is called a selection effect. The difficulty with Dawkins's argument is exposed by philosopher John Leslie. Leslie asks, suppose a massive terrorist bomb explodes a few feet away from you. Given the extremely low odds of survival, wouldn't you be amazed to find yourself still alive? How impressed would you be with Dawkins's contention that there was nothing to warrant surprise; obviously you had to have survived, because if you hadn't you wouldn't be here to discuss the subject. Leslie's point is that your survival under the circumstances remains highly improbable and in need of explanation.[11] Fine tuning is even less likely than the odds of me buying a lottery ticket in all fifty states and winning every time. How clueless do you have to be to fail to recognize that something very strange is going on here?

The scientists know this. Ever since the Anthropic Principle was first proposed by astronomer Brandon Carter more than half a century ago, scientsists have been trying to avoid its theistic implications. The Big Bang was bad enough but now this! Physicist Leonard Susskind writes in *The Cosmic Landscape* that the Anthropic Principle is a "huge embarrassment" and an idea "hated by most physicists." The reason, according to Susskind, is that the principle points to a creator. Susskind too will have none of this. Rejecting "the false comfort of a creationist myth," Susskind writes that "real science requires explanations that do not involve supernatural agents."[12] Here again, the scientists are following the atheists by going into God-avoidance mode. This is not easy to do, because the evidence seems strong that the universe is tailor-made for life on earth. So how to get around the obvious conclusion, explicitly stated by astronomer Fred Hoyle, that a "super-intellect must have monkeyed with the laws of physics"?[13]

Let's return to Leslie's example about the bomb. If a single bomb exploded a few feet away from a man and he survived, that would indeed be astonishing. But let's say we are in a war zone. Bombs are exploding everywhere, killing people. When the bombing stops, a man reports that he survived a nearby bomb blast. Would this be so surprising? No, because out of the many lethal blasts it's quite possible to have one or two near misses. Sure, this particular man is very fortunate to have survived. It could easily have been someone else. And in such situations there is a selection effect: obviously we're going to hear from the one guy who did survive because the others who didn't are dead. Yet the event of one man's survival is not by itself surprising. In fact, probability itself dictates that out of a very large number of tries, there are likely to be many hits and a few misses.

This reasoning shows that there is a way to give a natural explanation of the fine-tuned universe, and not surprisingly some leading scientists have enthusiastically advanced it. Atheists, too, have been right there with them. Here is the solution the scientists propose: multiple universes. Multiple universes are supposed to offer a way out of the fine-tuning problem. And the logic is incontrovertible: if there is an infinite number of universes, then it would not be surprising if some of them permitted life. Even very unlikely outcomes do occur with a very large sample size and a very large number of tries. And then we have to allow for the selection effect: if just one or two universes permit life, obviously we're going to hear from the folks in those universes. In the other universes there is no one to hear from.

Where, then, is the empirical data for multiple universes? Do we have a shred of scientific evidence that points to the existence of a single universe other than our own? No, we don't. And now we are in a really comic situation. Basically we are in a fine-tuned universe, which looks like it was tuned by a creator, but science can't really admit the obvious, and so scientists have to posit many universes that they have no evidence for in order to explain why we have the one fine-tuned universe that we do inhabit. In fact, if you want to see the lengths to which science is willing to go, consider some of the proposals concerning multiple universes. Keep in mind as you read that they are completely made up and entirely lacking in evidentiary support.

One proposal posits a single Multiverse with trillions of daughter universes, ours being one of them. Another postulates an infinity of universes, each with its own separate laws. One physicist, Lee Smolin, has proposed a kind of Darwinian natural selection among universes, in which the fittest universes survive and others perish. Perhaps the most mind-boggling proposal is that whenever anyone makes a decision, the universe splits into two. For example, if you decide to go to Bali instead of St. Tropez on vacation, presto! The universe breaks into two universes. In one of them, you go to Bali; in another, an identical duplicate of you heads for St. Tropez.[14] No, the physicists who say these things aren't on drugs. They concoct such scenarios because they are the only way to get God out of their equations. Cosmologist Bernard Carr spells out the dilemma, "If there is only one universe, you might have to have a fine-tuner. If you don't want God, you'd better have a multiverse."[15]

Actually, I don't think that all these backward somersaults really eliminate the God problem. Multiple universes could help to account for our universe, but one could still ask: Yes, but who created those universes? Physicist Stephen Barr writes that the God hypothesis is quite consistent with the possibility of multiple universes.[16] But that's not where I want to go with this. Rather, I want to ask, what are the expected characteristics of those universes? Recall what we learned earlier about the laws of physics: they apply only to our universe. What this means, Carl Sagan notes, is that if there are other universes, "there may be different laws of nature and different forms of matter in those universes." For example, time runs forward in our universe—scientists speak of the "arrow of time"—but maybe time flows differently, or not at all, in another universe. And since other universes don't operate by our laws of physics, Sagan concludes that "we may never be able to plumb their secrets, much less visit them."[17]

Many readers at this point may have given up entirely on multiple universes, but I cannot deny that they are possible, and I confess I find them fascinating. In particular, the notion of universes with their own laws is not only interesting, but has some scientific plausibility. It seems absurd because it contradicts all experience;

experience tells us, for example, that time only moves toward the future; it cannot move any other way. Let's recall, however, that our experience is a very unreliable guide in these matters. Our experience misleads us about the rules of our own universe at the level of the very fast and the very small; surely we cannot take it as authoritative when we are examining universes other than our own.

We began this chapter by asking about the alternative realms of the afterlife, realms beyond space and time and ordinary matter. Could these conceptions of life after death be justified only by appeals to faith in the supernatural, or might they be possible naturally within the scope of our best existing scientific theories? Now we are in a position to conclude that the proposed scenarios for life after death are entirely consistent with respectable science. In fact, they stand proudly alongside the most important and cutting-edge ideas and discoveries, from relativity to quantum mechanics to dark matter to multiple universes. Atheists can no longer ridicule as unscientific the idea of eternal places beyond time, or of invisible matter that isn't like our matter, or of realms that have their own laws and their own modes of being.

In this context, astronomer Owen Gingerich considers the Christian notion of heaven. "Christians have long envisioned a world with which they have no physical contact, not the heavens, but Heaven, the empyrean. It is a totally other place, without evil and suffering, and where the inhabitants never grow old. It thus cannot be our present world remodeled, for the remodeling would strike at the very heart of all our physical understanding. To suspend the rules of our cosmos would be tantamount to being in another universe."[18] Gingerich's point is that if our universe were the only one, then the Christian scheme of heaven would seem impossible, or only possible through an appeal to the miraculous. If there are multiple universes, however, it is quite conceivable that one of them operates precisely according to the guidelines of the

Christian empyrean. "It is not automatically absurd to imagine other places with other, unfamiliar physical laws." Heaven now becomes a real possibility under the existing diversity of laws that govern multiple universes. Certainly it is not contradicted by anything that we know about modern science. The beauty of Gingerich's scenario is that it exploits the scientific escape route. Many physicists started down this intellectual path to avoid having to encounter God. In the process, they mapped out plausible scenarios for afterlife realms like heaven and hell.

So what does modern physics have to say about the Eastern and Western conceptions of life after death? In Newton's time, the verdict was decidedly negative. Today, however, the situation is completely different. Modern physics has expanded our horizons and shown how life after death is possible within an existing framework of physical reality. The materialist objection has proven to be a dud; in fact, modern physics calls materialism itself into question. In a crucial area, and sometimes against the intentions of the scientists themselves, modern science has proven itself not the foe of religious believers, but an unexpected ally.

Chapter Six

UNDENIABLE TELEOLOGY

The Plot of Evolution

The laws of nature are rigged not only in favor of life, but also in favor of mind. Mind is written into the laws of nature in a fundamental way.[1]

—Paul Davies, *The Fifth Miracle*

Having seen that there is nothing in physics to contradict life after death, we now explore whether this is also true of biology. Actually, I want to go further: it would be important for our investigation of life after death if we could find in nature some sort of a plan. The principle of fine-tuning might suggest a plan in physics, but now we're looking for a plan in biology, a plan for life and ideally for human life. We're seeking not just any plan, but a plan that shows a progression from perishable things to imperishable things. Yes, a plan that develops from something like inert matter to something like consciousness or the mind would do very nicely. We haven't yet explored

91

attributes of consciousness and mind, but here it's sufficient to say that they are different from those of the body. If you doubt that, ask yourself: how much does your mind weigh? What are the dimensions—length, width, and height—of your consciousness? There are no answers to these questions, and that tells us that consciousness and the mind have qualities different from those of bodies. It's possible that these qualities enable consciousness and mind to survive even after bodies perish.

The idea of a plan is called teleology. We are speaking here of natural teleology, a plan that is built into nature. Historically two groups oppose natural teleology: creationists and atheists. For many creationists, who reject evolution as a godless system, it is pointless to look for a plan in nature because any such plan would obviously be God's plan, as revealed in the Bible. And since God, being omnipotent, doesn't need a plan, we may as well look directly for a divine hand in the universe. If some believers are lukewarm to natural teleology, however, atheists vehemently hate the idea. And it must be said that most biologists agree with them. Since Darwin, the idea of teleology has been largely out of bounds in mainstream biology.

The conventional wisdom among biologists is that we are purely material creatures whose existence, like that of all living things, is the consequence of evolution. And since evolution is driven by chance and natural selection, there is no question of teleology—man's appearance on the scene is pure accident. Biologist Jacques Monod writes in *Chance and Necessity* that "chance alone is at the source of every innovation, of all creation in the biosphere." In *Wonderful Life*, paleontologist Stephen Jay Gould argues that if we could "wind the tape of life to its origin ... and let the tape play again from this identical starting point, the replay will populate the earth ... with a radically different set of creatures. ... Humans are here by the luck of the draw." Given that our lives are the material products of a random process, biologist William Provine knows what to expect when this process is completed. "When we die, we die, and that's the end of us."[2]

Interestingly, Darwin, who did not believe in God, did believe in teleology. When biologist Asa Gray in 1863 congratulated Darwin for showing a pattern of development in nature that reflected "striking contributions to teleology," Darwin wrote back, "What you say about teleology pleases me especially, and I do not think anyone else has noticed the point." At the same time, an enthusiastic Karl Marx declared that Darwin had "dealt a death blow to teleology." Some of Darwin's champions, including Thomas Huxley, agreed. The apparent contradiction can be resolved by distinguishing between a supernatural or divine plan, which Darwin rejected, and a built-in pattern in nature, which Darwin approvingly recognized. In the *Descent of Man*, Darwin wrote that nature's harsh struggle was responsible for weeding out "lower animals" and producing "higher animals." Darwin viewed this upward progression as also applying to human groups. "At some future period, not very distant as measured by centuries, the civilized races of man will almost certainly exterminate and replace throughout the world the savage races."[3] This may sound like an ugly plan, but it certainly is a plan. We may not approve of Darwin's teleology, but we can easily recognize it as such.

How can we tell whether Darwin was right and whether nature operates according to a plan? One way, of course, is to look for a planner. In this case, however, the planner has chosen to be invisible. Even religious believers have to acknowledge that the planner must be inferred from the plan itself. There is nothing wrong in this: it would be like inferring the existence of Shakespeare from the plot of *Macbeth*. But Shakespeare obviously exists outside the play. If the plot is what we seek, we don't require Shakespeare to establish that *Macbeth* has one; the sequence of events in the play

speaks for itself. Similarly, if life on earth has a plan, we can figure this out even without postulating a divine architect as long as
we can find the blueprints. The blueprints are sufficient by themselves to disclose the plan. So we have to look at the evolution of
life on the planet very closely to see if it offers evidence of a consistent pattern or blueprint.

To see how my arguments for evolutionary teleology might go,
imagine that we are detectives trying to figure out if a killing on
the street is a crime of passion or a premeditated murder. The evidence clearly shows random shots being fired, following a chance
meeting between the shooter and his victim. Even so, premedita-
tion could easily be established in three ways. First, we could show
that the whole situation could never have developed were it not
for a set of preexisting conditions that suggest a plan. For
instance, it would surely be significant if the assailant flew in from
Las Vegas the previous day; if he hadn't, none of this would have
happened. Second, let's say we found out that before arriving at
the scene, the suspect went to a gun store and obtained a weapon.
Our suspicions of a plot would be strengthened. Third, let's say
the sequence of events showed that while this particular meeting
may have been a chance event, the situation was such that the suspect and his victim were very likely to run into each other one way
or another. By now we have a strong case for a plot, and it does
not depend on us knowing the identity of the suspect. We intended
to show that there was a plan, and the evidence shows that there
was.

Now let's consider evolution. I intend to reveal the underlying
plan in three separate ways. First, I will show that evolution itself
depends on pre-existing natural conditions on earth. Evolution
cannot account for these conditions, and yet in their absence there
would be no evolution on this planet. From our previous analogy,
this would be equivalent to flying in from Vegas. Second, the evo-

lutionary process itself requires its own discharging weapon, in this case, self-replicating cells. These cells didn't themselves evolve, but without them the multiple life forms on earth would not exist. Finally, there is an obvious and undeniable pattern in evolution itself which belies the whole random chance argument. Like the "accidental" meeting of the killer and his victim that was actually a likely outcome, the seemingly random outcomes of evolution have a built-in directionality, if not inevitability. I intend to demonstrate that, taken together, these three findings are sufficient to show not only that there is a plan, but also what the plan is and its significance for the prospect of an afterlife.

In the previous chapter we saw how fine-tuned the universe is for life in general; now let us see how fine-tuned the earth is for human life in particular. This is the Anthropic Principle as revealed not in physics, but in chemistry and biology. Biologist Lawrence Henderson first made this case in the early twentieth century in his classic *The Fitness of the Environment*. Henderson's argument has been strengthened even further with new data from the sciences by astronomer Stuart Ross Taylor and biochemist Michael Denton. I can only give a brief summary of their case. But even that should be enough to show that while we may no longer regard the earth as the physical center of the universe, we are entirely justified in considering it as the biological center.

We humans require for our survival a much narrower set of environmental conditions than do other life forms. Scientists have found bacteria and microorganisms that survive in the extreme conditions of boiling geysers and frigid glaciers. But our species requires more temperate climates. For example, humans can only live within a Fahrenheit temperature range that is between, say, 50 degrees below zero and 120 degrees above zero. Most of the earth, for most of the year, has a temperature that is squarely within this range. That's in large part because the sun happens to be eight light minutes away from us. If the sun were farther away, we'd freeze. Mars is farther away, and the temperature there plunges as low as 200 degrees below zero. Yet we don't want the sun much closer to us either, or we'd bake. Venus is about a third closer to the sun than earth, and surface temperatures there are around 800 degrees Fahrenheit. Even at its current distance, the sun dispatches ultraviolet radiation that would be lethal for us. Fortunately, earth's upper atmosphere has an ozone layer that shields us from ultraviolet radiation while letting through the sunlight that is necessary for photosynthesis and warmth and just getting around during the day.

The moon, by contrast, seems to serve mainly as a facilitator of mood and romance. But in fact the moon also performs a number of practical functions. We all know that the moon's gravity is largely responsible for the tides, but few people know that the moon is also responsible for keeping the earth's rotation axis at a constant 23-degree tilt. Without this tilt there would be no seasons on earth; even worse, there would be sharp fluctuations in climate that would imperil food production and make human life much more difficult. The planet Jupiter, meanwhile, seems irrelevant to our existence until we discover that its mammoth size and gravitational force have served over millions of years to attract and intercept innumerable comets and meteorites that could easily have crashed into earth and obliterated all traces of life. "If Jupiter did not exist or was smaller," Stuart Taylor writes, "the earth would be bombarded with comets . . . . It seems unlikely that our species or life itself could survive such disasters."[4] Thanks, Jupiter!

Most of us recognize that creatures like us cannot survive without water. In fact, our bodies are made up mostly of water. In his book *Nature's Destiny*, Michael Denton shows that the properties of water are just right for human existence. Like most other substances, water contracts when it cools. But just before water freezes, it stops contracting and starts expanding, until it becomes ice. Most solids expand when they are heated, but ice expands on freezing. Now this is a strange way for water to behave, at least by the standards of other substances in nature, and yet if water didn't have these properties the oceans and lakes would be completely and permanently frozen. During the winter, water would freeze into ice, the ice would sink down to the bottom of the lake or ocean, and this process would continue until the entire body of water turned into ice. Once this process was completed, it would be essentially irreversible because even summer heat could not reach the depths of a frozen ocean. Fortunately, we don't have to worry about any of this. As a consequence of water's unusual properties, what we observe instead is that ice once formed floats on the ocean surface, while the lower depths remain largely unaffected.

Water has a second property worth considering here; it has the highest specific heat of any liquid except ammonia. This means that it takes a lot of heat to raise the temperature of water. If water had a lower specific heat, then the oceans couldn't moderate the temperature as effectively on land during the winter and summer. Moreover, the water temperature in our bodies could rise dramatically when we exert ourselves. Think of what happens when your body temperature goes up just a couple of degrees; you now have a fever. Without the moderating effect of water, your body temperature could easily rise by 20 or 30 degrees Fahrenheit, which would kill you. Denton outlines the various properties of water—its latent heat, its solvency, its viscosity, its thermal conductivity, and so on—and shows that they are marvelously adaptive for a whole set of life-sustaining ends. He writes that "water is uniquely and ideally adapted to serve as the fluid medium for life on earth in not just one or many but every single one of its known physical and chemical characteristics."[5] Without these properties, we humans certainly wouldn't be here.

We've focused here on just a few conditions, namely, the sun's distance from earth, the moon's gravitational force, the ozone layer in the atmosphere, and the various properties of water. We could add many others, such as the oxygen levels in the atmosphere, the strength of the earth's magnetic field, the presence of plate tectonics, the critical role of carbon compounds, and so on. While some of these conditions have changed over time, none have evolved in the Darwinian sense. On the contrary, the general stability of most of these conditions has been absolutely necessary to make Darwinian evolution possible. So, contrary to atheist boasting, evolution cannot provide an ultimate explanation for life because evolution itself presupposes specific environmental conditions and specific entities with specific properties. Having briefly surveyed some of these external entities and environments, let's now consider evolution's biggest prerequisite: the living cell.

The cell, writes biologist Franklin Harold in *The Way of the Cell*, is like a factory. "Even the simplest cell is an exceedingly complex mixture containing thousands of different molecules." Cells display "levels of regularity and complexity that exceed by orders of magnitude" any non-living object found in nature. Indeed, the cell's molecular machinery works in an intricate way that suggests a unity of function or purpose. "Cell components as we know them are so thoroughly integrated that one can scarcely imagine how any one function could have arisen in the absence of others." All by themselves, cells "break down foodstuffs, extract energy, manufacture precursors, assemble constituents, note and execute genetic instructions and keep all this frantic activity coordinated."[6]

Not only does the cell function as a kind of manufacturing plant, it also functions as a digital software program of unrivaled complexity. In fact, the information in a single cell is equivalent to that found in several encyclopedias, and the processing power of the cell is comparable to that of any existing supercomputer. All of this occurs in an infinitesimal structure thousands of times tinier than a speck of dust. Just as remarkably, the cell has the capacity to copy itself. As biologists like to say, the dream of every cell is to become two cells. The greatest accomplishments of human civilization don't compare with the creative and technical ingenuity built into every living cell. Human technology is not up to building a basic hammer that can work by itself and make little hammers, let alone constructing a living creature like a bee or a housefly. Yet in nature, bees, houseflies, and countless other creatures function autonomously and reproduce themselves with prodigious fecundity.

So how did we get cells? This is another way of asking how life began. Darwin didn't even attempt to answer this question. He recognized that there was no way to explain the integrated functionality of the cell by appealing to evolution or natural selection. Evolution itself presumes and requires cells that come fully formed with the capacity for metabolism and self-replication. No reproduction, no natural selection. Clearly the basic template of life came fully formed when life first appeared on this earth around 4 billion years ago. Michael Shermer, in *Why Darwin Matters*, admits that evolution is not a theory about the origin of life but only "of how kinds can become other kinds."[7]

Richard Dawkins conveys the impression that science is close to solving the problem. "We still don't know exactly how natural selection began on earth."[8] What he means, of course, is not that he doesn't know "exactly" but that he doesn't have any idea. Of course lots of theories have been suggested, but to date none seems even remotely persuasive. Here, for instance, is a suggestion from a Dawkins ally, the British chemist Peter Atkins. "Molecules did not aim at reproduction: they stumbled upon it. Accretion of complexity reached a point where one molecule was so structured that the sequence of reactions it could undergo ... led by chance to the formation of a replacement. That molecule naturally had the same reproductive ability."[9] Yes, naturally. Wonder why I didn't think of that before.

Atkins, like Dawkins, is an atheist of an especially virulent sort, and I don't mean to suggest that all scientific accounts are of this caliber. Even so, the more refined ones don't fare much better. The reason for this is that virtually every proposal requires some chance combination of chemicals to come together to produce cells. But the earliest fossils show that life started on earth around 3.5 billion years ago, relatively soon after the earth itself formed, and almost immediately after the planetary hydrosphere had cooled enough to support life. So there isn't a whole lot of time for random chemical mixing to have produced so unlikely an out-come as complex, DNA-coded, living cells. Indeed, this would be on the order of suggesting that grains of sand on the seashore might combine by chance to form a five-storey building, complete with columns and corridors, or that various metal pieces might randomly come together to produce a functional automobile. Biol-ogist Francis Crick writes in *Life Itself*, "An honest man, armed with all the knowledge available to us now, could only state that in some sense the origin of life appears at the moment to be almost a miracle, so many are the conditions that would have had to get satisfied to get it along."[10]

Crick's own solution is that life may have been brought to earth by intelligent aliens from another planet or galaxy. Dawkins him-self echoed this possibility in an interview featured in Ben Stein's movie *Expelled*. The proposal sounds a little nutty, but its prob-lem is not that things could not possibly have happened that way. Meteorites and other extraterrestrial objects have struck the earth for billions of years, and one of them could have carried some form of life. But even if things happened like this and aliens indeed brought life to earth from Alpha Centauri, that would solve the problem of life on earth, but not the problem of life itself. How, after all, did we get intelligent aliens on Alpha Centauri? Was life imported there too? From where? Another galaxy?

The common feature of all scientific hypotheses to explain the origin of life is the avoidance of miracles and supernatural explanations. Once again, this is not because there are too many atheists in science. The reluctance to admit the role of the supernatural on the part of biologists, just as on the part of the physicists, is more a product of the *modus operandi* of science. We religious believers simply have to accept this, and I have no problem in doing so. The quest for natural explanations is not a rejection of God per se, but is merely an attempt to show what natural processes cause a natural phenomenon. This approach says nothing about God one way or the other, and only excludes God if we let it. For this reason I willingly go along with the scientists and even the atheists who say that life probably had a natural origin, and that one day science may find it.

Still, let's be clear about what this entails. The natural explanation for life requires that atoms and molecules somehow assemble into cells, and then cells somehow assemble into ants, elephants, and humans. If this is achieved without miracles or supernatural intervention, then the capacity to achieve these results must be built into matter itself. Some scientists call these "emergent" properties, but that is just another way of saying that material substances can combine in ways that generate new properties unobserved in any of the original materials. In *Reinventing the Sacred*, Stuart Kauffman speaks of "an emergent universe of ceaseless creativity" that functions according to physical laws but produces outcomes that were not evident or predictable.[11]

In this case, as Kauffman would fully recognize, we are not just talking about hydrogen and oxygen combining into water; we are talking about carbon, hydrogen, and other elements combining into living beings that breathe, move around, and reproduce. In other words, matter must not only have the potential to produce new properties; it must also have the hidden potential to come alive! Matter must, under propitious conditions, be able to manifest itself in forms as diverse as ants that can find their way home across an unmarked landscape using the sun as their compass; or birds that can in winter recover hundreds of food items stored in the fall; or bats that can navigate and find prey in the dark using a form of sound signals called echolocation. Evolution can show why these capacities were selected, but it cannot account for how matter came to possess such capacities in the first place.

It seems incredible that mere atoms and molecules can achieve such results without external assistance, but this is the direct implication of the naturalistic explanation. Modern science has shown how nature works as a network of intelligent systems. Viewed naïvely from the outside, matter seems deceptively inert and stupid; beneath the surface, however, there is an intelligible script. This script is written in the language of mathematics. Matter functions in a manner that is describable by physical and natural laws. No legislature passed these laws, and as far as we know no material object ever breaks one of them. Somehow the quarks and electrons all play by the rules. Somehow these elaborately structured and comprehensively coherent rules govern the diverse operations of nature. What we have here, in other words, is a very sophisticated architectural and informational blueprint that is imprinted in the nature of matter. Physicist Paul Davies calls this the "cosmic code."[12]

Davies raises the question: who devised the code? This is the intelligent design question, a subject of interminable controversy.

But here I want to focus on a different question: what does the code reveal? In other words, is there a fundamental pattern that is discoverable in the code and the way that it manifests itself in nature? Of course there is, and the pattern is right before our eyes. We can see it not only in the pathways that lead to evolution, but also in the pathway taken by evolution itself. Yet most biologists are blind to it, for the simple reason that they are in principle opposed to teleology. This opposition dates back to Darwin's day, and it is an historical product of Darwin's own hostility to divine teleology. Yet as we have seen, Darwin himself championed natural teleology. Perhaps because Social Darwinism took such an unpleasant turn, resulting in forced sterilizations and in some respects even promoting Nazism, the very idea of teleology got a bad name in biology.

The plan that we are talking about, however, has nothing to do with Social Darwinism and is clearly distinguishable from divine teleology. Consider this passage from physicist Freeman Dyson's *A Many-Colored Glass*, "Before the intricate ordered patterns of life, with trees and butterflies and birds and humans, grew to cover our planet, the earth's surface was a boring unstructured landscape of rock and sand. And before the grand ordered structure of galaxies and stars existed, the universe was a rather uniform and disordered collection of atoms. What we see ... is the universe growing visibly more ordered and more lively as it grows older."[13]

This is a scientific description, not theological speculation. Consequently, the only valid objection to it is the scientific claim that the apparent progression is misleading. This is precisely what several leading biologists say: evolution is based on random accident, not on any kind of teleology. This position has been argued by several leading biologists, from Stephen Jay Gould to John Maynard Smith. In *Full House*, Gould points out that the earliest forms of life were bacteria. "Now we have oak trees, praying mantises, hippopotamuses, and people." Even so, bacteria haven't been eliminated in the struggle for survival; indeed they outnumber all the other species put together. Somewhat wryly, Gould writes that we live in an "age of bacteria" confirmed by global "bacterial domination." Gould concedes that one can trace a continuous lineage from one creature to another, but this, he argues, does not constitute "progress" of any sort. After all, "Invertebrates didn't die or stop evolving after fishes appeared." And similarly "fishes didn't die out or stop evolving because one lineage . . . managed to colonize the land." Mammals emerged later than reptiles, but reptiles are still around. On this basis Gould argues that it is mere arrogance for man to place himself at the top of the evolutionary ladder; in reality, we are the products of a fortunate series of accidents, just like every other life form.[14]

Gould's position was conventional wisdom in biology until a decade ago, but now some of the world's leading biologists are challenging it. Two of them are worth naming: Christian de Duve, who won the Nobel Prize for his study of cells, and Simon Conway Morris, who is a leading expert on the fossils of the Burgess Shale. Duve and Morris argue that all the talk about randomness and contingency is overstated. In fact, they insist that evolution among several species has followed predictable pathways. Eyes, they contend, have evolved on separate evolutionary lines on multiple occasions. Placental and marsupial mammals are not closely related, and yet they have developed with similar structures and forms. Morris writes that "each group has independently navigated to the same evolutionary solution."[15]

Duve and Morris don't deny the factor of chance, but they insist chance itself follows a largely predetermined trajectory. Paradoxically, chance mutations and varied environments nevertheless lead to evolutionary convergence. To understand how this might happen, think of tossing a coin several times; each toss produces a random result of heads or tails, but with many tosses one can predict with a high degree of certainty roughly how many heads and tails will occur. Or think of water descending from a mountaintop—there are many available tracks for it to follow, but they all point in the same direction: downward. So too, Duve and Morris view evolution as finding varied pathways toward convergent solutions. The clear implication is that if we could re-run the tape of evolution, we'd find a similar pattern emerging all over again.

Duve in *Vital Dust* and Morris in *Life's Solution* offer a plethora of examples to illustrate their point. For our purposes, it's enough to note the obvious plan suggested by evolution. Even though bacteria are still around, it's hard to deny that as we move through historical time, with all its disruptions and cataclysms, evolution shows a progression from more simple creatures to more complicated ones. Morris writes, "What we do see through geological time is the emergence of more complex worlds."[16] Duve's book features a diagram of a Tree of Life that has eubacteria and archaebacteria at the root, then simple eukaryotes, then more complex multicellular organisms, then fungi and plants, then fishes, then reptiles, then mammals, and finally humans. Strikingly, Duve speaks of an "arrow of evolution" that makes this progression virtually inevitable. Duve speaks of biological history as proceeding through successive ages, from the "age of chemistry" to the "age of information" to the "age of the single cell" to the "age of multicellular organisms" and finally the "age of the mind."[17]

The age of the mind: an arresting concept. It reveals that evolution has gone beyond increasing complexity; it has provided the catalyst for a new order of being in the world. Through the human mind, the cosmic code has finally produced a mechanism

for its own detection. Surely this is a fact of fundamental significance. Operating with the code, not only has matter somehow
generated life, it has also generated awareness and understanding.
In other words, evolution has, through a kind of historical
inevitability, produced a special kind of being that can discover
evolution. In addition to ensuring survival, the universe has
ensured its own comprehension. Nature has unfolded a plan for
nature itself to become known. The progression of evolution on
earth shows an unmistakable trajectory from matter to mind.

The mind is our subject of exploration in the next two chapters. Here we are concerned with showing an undeniable teleology that opens up a tantalizing possibility. The teleology is the
progression, neither random nor accidental in its overall direction,
from the simple to the complex, and from physical matter to non-
physical mind. Now the mind may have arisen out of the material, but it is manifestly immaterial. Consequently minds have
attributes—such as thoughts and ideas—that are different from
those of material things. In particular, material things like bodies
are perishable but immaterial things like ideas aren't. In showing
that perishable matter has within itself the capacity to generate
imperishable ideas, nature provides a powerful clue to unique
creatures such as us who can read nature's laws and patterns. Just
as nature is part material and perishable, and part immaterial and
imperishable, so are we. And it is possible that our individual destiny might follow nature's destiny in moving from one type of
existence to another. We, like nature, might have a built-in progression from physical substance to non-physical ideas, from perishable matter to imperishable mind. The time will come when our
bodies will irretrievably break down, but it is possible, indeed suggested within the script of nature, that a part of us might outlast
these mortal coils.

Chapter Seven

THE SPIRITUAL BRAIN

Finding the Soul within the Body

You, your joys and sorrows, your memories and your ambition,
your sense of personal identity and free will, are in fact
no more than the behavior of a vast assembly of nerve cells
and their associated molecules.[1]

—Francis Crick, *The Astonishing Hypothesis*

Having seen an evolutionary transition from matter to mind, we now begin our probe of the mind. In this chapter and the next one, we examine the findings of psychology and brain science. Here we tackle reductive materialism at its core. The question we explore in this chapter is whether the mind can be reduced to the operations of the neurons in the brain. In other words, is the immaterial realm simply one branch of the physical realm? I will consider materialism's strongest arguments and show why they fall short. Our minds simply cannot be accounted for exclusively in terms of our neurons. In fact, we will discover here a deeper problem with science: it can comprehend objective things like neurons, but it cannot comprehend subjective things like thoughts.

Let's begin with a fundamental distinction. Human experience is of two kinds. We experience physical things, such as trains, lakes, pebbles, and staplers. We also experience mental things, such as thoughts, ideas, feelings, decisions, and awareness. The physical things are products of what may be called "outer" experience, the experience of the world out there. And in outer experience we find things that have mass, weight, and dimension and can also be observed and experienced by other people. When we turn our mind's eye within, however, we discover an entirely different world. This is the world of "inner" experience, and it is constantly churning with new thoughts and emotions. "I'm a little bored today. . . . I wonder if I should go to the movies. . . . Well, there's probably nothing worth watching; too bad they haven't done a sequel to *My Cousin Vinny*." These ideas and sentiments are exclusively ours—if we keep them to ourselves, they are invisible to others—and yet we experience them with the same force and directness that we experience the outside world.

The view that humans inhabit two separate and distinct realms—the physical and the mental—is called dualism. Plato was a dualist, although dualism's most famous champion is the philosopher René Descartes. Descartes argued that humans are an unlikely amalgam of material bodies and immaterial minds. Our bodies, he said, are physical things and function according to the laws of physics that govern all material objects. Our minds, however, are not physical and are therefore exempt from those laws. Cartesian dualism holds that we are our minds, but we possess physical bodies. Dualism reigned unchallenged in Western thought until recent times, and the founders of modern neuroscience, Charles Sherrington, Wilder Penfield, and John Eccles, were all dualists. Indeed, most people in the world are and have always been instinctive dualists, because dualism seems to accurately describe our everyday experience.

If dualism is true, then life after death is not only possible, but plausible. That's because our immaterial minds are distinct from our material bodies, and the mortal fate of our bodies in no way implies the death of our minds. Even more than this, the death of the body becomes a kind of emancipation for the mind, because during life our minds are inextricably bound to our bodies. Think of a vapor or gas that is sealed inside a bottle. Smash the bottle and you haven't smashed the vapor; you have released it. The fate of the vapor is not tied to the fate of the bottle as long as vapors and bottles are different kinds of stuff. Both Plato and Descartes advanced arguments along these lines for the immortality of the soul, and given their underlying assumption, their arguments are strong ones.

But is the assumption valid? Dualism has a problem that has caused most philosophers today to abandon it. We can see the problem by asking a simple question. How does a mind act upon a body? Specifically, how does a thought cause movement in a finger or a hand? At first glance these seem like monumentally stupid questions. Here, look, I think I'll wiggle my finger and see, I've done it. So that's how. But this is not an adequate explanation. You did it, so it must be possible, but how is it possible? Consider this: the world operates according to physical laws. It takes force acting upon an object to cause the object to move. Let's say that we have a billiard ball on a table. You can stand alongside the table, but no matter how hard you think and hope and wish, you cannot through sheer force of thought or will cause the billiard ball to move. "Move, ball, come on, you can do it!" Sorry, Charlie, and don't think that your psychic aunt can do any better. Moving the ball requires the impact or force of another physical object, say another billiard ball.

Descartes recognized that the billiard ball problem posed a formidable challenge to dualism. He understood the persuasive power of the scientific view of the world, according to which everything operates in accordance with fixed laws. Descartes conceded that if human minds regularly act on bodies in the way that common experience suggests, then there must be some physical link between the two that mediates this interaction. Descartes speculated that the pineal gland in the brain is the place where immaterial minds and material bodies have their secret rendezvous. Today we know that Descartes was wrong about the function of the pineal gland. But the bigger problem for philosophers is not where minds and bodies interact; it's how they possibly could. Minds are like ghosts and bodies are like walls; so how can a ghost move a wall when it is in the nature of ghosts to go through walls?

The apparent insolubility of this problem has led most contemporary philosophers and scientists to embrace materialism, which is the main alternative to dualism. Neuroscientist V. S. Ramachandran states the materialist view bluntly: "All the richness of our mental life—all our feelings, our emotions, our thoughts, our ambitions, our love lives, our religious sentiments, and even what each of us regards as his or her own intimate private self—is simply the activity of these little specks of jelly in our heads, in our brains. There is nothing else."[2] It should be obvious from this description that materialism poses a serious obstacle to the possibility of life after death. No one denies that when we die the physical stuff that we are made of disintegrates. So if the death of the body is the death of us, then there is no way that any part of us can outlive our bodies. From the materialist point of view, there is nothing left to continue on.

As we have seen, atheists find materialism to be a very congenial philosophy, but many brain scientists do also. Atheists like it because, as philosopher Owen Flanagan puts it, if humans are material beings through and through, then "there is no longer any place for the soul to hide," and we are "without prospects for an afterlife." In philosopher Paul Churchland's words, we are nothing more than "suitably organized matter," or as Carl Sagan put it, "a particularly complex arrangement of atoms, and not some breath of divinity."[3] But neuroscientists, too, tend to be materialists, in part because of the nature of their jobs. They study the physical brain, and yet they also want to understand the nonphysical mind. If the mind can be reduced to the workings of the brain, then neuroscience has the chance to master both. Consequently, neuroscientists routinely seek to reduce mental transactions to physical transactions, and this of course is the essence of reductive materialism. The prevailing attitude in the field was expressed by a nineteenth-century Dutch physiologist who famously said that "the brain secretes thoughts as the kidney secretes urine."

Thoughts, however, cannot be collected in a vial like urine, nor can they be weighed, measured, or sniffed. Scientists recognize this, but they are attempting to trace a direct causal relationship between the brain and the mind. This has been going on for more than a century now. In the nineteenth century, language centers were identified in what we now call Broca's area and Wernicke's area. Around the same time, scientists also discovered that damage to one side of the visual cortex results in blindness on the opposite side. In recent decades, aided by technologies such as PET scans and resonance imaging (fMRI), scientists can monitor brain activity in real time while specific mental functions are being performed. The prefrontal cortex is the thought center of the brain where ideas are generated and decisions are processed. The limbic system is now recognized as the emotional center of the brain, with a structure called the amygdala serving as its entrance point or gateway. The hippocampus is in charge of memory, and damage to the hippocampus prevents the transfer of information from short-term memory to long-term memory.

Neuroscientists such as Ramachandran and Antonio Damasio have written best-selling books showing that damage to particular parts of the brain can produce exotic ailments such as Cotard's syndrome, in which patients who are alive nevertheless insist they are dead; or Capgras delusion, in which patients believe that their family members are actually impostors; or pain asymbolia, in which pain is now experienced as amusing, and the patient actually responds to blows with giggling and laughter. Ramachandran has successfully treated patients who feel pain in "phantom limbs"; these are cases in which the limb has been amputated but the patient experiences pain as if the limb were still there. Ramachandran says in these cases, the brain is still receiving pain signals from the surrounding area and somehow interprets them as coming from the missing limb. So the limb hurts even though the patient knows it isn't there. Using mirrors and illusions, Ramachandran makes the patient "see" that the missing limb is back and can now be treated; remarkably, the pain goes away. All of these instances would seem to show, with a wealth of corroborative detail, that our mental life reduces to physical transactions, and that the brain produces the mind in the same way that the stomach produces digestion.[4]

No one would dispute the actual and potential medical benefit of this research, but the general point it makes is not exactly new. In fact, it has been known since classical antiquity. The Greek philosopher Lucretius in the first century BC pointed out that the mind weakens as the body ages, and that disease and injury can disrupt mental functioning. The physician Hippocrates recognized that brain deterioration destroys sanity. Galen discovered that lesions and cuts in the brains of animals can produce both blindness in some cases and paralysis in others. The findings of modern science are confirmed in the experience of everyone who feels tired after a big meal, or who can't think clearly after imbibing several glasses of wine. Without being a neuroscientist and without performing any experiments, I offer the bold prediction that if you remove a man's brain, he will be unable to think.

All of this clearly shows that brain states and mental experience are correlated. It also shows that mental experience is in many cases dependent on brain states. But does it show that brain states cause mental states? To answer this question, let's consider a series of analogies. If I want to listen to Mozart, I need my radio or CD player. Without them, I couldn't listen to a particular Mozart symphony. Destroy the player, and Mozart stops playing. But does it follow that the radio or CD player causes the music itself? Of course not. These are merely instruments for the expression of sound waves. If the player goes dead, the music can easily be heard on another one, or perhaps in an open-air concert. Similarly, software programs require computer hardware, but it doesn't follow that the hardware somehow causes the programs. The programs are actually distinct from the hardware, but they utilize the hardware to function. Moreover, a given software program may be compatible with several types of computer hardware. Fine paintbrushes are required to produce detailed paintings; damage the brush and the painting will be ruined; still, paintings are not caused by fine brushes, but by artists who use fine brushes. Olympic tracks are highly correlated with sprints and hurdles; without tracks, you can't have these sprints and hurdles; even so, tracks are not the cause of these events, but merely the venue where they occur.

I could go on. We cannot assume that brain states cause mental activity, because there is a second possibility. This is that the brain is a kind of gateway or receiver for the mind. William James, the founder of modern psychology, explored this idea in an important essay titled "Human Immortality." James argued that the brain serves not as a causal but as a transmission vehicle for the mind. Just as a prism or a lens allows light to pass, just as the keys of an organ channel wind and air in various ways, so the brain is an apparatus for channeling feelings and thoughts. Sure, James conceded, when the human brain dies, those feelings and thoughts, and their underlying consciousness, can no longer be expressed in that way. "But the sphere of being that supplied the consciousness would still be intact." In other words, James hypothesized the existence of a cosmic immaterial realm that, even while we are alive, supplies consciousness through our brains. When our brains die, this consciousness goes on, not because it enjoys life after death, but because it never died in the first place. We perish, but our consciousness endures, perhaps all by itself, perhaps in other instantiations. There is nothing in science, James argued, that undermines this alternative possibility.[5]

How do we adjudicate between these two possibilities? Let's begin by considering the materialist argument in its full force, and right away we confront a serious problem, comparable to the one faced by dualism. The problem for dualism was to explain how immaterial minds can move material objects. This was indeed a problem, but now materialism poses a challenge no less daunting. How do material objects, such as neurons with their associated apparatus of axons and dendrites, cause immaterial outcomes such as sensations, emotions, and ideas? Descartes is much ridiculed today for his idea that a mere gland in the brain provides the mysterious link between such radically distinct domains as the material and the mental. But materialism now seems to contend that the brain itself serves as a kind of pineal gland. Materialism suggests that the brain manufactures the entire repertoire of our mental lives. But how do we know this is true? How can we be confident that the brain is a manufacturing plant for the mind and not merely a gateway or transmission belt?

Materialists have produced a frantic flurry of proposals, each of them attempting to reduce mental states to brain states. One idea is that the mind is an epiphenomenon of the brain. This means that the mind is a kind of shadow that rides alongside the brain. The brain produces the mind in the same way that fire produces smoke. But epiphenomenalism holds that just as shadows and smoke are accompaniments that don't really do anything, neither do minds. This view was quite popular in the nineteenth century—Thomas Huxley was one of its advocates—but today it has few defenders and has fallen into disrepute. The main objection to it is an evolutionary one. If minds are shadows that don't do anything, why do we have minds? Evolution equips us with bodily functions in order to survive and thrive in the world, so it seems more than unlikely that evolution would provide mental functions if they were irrelevant.

A second position, called eliminative materialism, asserts that the entire mental world does not in fact exist. There are no mental states, only physical states. This seems a little crazy, but it has been energetically defended by neuroscientists Paul and Patricia Churchland.[6] The Churchlands argue that we imagine ourselves to have thoughts and feelings, but let's recall that our forbears imagined themselves to be standing on a stationary earth. The Churchlands call such beliefs "folk psychology." Science has now shown, they say, that the earth isn't stationary even though we feel it to be so. Similarly, they contend, science will one day show that our entire mental world is an illusion. They anticipate that a much better scientific description is coming of what's really going on.

I have never found such promissory materialism—"one day science will figure everything out"—very convincing. But that aside, eliminative materialism is a theory that undermines itself. After all, if all thoughts and beliefs are illusions, what does this say about the Churchlands' thoughts and beliefs? Even the analogy between a stationary earth and having a belief or a sensation is a flawed one. I may be wrong about the sun and the world around me, but I cannot be wrong about having an itch. Have you ever gone, "That really itches! No, wait a minute. I was wrong about that. That didn't itch at all." Each of us is an unimpeachable expert on our own itches. Even a scientific description of an itch would only account for what makes me scratch; it wouldn't show an itch itself to be illusory. And if it did, well, most people's reaction would be to tell the Churchlands, "To heck with your science!" As Samuel Johnson once said to Boswell, "If a man should give me arguments that I do not see, though I could not answer them, should I believe that I do not see?"[7] My conclusion is that, without being aware of it, the Churchlands have lost their minds. This, however, should not disturb them very much since they don't believe they have minds in the first place.

We now come to the two most widely held contemporary theories of materialism. The first, bluntly expressed by philosopher Daniel Dennett, is that "the mind . . . is the brain."[8] This is perhaps the classic case of reductive materialism, and it is called identity theory. Two things—brain and mind—appear different but are in fact identical. Consider this: light isn't caused by electromagnetic waves; light simply is an electromagnetic wave. The morning star and the evening star appear different, and were for centuries considered two different stars, but now we know that they are two different names for the same star. By the same token, mental states simply are brain states. Identity theory is an improvement over the theories earlier mentioned in that it doesn't seek to diminish or do away with mental events. It fully concedes them, suggesting only that they are nothing more than physical events. Your thoughts about Edna Millay's poem or your feelings about a succulent dinner aren't caused by particular brain states; they just are those brain states. Your pain isn't produced by the firing of C-fibers in your brain; it actually is the firing of the C-fibers. Psychology is the same thing as neurobiology.

Identity theory can be tested by a famous principle suggested by the mathematician and philosopher Gottfried Leibniz. The principle—called the identity of indiscernibles—simply says that if two things are identical, then everything that is true of the first will also be true of the second. This seems obvious: if a man shows up at your door claiming to be Barack Obama, then everything that is true of Obama should be true of that man. If you can find things that are true of Obama that are not true of the man, then clearly the man is not Obama. Let's apply the test to find out if mental states really are the same thing as brain states. Now imagine that I have the mental state of thinking that George Washington was our greatest president. Identity theory says this mental state is the same thing as my current brain state. But my mental state is private, known only to me. By contrast, my brain state is not private; it can be observed and registered on a brain scan. Moreover, my mental state cannot be spatially located—the materialist can say it's in my head, but he can never find it there—while my brain state certainly can be found. In addition, my mental states are about something; they intentionally refer to something external to themselves. This is not true of brain states. Brain states aren't "about" anything; they just are. Finally, we are in a sense infallible about mental states; we can't really be wrong about them. If I think Washington was the greatest president, I may be mistaken about the facts, but I cannot be mistaken about my own thoughts. But of course I could easily be mistaken about my brain states, which are better known to a neuroscientist than they are to me. Thus we have identified four things—privacy, absence of specific location, intentionality, and infallibility—that are true of mental states but not of brain states. Identity theory fails the Leibniz test.

Further, consider my friend Harry Crocker, who also thinks that George Washington was our greatest president. Since mental states are held to be brain states, this means that when Harry and I have the same thought, we must be in the identical brain state. In fact it follows that everyone who thinks that Washington was the greatest president must share the same specific brain state. But neuroscience itself tells us that this is absurd, because human brains are wired differently from one person to another. Or imagine that my nephew Warren comes over to my house for dinner, bringing a female date who is actually a Martian. (This is not a real situation, but close.) My dog, taking an instant disliking to the Martian, bites her on the leg. She screams, "Oh my God! I'm in pain. Get me to a hospital." If Warren and I are identity theorists, we will say, "Actually, you are not in pain. Pain is the firing of C-fibers, and since you don't have any C-fibers, clearly you can't be in pain." Such a response would not only be cruel, but also foolish. It certainly seems possible that pain can be felt by creatures, whether earthly or Martian, who have brain states different from our own.

The problems facing identity theory, as well as other attempts to reduce the mental to the physical, have led many materialists to their last refuge, which is called functionalism. Indeed one sees in the work of the Churchlands and Dennett a drift toward functionalist arguments. The functionalists want to get away from problematic efforts to completely dismiss mental states or to equate the mental and the physical. So they content themselves with giving a descriptive account of the mental. Their argument is that mental states can be apprehended by their functional purposes. A mousetrap, for instance, is defined by what it does; it is any kind of device that catches mice. A fist is not something added to the hand; it is a particular configuration of the hand that serves certain purposes. By the same token, functionalists argue that a mental state like "being in love" can best be understood in terms of its behavioral results: writing poems, sending flowers, and so on. Note that functionalism is also a form of reductive materialism: the mental is reduced to its physical consequences. So here is the functionalist credo: the mind is what it makes you do.

The obvious defect of this theory is that it clearly falls short in explaining mental states. The feeling of being in love is hardly explained by love's behavior, because even if we subtract the behavior the feeling remains, and it seems churlish at best to say, "Well, you are obviously not in love because you aren't writing poems and you haven't sent flowers." We all know that there is something that it feels like to be in love, just as there is something it feels like to watch a sunset by the ocean, or to smell fresh-brewed coffee. Philosophers call such sensations "qualia," a term that refers to the inner quality of an experience on the part of the one who is having it.

It seems that no amount of scientific and functional analysis can capture this inner quality, this "what it is like" to have a particular sensation. To demonstrate this point, philosopher Thomas Nagel wrote a famous essay in 1974 with the provocative title, "What Is It Like to Be a Bat?"[9] This may seem a damning indictment of how philosophers spend their time, but Nagel wasn't sitting around thinking, "What would it be like for me, Thomas Nagel, to be a bat? I wonder how I'd feel if I had wings and could navigate by echolocation." Rather, he was asking what it was like for a bat to do those things; what it was like for a bat to be a bat. Nagel's point was that there is something that it is like to be human, or male, or a dog; by the same token, there must also be something that it is like to be a bat. But however much we learn about bat physiology and bat brains and echolocation, can we ever fully understand what it's like to be a bat? Nagel doesn't think we can, and if he's right, it's a big problem for any theory of the mind that equates physiology with mental states. Here is a case where a full understanding of the bat's brain physiology still gives virtually no indication of the contents of the bat's mental state.

In 1986, philosopher Frank Jackson broadened Nagel's argument into a refutation not only of functionalism, but of any attempt to explain mental states purely in physical terms. In what has come to be called the "Mary problem," Jackson envisioned a brilliant scientist named Mary who is locked in a black and white room from which she investigates the world by way of a black and white television monitor. As a specialist in the neurophysiology of vision, Mary knows everything there is to know about color. She understands how different wavelengths of light stimulate the retina, and how those are channeled to the visual areas in the brain, resulting in such statements as "the sky is blue" and "tomatoes are red." Now here's Jackson's question. Suppose Mary finally gets a color TV monitor or is released from her black and white room into the outside world. Will Mary learn something that she didn't know before? Jackson says she obviously would. She would for the first time know what it's like to see the blue sky or red tomatoes. These experiences would teach her something about color that all her previous knowledge could not.[10]

The materialist philosopher Daniel Dennett knows where this is going, and he has attempted to dispute Jackson's interpretation, arguing that if Mary really knew everything about color, including, as Dennett puts it, "ten billion word treatises" on the subject, then she actually would know what it was like to see the blue sky and red tomatoes. Dennett knows this is counterintuitive, but he contends that intuitions are not always our best guide.[11] I agree with him on that, but on balance I have to go with Jackson here.

It defies not only intuition but also reason to say that Mary wouldn't, on being liberated from her black and white world, discover something new. Her extrinsic information about color would now be supplemented by intrinsic knowledge. But if this is so, then it is hard to resist Jackson's conclusion that all attempts to reduce mental states to physical states must fail, because Mary had all the pertinent data, and yet her prior knowledge was incomplete.

Despite its problems, functionalism remains the leading approach in neuroscience, and this is in large part because of computers. Computers, like mousetraps, are defined by their function, by what they do. Functionalists have equated what minds do with what computers do, saying in effect that the mind is a kind of carbon-based computer. In *How the Mind Works*, cognitive psychologist Steven Pinker gives this argument an evolutionary thrust. He writes that since "thinking is a kind of computation," we can understand the mind as "a system of organs of computation designed by natural selection to solve the kind of problems our ancestors faced in their foraging way of life."[12] But if this is so, then it should be possible, at least in principle, to build computers that can do what minds do. It should be possible for computers, like minds, to think. So the functionalist claim is that computers do not merely resemble minds in certain respects; they actually are minds. If this is true, it would be a dramatic confirmation of materialism because a material object, namely a computer, would be shown to be the functional equivalent of an immaterial mind.

Oddly enough, materialism in this form does not completely outlaw the possibility of life after death. Think of the mind as a software program instantiated in the hardware frame of the body. There is no reason that the software should not be able to find new instantiations when the hardware breaks down. Indeed, futurists argue that humans might be able to pursue immortality on earth by, in effect, "downloading" their minds onto computers, updating them with new software, and continuing that way indefinitely. Physicist Frank Tipler makes a provocative case along these lines in his book *The Physics of Immortality*. Even so, functionalism does imply that minds are nothing more than computer programs. Certainly it is hard, in this framework, to envision life after death in any of the mainstream philosophical and religious scenarios earlier outlined in this book. So we need to investigate with an open mind the claim that computers, like people, are intelligent and can think.

This premise that computers can think intelligently guides a whole school of artificial intelligence called "strong AI." This group seemed to be stunningly vindicated in 1997 when the IBM computer Deep Blue managed a 2–1 victory with three draws against world chess champion Garry Kasparov. Computers seem on their way to passing the Turing Test, the famous test proposed by Alan Turing to figure out if a computer is really thinking. Turing asked: How do we know when human beings are thinking intelligently? We talk to them. Well, Turing suggested, let's try that with the computer. He proposed that we place a human being and a computer in a room out of sight of a group of interrogators. The interrogators would pose questions to which the human and the computer would respond indirectly, say through a teletype machine. Turing wrote that if the interrogators could not from the answers distinguish the human and the computer, then the computer could reasonably be said to be thinking in precisely the same way that humans do. Turing of course recognized that in thinking this way the computer would not be conscious in the way that humans are. But, he argued, so what? When we deal with other people, we can't be sure that they are conscious either. We don't see their inner consciousness; we only perceive what they say and do. Turing concluded that, for computers as for humans, intelligent thinking could be evaluated through a functional test.[13]

No computer as of today can pass the Turing test. But this is not really decisive, because computers are getting faster and better, and I suspect that we will be handing Turing medals to computers in the not-too-distant future. Still, would a computer that passed the Turing test actually be thinking? Philosopher John Searle says we can answer this question by entering his Chinese Room to play a very interesting game. The Chinese room has a single individual in it—let's say you—and a whole bunch of cards with Chinese ideograms on them. Now assume you don't know any Chinese; you couldn't even recognize Chinese if you saw it. Someone passes you new cards on which you find more incomprehensible ideograms. Fortunately, you have a code book, written in English, which gives you detailed instructions of the sort: when you see this kind of symbol, correlated with that kind of symbol, look for the following set of symbols. Based on the rules of the book, you respond to the cards you are given by handing back cards from your pile. Unknown to you, the people who are conducting the experiment call their cards "questions" and your cards "answers." In effect, you are taking and answering questions based on a detailed code of rules. Let's say you get so good at this that after a while you can give answers indistinguishable from those of native Chinese speakers. In short, you pass the Turing test. Even so, Searle asks: do you understand Chinese? Obviously not! Even though you are giving the correct answers, you still don't know a word of Chinese! But what you have just done, Searle writes, is exactly what computers do. They merely manipulate symbols. Consequently, they may give appropriate responses, but they have no comprehension of what they are doing. Computers cannot understand anything, not even the programs they run on.[14]

In his analysis, Searle distinguishes between syntax and semantics. Syntax refers to grammar or functional rules, while semantics refers to content and meaning. Searle's point is that a computer can do syntax but it cannot do semantics. Of course we use computers, as we use slide rules and calculators, to perform mental tasks. But calculators don't think mathematically; we think mathematically with the aid of calculators. Similarly computers don't think or understand anything; we do with the help of the symbol manipulation that computers perform. Even this symbol manipulation has been programmed into the computer by human beings. If a computer seems intelligent, that's no surprise, because human intelligence created it. In this sense, a computer didn't defeat Kasparov; he was actually playing against a whole group of programmers and chess grandmasters whose collective acumen was further enhanced by a machine that could perform millions of symbol manipulations every second. The power of Searle's argument is in its long reach. It doesn't merely show the limits of this or that computer. It shows that no computer, no matter how complex, will ever be able to think. And with the failure of computers to think we see that functionalism loses its best argument and much of its appeal.

Where does this leave us? We began this chapter by asking whether there are two kinds of things, the mental and the material, or just material things. We identified the problem with dualism—how can mental states cause material states?—and provisionally abandoned it to consider the alternative, materialism. We have seen however, that even the most sophisticated attempts to uphold materialism have failed. In fact, the materialist argument has boomeranged on itself: it began by trying to reduce the mind to the brain, and it only succeeded in showing its own limitations. Science itself has shown its "blind spot": its operations are confined to a restricted domain. Modern science operates according to what biologist Jacques Monod called the "postulate of objectivity."[15] This means that science is limited to the study of material things that are objective and publicly observable. But by Monod's criterion, the subjective domain, which is the domain of the mental, remains largely outside the reach of science. Consequently, the scientific argument against the soul collapses, because the soul is not material or objective. The scientific quest for the soul becomes another pathetic case of looking for the car keys only where the light is good. Does this make life after death reasonable? Not yet, but it does make it plausible. The best evidence of contemporary neuroscience is that the mind cannot be equated with the brain, and while deterioration of the brain might impede the operation of the mind, the two are separate, which makes it possible that our immaterial minds and consciousness might survive the termination of our physical frames.

Chapter Eight

THE IMMATERIAL SELF

How Consciousness Can Survive Death

Brains are automatic, rule-governed, determined devices, while people
are personally responsible agents, free to make their own decisions.[1]

—Michael Gazzaniga, *The Ethical Brain*

Now it is time to ask whether life after death is not
merely possible but actually reasonable. We will first
reconsider dualism and see how it has made a remarkable scientific comeback. We still won't be able to fully understand how minds interact with bodies, but we do have the
beginning of an answer to what seemed like an impossible problem. Dualism, as we have seen, enables life after death, but it
doesn't confirm it. That's because minds may still depend on
earthly bodies for their instantiation, in the same way that software programs require certain types of hardware in order to run.
Therefore, we need to explore whether there are parts of our

mental lives that are completely independent of bodies, indeed independent of the laws of nature that govern material bodies. If this is so, then minds can be expected to live on past death either by themselves, as Socrates believed, or in union with some greater mind, as the Hindus and Buddhists hold, or in different kinds of bodies, as the Abrahamic religions affirm. By examining two crucial features of mental life—consciousness and free will—I will show aspects of our minds that are irreducible to material bodies or to the laws that describe them. The argument, if sound, will provide my first proof of life after death.

Dualism as a philosophy is supported by everyday experience. We speak as if our mind is distinct from our physical brain. We say, "Greg made up his mind to go to the concert," not "Greg's brain circuitry caused him to go to the concert." Descartes, however, did not merely rely on intuition to make his case for dualism. He advanced several arguments, and here I focus on one that oddly enough does not appear in Descartes' writings but was attributed to him by the philosopher Antoine Arnaud. Descartes' argument goes as follows. If the mind is independent of the body, then we should be able to assert something about the mind that is not true of the body. (Recall Leibniz's law of indiscernibles, which is a formal statement of this principle.) But what might this be? We are all familiar with Descartes' famous principle of doubt. Descartes raised the question of how we can know anything for sure. How can we know that our senses aren't deceiving us? How can we know that our life is not lived as a dream? I think I see some palm trees over there, but how do I know it's not a mirage? I think I have a brain, but how do I know that an evil demon hasn't manipulated the evidence to deceive me about this?

From these doubts themselves, Descartes realized there is one thing beyond doubt. It is that Descartes doubted, and that means he must be thinking. Even if Descartes was deluded—even if he thought wrong—he was still thinking about something. This is Descartes' famous *Cogito*: "I think, therefore I am." But if Descartes knows he is thinking, then he can be certain of something concerning the mind that he cannot be certain of concerning the brain. Consequently, the mind must be distinct from the brain.

Despite the ingenuity of Descartes' argument, it hasn't persuaded most philosophers. Even so, in recent years, dualism is gaining new respect and new adherents among both philosophers and scientists. Although most philosophers still consider themselves materialists, several of them have realized that the supposedly invincible objection to dualism—how can the mind move the body?—is not so strong after all. The objection relied on the authority of science: since the world is governed by physical laws, how can immaterial thoughts, beliefs, and desires produce physical outcomes? But of course the objective approach of science cannot even reach the subjective, immaterial realm of thoughts, beliefs, and desires. It is only the material world that is governed by physical laws. So the failure of science to explain how the immaterial realm affects the material realm is more of a commentary on the limited scope of science.

Dualism's comeback in science is largely due to recent developments in medicine. They show that mental activity not only affects physical outcomes, but also that it reconstitutes and reprograms the neurons in our brains. In *The Mind and the Brain*, physician Jeffrey Schwartz describes his work with patients suffering from obsessive compulsive disorder (OCD). OCD is a disorder of brain chemistry that provokes patients to such behavior as washing their hands every few minutes, or running away from spiders that are allegedly after them, or waking up every morning in fear that they will find excrement on their face. For decades, OCD was treated with drugs supplemented with behavioral techniques aimed at

forcing the patient to "face the fear." Thus if you had a paranoid
fear of spiders or of being covered in excrement, part of your
treatment would involve having spiders crawl all over you, or having your face shoved in a mound of manure.

These treatments had only modest success rates. Not surprisingly, many patients found them humiliating and refused to follow them at all. Schwartz developed what he terms "cognitive
therapy," in which patients learn to refocus their minds away from
the compulsion and to redirect their thoughts and actions to some
activity, ideally something more pleasant. Not only did these treatments show impressive results, Schwartz also found that they had
the effect of re-wiring the patient's brain so that he no longer experienced the paranoid and destructive OCD urges. In other words,
patients weren't just modifying their obsessive thoughts, they were
actually modifying their disordered brains.[2]

In a sense, Schwartz's discovery that minds can change brains
was not new. Doctors have known for a long time that mental
stress can contribute to high blood pressure. Moreover, as neuroscientist Mario Beauregard points out, one of the most widely
attested phenomena in medicine is the placebo effect, in which
doctors who administer placebos or sugar pills find their patients
get better. The patients think they are getting medicine, and their
bodies respond as if they actually did. A less-known but comple-
mentary phenomenon is the "nocebo effect," which refers to what
happens to a person's body when he believes it has been infected
or contaminated. Patients who are convinced that a particular pill
will give them nausea report feeling nauseous, even though the pill
they have taken is not the one they expected but actually a sugar
pill. Similarly medical students sometimes display symptoms of
the diseases they are studying, and patients who believe they are
going to contract new ailments in the hospital do exhibit those
particular symptoms.[3]

All of this shows that mind can and does affect the body. But until recently the neural wiring of the brain was thought to develop in infancy and from that point to be largely immutable. Schwartz's research showed that brain systems can be re-wired, and sometimes re-wire themselves, in response to mental activity. Nor is Schwartz alone; neuroscientist Fred Gage has shown that in response to environmental influences, brains regularly produce new neurons and activate dormant ones. Today the phenomenon of "neuroplasticity" is widely accepted in the medical community and is producing a new range of therapies. In *The Brain That Changes Itself*, psychiatrist Norman Doidge shows how leading doctors are using cognitive treatments to help children to overcome learning disabilities, senior citizens to improve their memories, and even paralyzed stroke victims to move and speak again. In each case, Doidge reports, the treatment trains the brain to refocus or "change the channel" so that a new part of the brain takes over from a disabled or dysfunctional part. Doidge found that as a result of such treatment one stroke victim showed "massive brain reorganization," in which the right hemisphere of the brain took over from the left. Even mental tasks normally performed with the patient's left brain were now executed through the right brain.[4] This is not the brain reprogramming itself, but the mind of the patient, with help from others, reprogramming the brain.

The implications of this research are profound not only for dualism, but also for life after death. If your mind is independent enough to create changes in your body and your brain, it seems reasonable enough to suppose that it can survive the dissolution of your body and your brain. Schwartz, in conjunction with physicist Henry Stapp, has advanced a bold theory addressing the big question of how mental states can influence physical states. Schwartz and Stapp say the answer lies in one of the most important discoveries of quantum physics, the finding that subatomic particles only reveal their precise position when we measure them. In the Copenhagen interpretation of quantum mechanics, formulated by Niels Bohr, Werner Heisenberg, and others, the problem is not the inadequacy of measurement; rather, particles have no location until we measure them. It is the act of measurement that actually compels the particle to move from an indeterminate or "superposition" state into a determinate and actual state. In other words, as physicists Paul Davies and John Gribbin write, "The observer seems to play a central role in fixing the nature of reality at the quantum level."[5]

Now this may seem very surprising, and it is. But over nearly a century the surprise has worn off a little, and physicists today say there is no point in asking how such things can be; put them down to quantum weirdness and accept that this is the way that the world seems to operate. (Quantum physics is regarded as the most widely-tested theory in science and has yielded a plethora of new technologies including transistors, lasers, brain imaging machines, and semiconductors.) Schwartz and Stapp argue that cognitive therapies exploit quantum physics by teaching patients to focus their consciousness on productive mental states rather than dysfunctional mental states. In effect, consciousness operates at the quantum level to create a physical force that increases the probability of realizing preferred states. In this way the patient can, through trained volition, fix the position of subatomic particles and thus transform the physical reality within the brain.[6]

Schwartz and Stapp's theory is controversial and requires further testing and analysis, but at least it provides a plausible starting point for understanding how mental states could affect physical states. Besides, in identifying consciousness as the "missing link," Schwartz and Stapp have raised a critical subject for our purposes. If there is life after death, it is presumably consciousness that survives, either all by itself or somehow reunited with a new kind of body. Yet consciousness is probably the most perplexing subject in science. This seems ironic because to the ordinary person nothing could be more obvious than consciousness. Consciousness is something we all have and know more directly than we know anything else. We are on such intimate terms with consciousness that we happily relinquish it every night, only to get it back again in the morning. Even so, from a scientific point of view, consciousness seems inexplicable. As far as consciousness goes, cognitive psychologist Steven Pinker writes, "We have no scientific explanation." Philosopher David Chalmers adds, "We know consciousness far more intimately than we know the rest of the world, but we understand the rest of the world far better than we understand consciousness."[7]

Consciousness was recognized by the philosopher John Locke both as a great mystery and as somehow central to personal identity. In his *Essay Concerning Human Understanding*, Locke famously asks us to consider a Prince and a Cobbler who retire for the night. While they are sleeping, the contents of their respective consciousnesses are exchanged. The question Locke asks is, when each wakes up in the morning, will he be the same man? To this Locke answers yes. Both Prince and Cobbler have their same physical bodies. But then Locke asks, are they still the same person? Here he answers no, because each will now have the memories and inner consciousness of the other. So in this respect the Prince has become the Cobbler and the Cobbler has become the Prince. Personal identity, Locke insists, is not identity of substance but identity of consciousness.[8]

Today philosophers discuss consciousness less in terms of princes and cobblers and more in terms of zombies. Yes, we are talking about those strange creatures in Hollywood movies such as *Night of the Living Dead*. Zombies are like people, but they have no inner life. They act like humans but lack consciousness.

Hollywood is enthusiastic about zombies and has produced a range of zombie characters, but the philosophers' zombie is much more interesting. This zombie is a material replica of a person. Its physical structure matches that of the human being in every respect, organ for organ and cell for cell. Not only that, but this zombie acts in a manner indistinguishable from its human counterpart. It eats chili dogs, cheers at baseball games, and snores at night. Admittedly no one has ever constructed such a zombie, but the philosophical question is: is such a creature possible? If so, we have a being physically and functionally identical to humans and yet lacking the human attribute of consciousness. The unavoidable implication is that human consciousness has no physical explanation.

The zombie example is purely theoretical, but the fact is that consciousness has been studied for decades now and has so far eluded all scientific explanation. Put consciousness under the microscope and you see, well, nothing. Ask a brain scientist whether you are conscious, and he has no way of knowing unless you tell him. There are no physical facts or scientific laws that lead to the prediction or expectation that there should be consciousness. Consciousness has no good evolutionary explanation either. Psychologist Nicholas Humphrey argues in *Consciousness Regained* that consciousness helps us to be aware of how others are thinking so that we can better cooperate with them in getting food and avoiding predators.[9] But millions of other creatures, from amoebas to bacteria to insects, manage to survive without, as far as we can tell, being conscious. In fact, consciousness is not required for any of the activities that humans need for survival and reproduction. Consciousness doesn't even help us with figuring out other people, because we have no access to their consciousness, only to our own. You might say we can respond to them through their actions, but this is precisely the point; we can collaborate with others in the absence of anyone having inner states. This is what ants seem to do, and if they can do it, we presumably can. Odd though it seems, biologists tell us we could live our lives exactly the way we do and yet have no inner consciousness at all.

Philosopher Daniel Dennett has made perhaps the best sustained effort to explain consciousness from a scientific point of view. In *Consciousness Explained*, Dennett's considered conclusion is that consciousness does not exist. If this seems like a philosopher's joke, it isn't. I've debated Dennett twice, and the man does not even attempt humor. Dennett discusses at length the philosophers' zombie and concludes that no such creatures are possible. But then he refutes himself by declaring that the inner life of humans is illusory so that we actually are zombies. Recognizing how ludicrous this sounds, Dennett argues for what he calls the "intentional stance." Although people aren't conscious and consequently have no feelings or intentions, we should treat them as if they were conscious and did have feelings and intentions.[10]

But of course if we are really zombies, why pretend otherwise? Why not dispense with the wannabe stance, be happy with who we are, and announce "Zombie Pride Week"? Besides, the very act of pretending clearly suggests that we do have goals and intentions, and this means that we are conscious after all. Far from reducing the absurdity of his position, Dennett has heightened it. The real question is why an intelligent man like Dennett would say this. The reason is that Dennett is committed to a materialist, objective view about the world, and consciousness is irreducibly immaterial and subjective. Since Dennett holds that everything in the world is material and objective, he is ideologically compelled to deny the existence of immaterial, subjective things. Therefore, even though he knows perfectly well that he is not a zombie, he must nevertheless with a straight face declare that he is.

The problem for materialism, and for modern science more generally, is that human subjectivity is a fact of nature no less than planets, rocks, and trees. And subjective consciousness is a very special kind of fact because it is the fact in which all the other facts are located. Consciousness is our window to reality, not only the reality of the world out there but also the reality of our own existence. We recognize consciousness because we are unmistakably aware of it and because through it we are aware of everything else. There is no way to understand consciousness completely from the outside because consciousness operates entirely on the inside. Psychological attempts to "get around" or "get behind" consciousness are equally hopeless; I would give far better odds to the chance of seeing through the back of my head.

Philosopher David Chalmers argues that we should simply accept consciousness, as we accept matter and energy, as an irreducible element of reality.[11] In this case, consciousness would be like magnetism or energy or gravity, something with its own laws and properties that could not be explained in terms of something else. Moreover dualism would be fully vindicated, because we would have to recognize both physical things and mental things as distinct realities in the world. But whether Chalmers is right or not, we are quite safe in concluding that consciousness lies beyond all known scientific laws and explanations. The startling conclusion is that a central feature of our identity and humanity operates outside the recognized physical laws of nature. One of those laws is, of course, mortality for all living bodies. But consciousness is not part of the body. Nor is consciousness "in" the body in the same way that nerves or neurons are. Consciousness merely comes with the body and operates through the body. The body serves as a kind of receiver and transmitter for consciousness, not its author or manufacturer. What William James termed the "transmissive" doctrine of consciousness, in which our individual consciousness is derived from and dependent on an outer cosmic source, now seems far more plausible than the materialist alternative.

It might seem so far from our discussion that consciousness is unique. But there is another fundamental aspect of our humanity that also seems to defy scientific explanation and to operate without regard to known physical laws. This is our free will. We have the same direct experience of free will as we do of being conscious, but there is an important difference. Consciousness describes my experience of being aware; therefore, I cannot be wrong about being conscious. If I think I am conscious, I am conscious. But this does not apply to free will. That's because I no more have access to what's going on inside my brain than I have access to what's going on in my digestive or circulatory system. So my behavior could be mechanistically caused by my inner brain states without my knowledge. I would still believe I had free will, but I would be mistaken. I would be a live puppet feeling very pleased about my performance but actually dancing to the tune of the mighty neurons.

Leading materialist thinkers argue that this is precisely what happens. Philosopher Owen Flanagan writes, "That the will seems to be self-initiating is an understandable illusion. We are not in touch with most of the causal factors that contribute to who we are and to what we do." In *The Illusion of Conscious Will*, psychologist Daniel Wegner says we should not confuse our phenomenal will with our empirical will. The phenomenal will is the feeling of free will, a kind of "authorship emotion." But empirical will is the will as actually caused by antecedent forces that are invisible to us. "Each of our actions is really the culmination of an intricate set of physical and mental processes." Biologist E. O. Wilson writes that "the hidden preparation of mental activity gives the illusion of free will."[12]

The argument against free will comes not from biology or neuroscience but from physics. In fact, it was stated two centuries ago by the French physicist Pierre Laplace. He wrote that if we could know the position and momentum of every particle in the universe, we could in principle predict all future events. Not only that, but we could reason our way back and know everything that happened in the past. Laplace's point wasn't that someone could actually figure all this out, but that everything that happens is determined by the laws of nature. We are part of nature and made up of atoms and molecules just as everything else. Consequently, our thoughts and actions are caused by forces that have operated since the origin of the universe. There is no room in this picture for free will.

In recent years, the work of psychologist Benjamin Libet has provided experimental support for the proposition that we are not as free as we like to believe. Libet asked volunteers to perform simple actions, such as flicking their wrists or moving their fingers, and to record precisely when they made a decision to act. He also used an electroencephalograph (EEG) to monitor brain activity during these transactions. Libet wanted to find out which came first, the decision to act or the relevant neural firings in the brain. Remarkably, Libet found that the brain lights up a few milliseconds before the reported decision to act. What Libet calls the brain's "readiness potential" precedes conscious will. In later experiments Libet found that for some kinds of decisions the brain goes into action a full half-second before conscious decision-making. Libet does not interpret his results as invalidating free will. Rather, he says the brain proposes a course of action, and the will has a brief interval to exercise its veto power. Even so, Libet gives free will a limited jurisdiction. His work seems to suggest that free will is overrated—the main part of our behavior is predetermined by brain states that go into motion a measurable time prior to the will getting into the act.[13]

Consider the far-reaching implications if we didn't possess free will. In the absence of free will, none of the decisions that you believe you made in your life were actually made by you. Remember that girl you asked to the prom? Or how you turned down law school to write short stories in Spain? Or just earlier today when you told your spouse how much you loved her? Or what you have been planning do in retirement? Sorry to break this to you, Pierre, but none of those choices were yours to make. If there is no free will, the entire literature of Western civilization becomes incomprehensible, because every single character from Oedipus to Gatsby was merely acting in response to uncontrolled brain states. Sure, the Greeks believed in fate shaping our final destiny, but this did not amount to a denial of choice or responsibility: Oedipus' fate is only tragic because he resolves no matter what the cost to pursue the question of who his parents are.

Without free will, even collective decisions become involuntary. If there is no free will, the American founders didn't choose to adopt a Constitution in Philadelphia. Nor did Americans elect Barack Obama president. Nor is there anything we can decide to do to improve Social Security or Medicare. If free will is an illusion, then there are no good deeds or bad deeds because no one has any choice in the matter. Hitler cannot be blamed for killing the Jews. Abraham Lincoln labored under a delusion when he declared slavery wrong, and the Southern slaveholders were not guilty of buying and selling human beings. In opposing segregation Martin Luther King was merely conforming to his brain states at the time. Even heinous criminals cannot be held responsible for their actions because even premeditated murder is beyond the control of those who have no choice. Not only our criminal

justice system but our systems of self-government, economic contracts, civil liberties, education, marriage and social reform all presume free citizens making free choices; if that presumption is
wrong, all those institutions are a sham and the whole structure
of modern society should be revised.

Some materialist thinkers like Daniel Dennett and Owen Flanagan realize the preposterous pass to which they have led us. Consequently, there is a movement among philosophers to show that
free will can be compatible with the materialist view of the
world.[14] Of course this isn't free will as classically conceived. But
it is an attempt to reassure people that they still do enjoy a measure of autonomy and choice in the world. Now how in a materialist framework is this possible? Here philosophers distinguish
between two kinds of free will. The first kind is called libertarian
freedom. This means your action is free if it is undetermined, if
you could have chosen to do otherwise. Freedom of this sort does
not preclude other factors influencing your choice, but the choice
remains yours to make. Dennett and Flanagan say that this kind
of freedom is impossible in a lawful universe. The other kind of
freedom is absence of constraint. This means you have free choice
if nothing is standing in your way. Sure, your actions may be
caused or determined by brain states beyond your control, but
these are your brain states; as long as no external impediment prevents you from acting, you are free in at least this qualified sense.
So Dennett and Flanagan say you can choose what you will,
although you cannot will what you will.

Does this attempt to reconcile choice and determinism really
work? I don't think it does. Imagine a remote controlled car which
moves around a room without anything coming in its way. It
seems absurd to say that the car has free will simply because there
is nothing for it to crash into; in reality, the car is being entirely
manipulated by the guy with the switch. Even at the human level,

it is preposterous to suggest that sleepwalkers or heroin addicts are exercising free choice merely because no one is holding them back. If a mad neuroscientist manipulates your brain and programs you to go on an assassination mission, are you acting freely? Of course not. This is not what we mean by freedom at all. If we humans are to have autonomy and self-determination, then we require a kind of freedom that goes beyond the absence of external constraint.

Let's return to Laplace's argument. While Laplace based his rejection of free will on the Newtonian world view, that paradigm has been rendered obsolete by modern physics. As many physicists have noted, quantum physics, in particular quantum uncertainty, does create room for free will. The logic of this is very simple. If the universe is deterministic, there can be no free will; the universe is not deterministic, so there can be. As physicist Stephen Barr concludes, "There is nothing in the laws of nature... as they exist today which is logically incompatible with free will."[15]

The case for free will becomes even stronger when we realize that all attempts to refute it are incoherent. In his book *Possible Worlds*, the evolutionist J. B. S. Haldane wrote, "If my mental processes are determined wholly by the motions of atoms in my brain, I have no reason to suppose that my beliefs are true... and hence I have no reason for supposing my brain to be composed of atoms."[16] The man who denies free will is the intellectual equivalent of the man who drives himself off a cliff.

One of the first thinkers to see the full depths of the problem was philosopher Immanuel Kant. In his book *Religion within the Limits of Reason Alone*, Kant produced a proof of free will that is surprising both in its originality and direction. Kant argued that morality is an indispensable part of being human. No human culture has existed without morality. In fact, no normal human being can altogether reject morality; people who are unable to distinguish right from wrong are considered psychopaths. Treat any materialist with inhumane brutality—not as a person but as an object—and he will indignantly protest, "You shouldn't have done that!" Try as he might, the materialist cannot completely get away from morality. Morality is an incontrovertible fact in the world no less real than any other fact.

Even materialists who deny free will typically think and act in moral terms, just like everyone else. Earlier in this chapter I cited biologist E. O. Wilson insisting that free will is an illusion. So let's see how consistent Wilson is on the issue by consulting one of his recent books, *The Creation*. An ethical argument for environmentalism, Wilson's book is subtitled, "An Appeal to Save Life on Earth." In it, Wilson frets that "we took a wrong turn" when we began to abuse the environment but "it is not too late for us to come around." He offers "time tested suggestions for parents and teachers." He provides what he terms a "compelling moral argument . . . for saving the creation." He recommends that we "be careful with pesticides." It would be, he warns, a "serious mistake to let even one species . . . go extinct." He insists that "the time to act . . . is now."[17] Now ask yourself, how much of this is intelligible if we cannot choose freely? The answer is, none of it. Everything Wilson writes about the environment—our responsibility for the problem, his case for preservation, his recommendations for policy and behavior, our ability to endorse and follow his advice—only makes sense if we possess free will.

It's easy to dismiss Wilson as a hypocrite who is writing in bad faith, but Kant takes us in a much more interesting direction. The fact that we cannot get away from morality is significant, he argues, because morality by its very nature presumes free choice. Wilson's own analysis illustrates the point. The fact that Wilson thinks we ought to do certain things implies that there is a way for us to do them. And this is true of all moral counsel of any sort.

If you say to someone, "You should have told the truth," it follows that the person could have told the truth. If you tell your child, "You must not cheat on the exam," that means that your child can refrain from cheating. When it comes to morality, Kant writes, "We ought to conform to it; consequently we must be able to do so." When we become upset or indignant at someone for acting a certain way, our behavior only makes sense if they could have acted in some other way. Even regret and remorse as emotions are incomprehensible to us in the absence of freedom; we are sorry for what we did; therefore it has to be the case that we could have done otherwise. Yet if all this is true, then humans do, at least on some occasions and to some degree, have free choice.

Now we can turn Laplace's argument on its head. Laplace argued that since we are merely material objects in a lawful universe, free will is impossible. His argument, like all arguments, depends on the strength of its premise. If the premise is valid and the reasoning is sound, the conclusion inevitably follows. Conversely, if the conclusion is false, then the premise must also be false. We have seen with Kant's help that free will exists, and therefore it follows that we are not merely material objects in a lawful universe. The startling conclusion is that there is a part of human nature that transcendentally operates outside the physical laws of governing material things.[18]

What are the implications of this discovery? We started this discussion by asking whether there are aspects of our humanity that are not subject to the material restrictions of this world. We have now found two central features of human nature—consciousness and free will—that are irreducible to matter and appear to be independent from it. Even more remarkable, consciousness and free will have no natural explanation and seem to function beyond the bounds of physical law. Things that are defined by physical law, such as human bodies and human brains, are perishable or

destructible. Consciousness and free will, unbound by those constraints, are not. Moreover, consciousness and free will are the
defining features of the human soul, which requires awareness and
choice in order to discriminate between right and wrong. The
implication is that whatever happens to our bodies and brains
after death, our souls live on.

Chapter Nine

OUT OF THIS WORLD

Philosophy Discovers the Afterlife

The sense of the world must lie outside the world.[1]

—Ludwig Wittgenstein, *Tractatus Logico-Philosophicus*

We saw in the previous chapter, drawing on the brain sciences, how consciousness and free will seem to operate outside of physical laws, making life after death a reasonable prospect. Now I will offer a second, completely independent proof of the afterlife. I will also draw on some of the most powerful philosophy of the last two centuries to locate an eternal realm that is beyond physical law. Both Western and Eastern doctrines of immortality require such a realm, and I will vindicate their expectation that there is one. Then I will show that there is an eternal part of us that inhabits this realm now and will rejoin it when we die. Remarkably our guide will be the atheist philosopher Arthur Schopenhauer. Just as Virgil was Dante's spiritual guide through the circles of hell, purgatory, and heaven, Schopenhauer will be our intellectual guide, showing us the way to the world beyond science and beyond our senses.

Schopenhauer was the first great philosopher of the West to be an outspoken atheist. Others, such as Hobbes, Hume, and Diderot rejected God but never explicitly admitted to atheism. Schopenhauer, in a sense, began a tradition of public atheism that continued in philosophy through Nietzsche, Heidegger, and Sartre. Born into one of the richest families in Germany, Schopenhauer developed a personality that was both colorful and eccentric. He was a pessimist in outlook, an elitist and misogynist in social relations, and a reactionary in politics. When a group of revolutionaries attempted to storm the German parliament in September 1848, Schopenhauer offered soldiers the use of his apartment so they could shoot at the mob through his window. He even provided his opera glasses, so the snipers could take better aim. Although Schopenhauer was hugely influenced by Immanuel Kant, fortunately he did not adopt Kant's somnolent style of writing; rather, his prose is clear, vigorous, and enlivened with memorable turns of phrase.

Schopenhauer was not recognized as a great philosopher during his lifetime. Rather, the best-known German thinker in the early nineteenth century was G. W. F. Hegel, whom Schopenhauer considered a poseur and a "common charlatan." Schopenhauer was baffled that people read Hegel when, as he put it, they could hear the same sort of talk in a lunatic asylum. Convinced that Hegel was corrupting a whole generation, Schopenhauer went to Berlin and announced he would lecture at the university at the same time as Hegel. The strategy misfired; no one came to Schopenhauer's events. Schopenhauer also submitted an essay on the origins of morality for a contest held by the Royal Danish Society of Scientific Studies. Even though his was the only entry, the judges refused to give him the award, in part because of his scornful dismissal of Hegel and other thinkers. Schopenhauer then published his essay with a caption below the title, "*Not* Awarded a Prize by the Royal Danish Society of Scientific Studies."[2]

Despite these antics, Schopenhauer was a man of immense philosophical and moral seriousness, and today he is recognized as one of the world's most powerful and original thinkers. Over the last 150 years, he has had an enormous impact both in Continental philosophy and in the arts, influencing among others Friedrich Nietzsche, Richard Wagner, and Ludwig Wittgenstein. His reputation rests on a single book, *The World as Will and Idea*, published in 1819. Of this book, Schopenhauer said that it provides "the real solution of the enigma of the world."[3] All educated people should read this book; in Germany, all educated people have. It is a genuine classic, equal to anything by Locke, and in an entirely different league than Machiavelli's *The Prince* or Rousseau's *Social Contract*. Even so, in America and Britain Schopenhauer is not known or taught as widely as Machiavelli, Locke, or Rousseau. Nor, for that matter, is Kant, even though Kant is widely acknowledged to be the greatest of modern philosophers, rivaled in the ancient world only by Plato and Aristotle. The main reason for this neglect, I believe, is that Schopenhauer and Kant pose a mortal threat to a whole set of premises and assumptions that lie behind Anglo-American philosophy and science. Schopenhauer and Kant probe these "self-evident" premises to reveal, beneath them, even more fundamental premises that cannot withstand rational scrutiny. If Schopenhauer and Kant are right, then much of educated opinion in today's West is constructed on quicksand and requires a completely new foundation in order to be considered rational.

For nearly two hundred years, the prevailing outlook of elites in Britain and America has been empirical realism. Empirical realism is a close cousin of materialism, and most materialists are also empirical realists, as are most leading scientists. Empirical realism is based on a premise that many people would consider obvious: there is a real world out there, and we come to know it objectively through our senses and through scientific testing and observation. This is sometimes called the correspondence theory of truth, because it presumes a correspondence between the real world and our sensory and intellectual apprehension of that world. Of course sophisticated people recognize that our senses can sometimes mislead us, as in the cases of mirages and sticks that look bent in water. But making allowance for these exceptions, and with appropriate qualifications, they still believe that our minds and our senses can give us a reliable and accurate picture of reality.

Empirical realism is clearly evident in the statements of leading atheists. Biologist Francis Crick writes that "there is an outside world . . . largely independent of our observing it," and science can find out about it "by using our senses and the operations of our brain." Physicist Steven Weinberg writes that "the working philosophy of most scientists is that there is an objective reality" that scientific techniques can investigate. Biologist E. O. Wilson says that modern progress is based on the Enlightenment principles of "objective truth based on scientific understanding." So obvious does he consider the truth of empirical realism that Wilson writes, "If empiricism is disproved . . . the discovery would be quite simply the most consequential in human history."[4]

So let's rise to the occasion by disproving empirical realism, or at least showing its irrational foundation. Here are a few empirical observations. "Look! There's the Empire State Building." "Hey, could you pass the butter?" "Just take in that ocean air." Now let's ask where exactly these objects are located. Do I see the Empire State Building somewhere out there? Actually no; I see it in my own mind. It would be ridiculous to suggest that the actual

Empire State Building has physically entered my head; rather, my mind forms a picture or representation of the Empire State Building. And that's what I really have in my mind, not the building itself but an image of it. And of course the same is true of the butter, the ocean, the air, and every other sensory apprehension.

Now we ask a question that lies at the heart of modern Western philosophy: How do we know that the representations of reality that we have in our minds correspond to reality itself? This is a deep question, because it goes against the inborn realism that we are born with, educated into, and that is the operating premise of daily life as well as modern science. Virtually all of us, whether we are scientists or scholars or ordinary folk, simply assume that reality must be pretty much the way that it presents itself to our mind and our senses. This unquestioned realism is the common-sense foundation for bringing our understanding into line with reality. It takes reflection of a particularly refined kind to wonder how this is possible.

The first thinker to grasp the full force of the question was the English philosopher George Berkeley. Berkeley, too, is not well known, and probably for the same reason as Kant and Schopenhauer. Admittedly the town of Berkeley, California, is named after him, and so is the University of California at Berkeley. But even most students at UC Berkeley probably know very little about George. That's a pity, because although Berkeley had only a single idea, it is one of the most disconcerting ideas that anyone has ever had, comparable to Darwin's idea about evolution. While Darwin's idea was about how we got here, Berkeley's idea was about what we actually perceive and know. "The only things we perceive," writes Berkeley, "are our perceptions." Berkeley notes that humans have assumed for millennia that there is a freestanding reality out there, and we know it because we can reconstitute a picture of it in our minds. But if we are honest, Berkeley says, we have to admit that we cannot place the picture and the reality side by side to see if the two are the same or even similar. That's because we don't have access to both things, only to one. We only have the picture, and not its corresponding reality. In fact, Berkeley says we have no reason to believe that anything exists other than the picture. We presume our experiences in some way reflect reality, but our experiences are all that we know or have ever known. Therefore, says Berkeley, to posit some reality beyond them is a superfluous hypothesis, or pure make-believe. Berkeley's stunning conclusion is that the material world outside our senses simply does not exist.

Berkeley's reasoning is a devastating blow not only to empirical realism but also to materialism. In fact, it undermines the distinction that we have been making throughout this book, a distinction between the physical and the mental. The argument so far is that while the subjective mental realm is largely outside the sphere of science, nevertheless science has made impressive progress in understanding the objective physical realm. Berkeley's argument is that this distinction doesn't hold; even what we call the objective physical world is apprehended through subjective mental experiences. Everything you see and hear and touch seems indisputably material and physical, and yet those experiences are indisputably mental. To borrow an example from Samuel Johnson, consider a rock. What could be more real and solid than a rock! Now go ahead and kick the rock. Clearly there must be a rock, because you felt it with your foot, and you feel the pain from kicking it. But Berkeley's argument is that the entire experience—the image of the rock, the sensation of pain, the slight gasp you heard yourself make—has occurred in your mind. Apart from this experience, there is no "real" rock. The rock is nothing more than your experience of it. So all we have are experiences, yet we persistently confuse them with some invented and non-existent reality that we presume exists apart from our experiences.[5]

Confounded by Berkeley's argument, empirical realists have labored for more than two centuries to refute it. Let's consider a couple of their best attempts, the first by philosopher Karl Popper. Popper argued that we can test Berkeley's premise that the sun, the stars, or trees exist only in the mind. We can set up a camera or recording device and then leave the room. When we return, the camera has taken a picture of the sun, the star, or the tree. So clearly these objects have been there even in our absence; therefore they don't exist only in the mind. Yet reflection will show that what Popper termed an "excellent refutation" of Berkeley is no refutation at all.[6] Consider the crucial piece of evidence, namely, the photographs. Now where are those photographs located? Ah yes, you like Popper assumed their independent existence, didn't you? But Berkeley's point would be that the photographs, no less than the sun, the stars, and the tree, all exist in your mind. Where else do you apprehend them? So the refutation of subjectivism fails because it relies on the hidden presumption of realism, the presumption of objects with an independent existence outside the mind.

Another attempt to refute Berkeley is by cognitive psychologist Steven Pinker. Pinker begins by addressing Berkeley's claim that the chairs we perceive in a room are nothing more than the collection of images and sensations we experience; take away those perceptions, and there are no chairs. According to Pinker, "Berkeley's suggestion never did work. Imagine a room with two identical chairs. Someone comes in and switches them around. Is the room the same or different from before? Obviously everyone understands that it is different. But you know of no feature that distinguishes one chair from the other. . . . Your knowledge of the properties of two objects can be identical and you can still know they are distinct."[7]

Now this is a crafty experiment, so let's follow it very carefully. Pinker begins with two identical chairs that are out there in a room. This seems like a safe start, but Pinker has already made a crucial assumption that Berkeley would dispute. Pinker assumes the independent existence of material objects outside the mind. Berkeley's point is that this premise is wrong. The chairs exist only in one place; they exist in our minds. Since all we have are images of chairs, there is no justification for positing the existence of chairs apart from those images. Concede Berkeley's point—and I don't see how it's possible to dispute it—and Pinker's whole experiment collapses. The original chairs, the fellows who came in to switch them, the new arrangement: everything has occurred in Pinker's mind. Yet Pinker cannot see that there is no basis for equating these mental images one the one hand with some freestanding reality on the other. Such is the obscurantist power of empirical realism that even a man of Pinker's caliber routinely confuses something he has access to, namely experience, with something he doesn't, namely freestanding reality. Pinker's failure shows the central fallacy of empirical realism: the inability to distinguish between experience and reality, and the chronic mistaking of one for the other.

Despite Berkeley's critique of empirical realism, it is a complete misunderstanding of his argument to suppose that he is in any way denying the validity of experience. On the contrary, Berkeley is the one who is being truly empirical. He is saying, let us see what we really have. Well, what we really have are experiences, and that's it. What Berkeley denies is not the world we experience, but rather the existence of a duplicate world of objects that correspond to our experience and yet exist apart from our experience. An amusing sidelight of all this is that Berkeley insists his philosophy would be completely obvious to the man in the street.[8] Show the man on the street the Empire State Building and ask him, "How do you know it's there?" His answer would be, "Well, obviously I can see it. I can get into the elevator and go to the top. I can touch it. And since it hasn't been cleaned lately, I can even smell it." In listing his sensory apprehensions, the man would have given a complete description of the Empire State Building. Never once would he pause to consider whether there was some "real" Empire State Building apart from his perceptions that provided the external basis for his experience. Rather, he would take the characteristics that he observed and experienced to be the Empire State Building. And in doing this, Berkeley says the man would be quite right. Remarkably, Berkeley's philosophy that seemed originally to be completely alien to common sense turns out upon reflection to be consistent with it.

For Berkeley only two things are real: experience and the experiencing subject. The philosopher David Hume radicalized Berkeley's argument by calling into question the experiencing subject. Hume conceded that there is experience, but he denied that there is any "I" that is having the experience. Where in experience, asks Hume, is this "I" to be found? There is laughter and the taste of horseradish and all kinds of other impressions and ideas, and that's all that experience provides. We automatically presume there must be some "I" that actually has those impressions and ideas, but Hume insists that is mere presumption; the "I" is, as it were, a fiction gratuitously added to the experience itself. Moreover, Hume pointed out that we are not justified in attributing causation to our experiences, even though we regularly do on the basis of custom or habit. In reality, our experiences come to us as a kind of procession, one after the other, some occurring more regularly in conjunction with others.[9] Hume's thoroughgoing skepticism calls into question what humans can know. According to

Hume, we don't have a rational basis for positing a world external to our experiences, we cannot make sense of those experiences, and we don't even know that we are the ones having them.

I would like to bring Schopenhauer to center stage at this point, but I have to introduce him through his predecessor and philosophical mentor, Immanuel Kant. It was Kant who set out to solve Hume's problem "in its widest implications." Kant is sometimes called a skeptic, but his stated goal is to overcome skepticism, what he termed the "euthanasia of reason." Kant is also accused of not believing that there is a real world out there, but he passionately believed that there is one, even if nobody prior to him could substantiate its existence. Kant is also, as we will see, a friend of empiricism, but he realized he had to save empiricism from its uncritical advocates. Sometimes Kant is even described as hostile to science, although he was himself a scientist who made important contributions to astronomy and physics.

Kant's philosophical approach, very different from any predecessor, was not to ask: Is there a real world out there? Is science a valid form of knowledge? Kant started from the premise that of course there is a world out there and of course science is a source of genuine knowledge. Then he asked: but how do we know this? In other words, how is any of this knowledge possible? In his masterpiece *The Critique of Pure Reason*, Kant carried out the most systematic reconstruction of human knowledge ever attempted. Schopenhauer regarded Kant as "perhaps the most original mind ever produced by nature" and said of the main body of Kant's philosophy, "It is so clearly established that to raise even an apparent objection to it has not been possible. It is Kant's triumph, one of the extremely few metaphysical doctrines that can be regarded as actually proved."[10] Schopenhauer recognized the full implications of Kant's ideas. He went on to extend them beyond Kant and built his own distinctive philosophy on the Kantian foundation.

Kant's refutation of skepticism begins by admitting the truth contained in skepticism. Since all knowledge is based on experience, Kant says that our knowledge of the world comes filtered through the apparatus of our senses, our brains, and our nervous systems. What we perceive and understand is what that human apparatus enables us to perceive and understand. And clearly this apparatus has limits. Dogs can hear sounds at frequencies that human ears cannot apprehend. Eels can derive information from electric signals in a way that we cannot. Bats use echolocation, a form of sonar, to navigate in the dark. We humans can't get around that way. So clearly there are forms of information and knowledge that are inaccessible to us because of the kinds of creatures we are.

We can appreciate these limits through the example of a video camera. A video camera can record images and sounds, but it cannot record smells or capture how an object tastes. We might say that a video camera is a two-channel instrument for apprehending reality. Now we humans have five senses, and in this sense we possess a five-channel system for apprehending reality. It follows of necessity that whatever cannot be captured by this system can never be reality for us. This is not to say that nothing else exists. In fact, we know from the examples of electric eels and bats that there most certainly are forms of perception and knowledge that are beyond our capacity. And certainly there could be many other forms of knowledge that are beyond the apprehension of any living creature. All creatures, after all, are in the same position that we are; they too are intrinsically limited in what they can perceive by their sensory apparatus.

So what is it that we can and cannot know? We can begin to answer this question by envisioning an apple. Ask yourself, where is the redness that we see? Is it in the apple? No, it is actually in our minds, which derive the impression from light signals processed in our eyes and in the visual system of our brains. Similarly the taste and smell and feel of the apple are all apprehended within our sensory and nervous systems. And obviously we all experience the same apple; that's because as humans we have the same kind of sensory equipment. Does it follow then that we are just imagining things and that there is no real apple? Of course not. There must be an apple, Kant insists, because these impressions in our minds are being produced by it. If there were no apple, there would be no such representations. For Kant, the apple is the "thing in itself" and what we see, taste, and touch is the phenomenal appearance of the apple. This is how it is with all our experiences.

On this basis, Kant said that we humans live in two worlds, the world as it is and the world as it can be apprehended through our mind and our senses. Kant called the world as it is the "noumenon." He called the world as it appears to us the "phenomenon." This is perhaps the most famous distinction in Western philosophy, so let us explore its significance. Kant argued that all human experience, including scientific knowledge, is knowledge of the phenomenal world. Because we can only experience what our senses and instruments are tuned to pick up, the phenomenal world is the empirical world, the world in which science has a say. So scientific knowledge and empirical knowledge are indeed possible. They are not, however, knowledge of reality itself, but only of reality as it is perceived by our senses. Science is the study of experience, not of reality as it exists apart from experience. Within the realm of experience, Kant insisted that science is the best method for gaining knowledge and consequently its authority is supreme. But as an empirical form of investigation, science is inherently incapable of making any claims whatever about the other world. For science to attempt this, Kant said, is to embarrass itself by asserting propositions that are obviously beyond the scope of its competence.

Kant noted that the phenomenal world, the world we experience through our senses and investigate through science, is a material world that is subject to material laws. This world exists in space and time. For Kant, however, space and time are not abstract entities out there in the universe; rather, space and time are modes of human perception, part of the furniture of the human mind. This may seem like an odd thing for Kant to say, but there are physicists who say they understand relativity and space-time in Kantian terms. Einstein was more of an empirical realist than Kant, but he too insisted throughout his life that the distinctions between past, present, and future were not objective facts in the world but simply represented a human way of ordering experience.[11] One telling implication of Kant's analysis is that space and time are both within the phenomenal world. Outside the realm of the phenomenal, there is no space and there is no time.

This brings us to the realm of the noumenal, the real world that is independent of our experience. Can we be sure that it exists? Of course we can, says Kant, because if it didn't exist we wouldn't have any phenomenal experiences at all. These are obviously experiences of something, and that something is in the noumenal realm. Based on our knowledge of the phenomenal realm, we can also say what the noumenal realm is not. It is a realm not bound by material laws. It is a world that is not confined within the frames of space and of time. It is also a world to which our reason and experience have no direct access. That is just about everything we can say about it. To say anything more would be to claim knowledge of a kind that we not only do not possess, but never will possess. Still, what has been established by Kant is that the world of our experience is not the only world. In fact, it is merely the manifestation of another world, a reality hidden behind the veils of human experience.

Remote though the noumenal realm seems from ordinary life, it helps to explain some of life's deepest puzzles. For instance, in the previous chapter we struggled to understand how free will can exist in a universe bound by physical laws. Kant's answer is that freedom must be understood "in a twofold sense." In one sense, freedom is a characteristic of the noumenal realm and is, as such, not subject to physical law. This is how we can make free or undetermined choices in the first place. But of course the consequences of free decisions, such as raising your arm to throw a ball, are manifested in the phenomenal world. That's why your arm and the ball do move according to the laws of motion. This is the sense in which freedom does operate in the phenomenal world, the world of experience.[12]

Schopenhauer regarded Kant's philosophy as unassailable in its central claims, and he took over where Kant left off. At the same time, Schopenhauer did not hesitate to correct Kant where he believed Kant had erred. Kant, for instance, wrote very little about the noumenal realm. This was consistent with Kant's claim that nothing can really be known about a realm that lies beyond all experience. But Schopenhauer distinguishes between *knowing* something and knowing *about* it. I don't know Verdi's operas, but I know about them. I don't know Bill and Hillary Clinton, but I certainly know about them, including a few things about Bill that I would rather not know. Schopenhauer says a good deal about the noumenon, and one thing he says is a departure from Kant and directly relevant to our purpose. Kant typically writes of the noumenal as a plural term, referring to things in themselves.

But Schopenhauer shows why that can't be right. For different things to exist, he writes, there has to be differentiation, and that's only possible in a world of space and time. If a material object is to be distinct from another, it has to be so either in space or in time, otherwise the two objects would be the same. Even abstract numbers and shapes have to be different in sequence or spatial configuration in order to be separate from each other. But as Kant himself notes, space and time are modes of human sensibility; they do not apply to the realm of the noumenal. Consequently Schopenauer contends that outside the realm of space and time there is no differentiation. In the realm of the noumenon, everything is immaterial and everything is one.[13]

Schopenhauer's concept of transcendental oneness is based on Kant, and yet is a significant advance because it develops Kant's thought in a way that Kant himself didn't. Schopenhauer also took up one of Hume's challenges that Kant did not address, namely the question of whether or not the self can be known to exist. "The world is my idea," Schopenhauer writes in the famous opening line of his *magnum opus*. What he means is that the existence of the world itself is dependent upon the idea of the thinking subject. The realist view considers this preposterous, so Schopenhauer asks his reader to consider the world and then subtract himself, the thinking subject. Now where is the world? Obviously it has vanished. There is no world without subjects in the world, and moreover the world itself is experientially located in the minds of those subjects. So subjectivity is the necessary ground of objectivity. Realism is false, writes Schopenhauer, because it attempts the impossible task of positing an object without a subject; materialism is equally false because it is "the philosophy of the subject that forgets to take account of itself."[14]

So Hume is wrong that no self exists. We know it to exist because it is presupposed by all our experiences. Yet Hume was right, in a way, that when we examine experience by itself, we cannot locate an "I." That's because the self is what has the experiences, but the self cannot itself be known independently of those experiences. Kant had made the point that the object in itself, say an apple, cannot be known apart from seeing and touching and tasting the apple. Schopenhauer says that the subject is in precisely the same position; we cannot know ourselves except through our experiences. But in our inner essence, we are also "things in themselves." In other words, the "I" cannot be experienced directly because it is part of the noumenal realm, and this should not be surprising because like every other material thing in the world, we too are material things in the world that simultaneously inhabit a phenomenal realm and a noumenal realm. This very subtle reasoning leads to the remarkable conclusion that reality consists of two different entities, mind and material things, both of which are in their inner nature noumenal and unknowable. All we can know is the middle world of interactions between them.

The test of a good theory is not only the validity of its reasoning, but also whether it helps to explain things that would otherwise remain mysterious. Schopenhauer argues that his doctrines help to make sense of morality, and specifically of human compassion. In contrast to Kant, Schopenhauer was not a moral philosopher. He never sought to justify morality, only to explain it. As we will explore in the next chapter, morality in general and compassion in particular are from the evolutionary point of view a conundrum, because evolution says that we are selfish beings preoccupied with surviving and reproducing in the world. It is not easy to see how sending money to children in Rwanda fits into this scheme. But Schopenhauer says that if the self is noumenal and the noumenal is undifferentiated, that means that whatever our phenomenal differences, we humans are, in the ultimate ground of our being, one. Perhaps at some level, Schopenhauer suggests, we recognize this. And this explains compassion, the ability of people to identify with each other, share each other's pain, and help even when it involves some cost or sacrifice. Schopenhauer's doctrine of a universal human connection implies that if we hurt each other we are, whether we realize it or not, hurting ourselves.[15] One fascinating feature of this argument is that whether or not it is true, humans certainly on many occasions act as if it were true. So Schopenhauer's philosophy has predictive power; it deepens our understanding of human behavior.

By now, the thoughtful reader will have noticed that Schopenhauer's ideas are virtually identical to those of Eastern religion and philosophy, notably the central teachings of Hinduism and Buddhism. For more than a thousand years, the sages of the East have professed that ultimate reality is one, that the world we perceive is not the world as it is, that phenomenal experience is a kind of appearance or illusion, and that humans are connected not only to each other but also to other living creatures. The close similarity between Schopenhauer's conclusions and those of Eastern thought has led many in the West, including some scholars, to suggest that Schopenhauer may have gotten his ideas from Hinduism and Buddhism or at least been significantly influenced by them. But as Schopenhauer's biographer Bryan Magee points out, in reality this was not so. Rather, Schopenhauer, like Kant, worked entirely within the mainstream of Western philosophy, in a tradition that begins with Parmenides and Plato and continues through Descartes, Locke, Berkeley, and Hume. When Schopenhauer reached his conclusions, he saw that they were very similar to those of Eastern thought, and this discovery amazed and delighted him. In his later writings, he emphasized these affinities, and he helped to bring the ideas of Eastern religion to a European audience. He also became one of the few Western thinkers to have a genuinely serious acquaintance with Eastern thought. But for Schopenhauer it was never an issue of the two traditions influencing each other; rather, he thought it remarkable that Western and Eastern thinkers had separately taken up the most important questions and traveled in complete independence from each other along quite different roads, and yet arrived at essentially the same place.[16]

So what does all this mean for life after death? Schopenhauer admits that when we die our bodies decay and our individuality is lost. Schopenhauer denies personal immortality of the kind that Jews, Christians, and Muslims believe in. When we die, the phenomenal world comes to an end for us. "As far as you are an individual, death will be the end of you." No wonder that death is perceived by us as annihilation. It scares us because it jeopardizes the will to live that Schopenhauer acknowledged to be the driving force of our terrestrial existence. But Schopenhauer contends that this fear of death is itself an illusion because the real or noumenal part of us cannot die. So far from denying the afterlife, Schopenhauer affirms it. "Your real being knows neither time, nor beginning, nor end. . . . Your immortal part is indestructible." In other words, at death we are fully integrated into the realm of the noumenal from which we originally came. For Schopenhauer, a pessimist about life in this world, death is a kind of liberation, a discarding of the veil of phenomenal existence and a discovery of our true oneness with each other and with infinite reality itself. When we die, our separateness is over and we live on as part of the absolute reality that is the only reality there is.[17]

Schopenhauer's afterlife is not the Christian one, but we should not miss the significance of his accomplishment. Schopenhauer, like Kant, is a thinker of incontestable greatness who formulated his ideas within the rational tradition that is the basis of Western thought. Schopenhauer was an atheist and Kant was a Christian, yet both men made secular arguments, without appeals to revelation or God, to show the existence and characteristics of the noumenon, the world behind the world. Christians, Jews, and Muslims, no less than Hindus and Buddhists, affirm the existence of this unseen reality. Ironically, Schopenhauer and Kant provide a rational route to the same destination that religious believers have arrived at by a very different route. In a sense, they provide solid intellectual grounding for what previously was affirmed only on the basis of faith. Our conclusion, then, is that there is good reason to believe in the afterlife. Schopenhauer, the first modern atheist, has shown through his philosophy that on this crucial point the atheists are wrong and the religious believers are right.

Chapter Ten

THE IMPARTIAL SPECTATOR

Eternity and Cosmic Justice

To feel much for others and little for ourselves,
to restrain our selfish and indulge our benevolent affections,
constitutes the perfection of human nature.[1]

—Adam Smith, *The Theory of Moral Sentiments*

Having presented two proofs of life after death, one from neuroscience and another from philosophy, I now offer a third proof, which is also a way of testing my hypothesis. This is called the presuppositional argument, and it requires a little clarification to show what kind of an argument it is and how it works. Imagine a detective who cannot figure out how his suspect could have committed the crime by himself. For instance, the suspect was indisputably in one location at the time when the body was dumped in another location. Our lieutenant Columbo puzzles over this and then it hits him: the man must have had an accomplice! Assume an accomplice and the otherwise inexplicable facts of the case now make sense. So there must have been an accomplice. And even without knowing anything about the accomplice, the detective's hypothesis is persuasive to the degree that it explains the known facts of the case.

Here's a second example. A woman is baffled by the fact that a man whom she has been dating for years keeps delaying his proposal of marriage. The man keeps telling her that he is waiting for the right time. She agonizes over the question, "Why won't he commit?" After a while the woman's friends tell her, "He will never marry you. He has no intention of marrying you." The girl-friends have no direct knowledge of the man or his real intentions. Their assessment is, in this sense, purely conjectural. But it has the merit of being able to explain things that the alternative hypothesis cannot explain. How believable is it that the man who has procrastinated for so long will propose at some unspecified "right time"? It is much more reasonable to suppose that he is simply making excuses because he doesn't want to get married, at least not to her. In this example there is a fact that is not directly known but is convincing because it makes sense of the facts that are known. The facts become, as it were, an empirical corroboration of the presupposition.

Here is my presuppositional argument for life after death. Unlike material objects and all other living creatures, we humans inhabit two domains: the way things are, and the way things ought to be. We are moral animals who recognize that just as there are natural laws that govern every object in the universe, there are also moral laws that govern the behavior of one special object in the universe, namely us. While the universe is externally moved by "facts," we are internally moved also by "values." Yet these values defy natural and scientific explanation because physical laws, as discovered by science, concern only the way things are and not the way they ought to be. Moreover, the essence of morality is to curtail and contradict the powerful engine of human self-interest, giving morality an undeniable anti-evolutionary thrust. So how do we explain the existence of moral values that stand athwart our animal nature? The presupposition of cosmic justice, achieved not in this life but in another life beyond the grave, is by far the best and in some respects the only explanation. This presupposition fully explains why humans continue to espouse goodness and justice even when the world is evil and unjust.

Notice what the presuppositional argument does not say. It does not say that because there is injustice in the world there must be justice somewhere else. Nor does it say that the human wish for a better world is enough by itself to produce another world that is better. Rather, it begins with the recognition that while science explains much of nature very well, there is a big part of human nature that science does not seem to explain at all. In particular, evolution does a good job in accounting for why we are selfish animals, but it faces immense challenges in accounting for why we simultaneously hold that we ought not to be selfish. Far from facing the facts of life, like every other animal, we cherish ideals that have never been and will never be fully achieved. We are flawed creatures who act as if we ought not to be. We know that we live in an unjust society where the bad guy often comes out on top and the good guy often comes to grief, yet we continue to hold that this is not how it should be. We say things like "what goes around comes around" even though we know that in this world it is not always so. Despite the harsh facts of life, we tirelessly affirm that it should be so. Our ideals, in other words, contradict the reality of our lives. It seems that we, uniquely among all living and nonliving things, seek to repudiate the laws of evolution and escape the control of the laws of nature.

Now why is this? Why do we continue to operate as if there is a better world with a better set of ideals that stands in judgment of this world? I will argue that the best explanation is that there is such a world. In other words, the presupposition of an afterlife and the realization of the ideal of cosmic justice makes sense of our moral nature better than any competing hypothesis.

Before we launch into our discussion, however, I want to answer an objection that will already be surfacing for a certain type of reader. Skeptics at this point may scorn my claim that certain features of human nature seem to defy scientific explanation. They will claim I am making a discredited appeal to the "God of the gaps." They will say that I am appealing to God and the supernatural to account for things that science has not yet explained. As Carl Sagan wrote in *The Varieties of Scientific Experience*, "As science advances, there seems to be less and less for God to do."[2] For the skeptic, the appeal to gaps is an illegitimate mode of argument; just because science doesn't have the answer now doesn't mean that it will not have the solution tomorrow or at any rate someday. In this view, the God of the gaps is the last desperate move of the theist, who searches for the little apertures in the scientific understanding of the world and then hands over those areas to his preferred deity.

Some creationists do employ this kind of "gaps" reasoning in order to posit a supernatural creator. For instance, they contend that science cannot account for the Cambrian explosion, so God must have directly done that. But there is no reason to think that the Cambrian explosion defies natural explanation, even if we don't have that explanation. So the skeptic's "gaps" critique works against this type of opponent. But it doesn't work with me, because I have not posited a God of the gaps; in fact, my argument so far has not relied on God at all. In addition, while the skeptic typically fancies himself a champion of science, his whole line of argument is just as unscientific as than that of the creationist.[3] For the skeptic, a gap is a kind of nuisance, a small lacuna of scientific ignorance that is conceded to exist as a kind of misfortune, and is expected soon to be cleared up. True scientists, by contrast, love and cherish gaps. They seek out gaps and work assiduously within these crevasses because they hope that, far from being a small missing piece of the puzzle, the gap is actually an indication that the whole underlying framework is wrong, that there is a deeper framework waiting to be uncovered, and that the gap is the opening that might lead to this revolutionary new understanding.

Gaps are the mother lode of scientific discovery. Most of the great scientific advances of the past began with gaps and ended with new presuppositions that put our whole comprehension of the world in a new light. The presuppositional argument, in other words, is not some sleight-of-hand way of postulating unseen entities to account for seen ones. Rather, it illustrates precisely the way that science operates and how scientists make their greatest discoveries. Copernicus, for example, set out to address the gaps in Ptolemy's cosmological theory. As historian Thomas Kuhn shows, these gaps were well recognized, but many scientists did not consider their existence to be a crisis. After all, experience seemed heavily on the side of Ptolemy: the earth seems to be stationary, and the sun looks like it moves. Kuhn remarks that many scientists sought to fill in the gaps by "patching and stretching," by adding more Ptolemaic epicycles.[4] Copernicus, however, saw the gaps as an opportunity to offer a startling new hypothesis. He argued that instead of taking it for granted that the earth is at the center of the universe and the sun goes around the earth, let's suppose instead that the sun is at the center and the earth and the other planets all go around the sun. When Copernicus proposed this, he had no direct evidence that it was the case, and he recognized that his theory violated both intuition and experience. Even so, he said, the presupposition of heliocentrism gives a better explanation of the astronomical data and therefore should be accepted as correct. Here is a classic presuppositional argument that closes a gap and in the process gives us a completely new perspective on our place in the universe.

Similarly Einstein confronted gaps in the attempt of classical physics to reconcile the laws of motion with the laws of electromagnetism. Again, there were many who didn't consider the gap to be very serious. Surely classical Newtonian science would soon figure things out, and the gap would be closed. It took Einstein's genius to see that this was no small problem; rather, the gap indicated a constitutional defect with Newtonian physics as a whole. And without conducting a single experiment or empirical test, Einstein offered a presuppositional solution. He said that we have assumed for centuries that space and time are absolute and this assumption has produced some seemingly insoluble problems. So what if we change the assumption? What if we say that space and time are relative to the observer? Now we can explain observed facts about electromagnetism and the speed of light that could not previously be accounted for. Einstein tested his theory by applying it to the orbital motion of the planet Mercury. Mercury was known to deviate very slightly from the path predicted by Newton's laws. Another gap! And once again there was a prevailing complacent attitude that some conventional scientific explanation would soon close the gap and settle the anomaly. But in fact the gap was a clue to the inadequacy of the entire Newtonian paradigm. Einstein recognized his theory as superior to Newton's when he saw that it explained the orbital motion of Mercury in a way that Newton's couldn't.[5]

In the last few decades, scientists have accepted the existence of dark matter and dark energy, again on the basis of presuppositional arguments. Here too the problem arose from some gaps. As we saw in an earlier chapter on physics, when scientists measured the amount of matter in the universe, it was not enough to hold the galaxies together. When they measured the amount of energy, it was not enough to account for the accelerating pace of the expansion of the universe. Of course these could be considered mere gaps, soon to be eliminated with some new observation or equation, but persistent scientists knew better. They recognized that we already know about the matter and energy that our instruments can measure, and these simply cannot account for the behavior of the universe and the galaxies. Consequently, there has to be some new kind of matter and energy, undetectable by all scientific equipment and following no known scientific law, to solve the problem. The gap, in other words, required a reassessment of the entire scientific understanding of matter and energy. On this basis leading scientists posited the existence of dark matter and dark energy, and despite initial skepticism, most scientists have accepted their existence because they help to explain phenomena that would otherwise remain largely unknown.

From these examples, we learn that science regularly posits unseen entities, from space-time to dark matter, whose existence is affirmed solely on the basis that they explain the things that we can see and measure. We also see that gaps are a good thing, not a bad thing, and the genuinely scientific approach is to ask whether they are clues that lead to a broader and deeper understanding of things. We also learn how presuppositional arguments work best, both in science and outside of science. The presupposition itself is a kind of hypothesis. It says, "This is the way things have to be in order to make sense of the world." We then test the presupposition by saying, "How well does it explain the world?" We cannot answer this question without considering whether alternative explanations work better. If they do, then we don't need the presupposition. If they don't, then the presupposition, unlikely though it may seem, remains the best explanation of the data that we have. We should accept what it posits until a better explanation comes along. My hypothesis on offer is, "There has to be cosmic justice in a world beyond the world in order to make sense of the observed facts about human morality." Let us now proceed to test it.

Morality is both a universal and a surprising fact of human nature. When I say that morality is universal, I am not referring to this or that moral code. In fact, I am not referring to an external moral code at all. Rather, I am referring to morality as the voice within, the interior source that Adam Smith called the "impartial spectator."[6] Morality in this sense is an uncoercive but authoritative judge. It has no power to compel us, but it speaks with unquestioned authority. Of course we can and frequently do reject what morality commands, but when we do so we cannot avoid guilt or regret. It is because of our capacity for self-impeachment and remorse that Aristotle famously called man "the beast with the red cheeks." Aristotle's description holds up very well more than two thousand years later. Even people who most flagrantly repudiate morality—say a chronic liar or a rapacious thief—inevitably respond to detection with excuses and rationalizations. They say, "Yes, I lied, but I had no alternative under the circumstances," or "Yes, I stole, but I did it to support my family." Hardly anyone says, "Of course I am a liar and a thief, and I don't see anything wrong with that." Morality supplies a universal criterion or standard even though this standard is almost universally violated.

Morality is a surprising feature of humanity because it seems to defy the laws of evolution. Evolution is descriptive: it says how we do behave. Morality is prescriptive: it says how we should behave. And beyond this, evolutionary behavior appears to run in the opposite direction from moral behavior. Evolution implies that we are selfish creatures who seek to survive and reproduce in the world. Indeed we are, but we are also unselfish creatures who seek the welfare of others, sometimes in preference to our own. We are participants in the game of life, understandably partial to our own welfare, while morality stands aloof, taking the impartial or "God's eye" view, directing us to act for the good of others. In sum, while evolution provides a descriptive account of human self-interest, morality provides a standard of human behavior that frequently operates against self-interest.

So if we are mere evolutionary primates, how to account for morality as a central and universal feature of our nature? Why would morality develop among creatures obsessively bent on survival and reproduction? Darwin himself recognized the problem. In *The Descent of Man*, Darwin argued that "although a high standard of morality gives but a slight or no advantage to each individual man and his children over the other men of the same tribe, yet . . . an advancement in the standard of morality will certainly give an immense advantage to one tribe over another."[7] Darwin's point is that a tribe of virtuous patriots, each of its members willing to make sacrifices for the group, would prove more successful and thus be favored by natural selection over a tribe of self-serving individuals. This is the group selection argument, and for many decades it was considered an acceptable way to reconcile evolution with morality.

But as biologists now recognize, the argument has a fatal flaw. We have to ask how a tribe of individuals would become self-sacrificing in the first place. Imagine a tribe where many people share their food with others or volunteer to defend the tribe from external attack. Now what would be the fate of individual cheaters who benefit from this arrangement but hoard their own food and refuse to volunteer? Clearly these scoundrels would have the best deal of all. In other words, cheaters could easily become free riders, benefiting from the sacrifices of others but making no sacrifices themselves, and these cheaters would be more likely to survive than their more altruistic fellow tribesmen. In *The Origins of Virtue,* Matt Ridley gives a more contemporary example. If everyone in a community could be relied on not to steal cars, cars would not have to be locked, and a great deal of expense would be saved on insurance, locking devices, and alarms. The whole community would be better off. But, Ridley notes, "In such a trusting world, an individual can make himself even better off by defecting from the social contract and stealing a car." By this logic, even tribes that somehow started out patriotic and altruistic would soon become filled with self-serving cheaters. The free rider problem doesn't apply to all situations—there are very limited circumstances in which group selection still works—but its recognition has pretty much sunk Darwin's group selection argument as a general explanation for morality within an evolutionary framework.[8]

In the 1960s and early 1970s, biologists William Hamilton and Robert Trivers offered a new and more promising approach, summarized in Richard Dawkins's *The Selfish Gene.* Dawkins argues that the basic unit of survival is not the individual but rather the gene. In one of his most memorable formulations, Dawkins writes that we individuals are "survival machines—robot vehicles blindly programmed to preserve the selfish molecules known as genes."[9] At first glance this seems like a crazy way to think about evolution, but Dawkins, employing a presuppositional argument of his own, notes that it explains morality in a way that previously seemed impossible.

The ingenious selfish gene theory explains morality not as a result of individual selfishness, but rather of genetic selfishness. "Altruism," writes biologist E. O. Wilson, "is conceived as the mechanism by which DNA multiplies itself."[10] This may seem cynical, but it does have a kind of cold logic. Think of a mother who runs into a burning building to save her two children trapped inside. An act of pure maternal unselfishness? Well, it looks that way. But William Hamilton reminds us that a child has 50 percent of the mother's genes. If two or more children are involved, then it makes rational sense for a mother to jeopardize her own survival if she can enhance the prospects of her genes surviving through her offspring. What looks like altruism from the individual point of view can be understood as selfishness from the genetic point of view.

Morality, in Hamilton's framework, is a form of nepotistic "kin selection." This idea helps us understand why certain insects, birds, and animals endanger their own welfare to promote that of their fellow creatures. Vervet monkeys and prairie dogs, for instance, give warning calls that signal approaching predators, sometimes at the cost of becoming the target of those predators. Why would they risk their lives in this way? Kin selection holds that it is because they are genetically related to those they are helping. So there is an evolutionary payoff: the risk-takers are maximizing not their individual chance for survival, but the chance for their genes to make it into future generations. From the gene's point of view, helping one's kin is simply a form of helping oneself.[11]

But of course kin selection is a very limited explanation in that it only accounts for why animals and people behave altruistically toward relatives. In life, however, humans and even some animals behave that way toward innumerable others who don't share their genes. Robert Trivers argued that this is because of "reciprocal altruism." A better term would be reciprocal bargaining: what Trivers means is that creatures behave generously toward others in the expectation that they will get something in return. Vampire bats, for instance, share food not only with relatives, but also with other bats that have recently shared with them. Other animals also practice this kind of give and take. Trivers does not suggest that animals engage in conscious planning or deliberation; rather, he argues that natural selection has rewarded with survival the instincts for engaging in mutually beneficial exchanges. And of course in human society we routinely exchange favors with neighbors and acquaintances; we even do business with total strangers, all motivated by the principle of "you do something for me and I'll so something for you." So here too altruism is understood as a form of extended or long-term selfishness.[12]

Even reciprocal altruism, however, cannot explain the good things we do that offer no actual return. A fellow gives up his seat in a bus to an 80-year-old woman. No, she isn't Grandma, nor is it reasonable to say that he's doing it because next week she will give him her seat. So neither kin selection nor reciprocal altruism provides any solution in this case. Moreover, altruism of this sort occurs on a regular basis throughout human society. Many people give blood without any expectation of reward. Others volunteer to help the severely disabled. Others donate money for malaria nets or to assist AIDS victims in Africa. Still others agitate against animal abuse in their own community or sex trafficking in Thailand or religious persecution in Tibet. Throughout the centuries there have been people who have devoted themselves to improving the lives of impoverished strangers, or risked their lives to benefit folks who are unrelated to them and cannot possibly reciprocate these sacrifices.

Some biologists concede that evolution is at a loss here. "Altruism toward strangers," writes biologist Ernst Mayr, "is a behavior not supported by natural selection."[13] Still, some diehard champions of evolution do try to accommodate such behavior within their evolutionary framework. Their best attempt is to argue that seemingly disinterested altruism toward strangers also has a well-hidden personal motive. Essentially it is performed in order to enhance one's social reputation. Reputation is valuable because it raises one's position in society and perhaps even improves one's mating prospects. Michael Shermer recognizes that it is possible to gain a good reputation by faking a dedication to the public welfare. He argues, however, that such schemes may well be exposed over time. According to Shermer, "The best way to convince others that you are a moral person is not to fake being a moral person but actually to be a moral person." Psychologist David Barash makes the same point, "Be moral, and your reputation will benefit." The motive here remains one of personal enhancement; we are helping others not for their sake but for our sake. Once again, morality is explained as the outward disguise of the selfish gene.[14]

But Shermer and Barash never really contend with the Machiavellian objection to their argument. Machiavelli argues that "the man who wants to act virtuously in every way necessarily comes to grief among so many who are not virtuous." A rich man who is habitually generous, Machiavelli remarks, will soon become a poor man. Much better, Machiavelli craftily counsels, to acquire the image of magnanimity while giving away as little as possible. In other words, it is preferable to seem virtuous than to actually be virtuous. "Everyone sees what you appear to be, few experience what you really are." Machiavelli insists that the people who prosper most in the world are the ruthless people who employ virtue only occasionally and instrumentally for strategic gain.[15] If Machiavelli is right, then under the rules of natural selection it is the moral pretenders, not the truly moral, who will prosper and multiply. And for empirical evidence Machiavelli could surely point to well-known successful connivers.

Of course if there is cosmic justice in the afterlife, then the bad guys ultimately lose. We see this in a beautiful example from Dante's *Inferno*, where in the circle of the fraudulent we encounter Guido da Montefeltro. Guido's martial prowess as a Ghibelline general had been largely due to his mastery of what he called the

"arts of the fox." He was highly successful in his scams and never
called to account. In short, he was a true Machiavellian. And late
in life he donned the robes of a Franciscan friar, not because he
repented of his earlier misdeeds, but in an attempt to fool God and
make it to paradise. "And oh, to think it could have worked!" he
says in one of the great lines of the *Commedia*. Unlike gullible
humans, however, God can't be duped, and so Guido gets his
comeuppance.[16] As we see from this example, cosmic justice
always evens the scales, but it simply defies reality to contend that
in this world the scales are always even. Terrestrial justice is
flawed and imperfect, and thus Barash and Shermer's claim that
morality always pays right here on earth isn't very convincing.

In any case, all these evolutionary attempts to explain morality
ultimately miss the point. They seek to explain morality, but even
at their best what they explain is not morality at all. Imagine a
shopkeeper who routinely increases his profits by cheating his cus-
tomers. So smoothly does he do this that he is never exposed and
his reputation remains unimpeachable. Even though the man is
successful in the game of survival, if he has a conscience it will be
nagging at him from the inside. It may not be strong enough to
make him change his ways, but it will at least make him feel bad
and perhaps ultimately despise himself. Now how do our evolutionary explanations account for this? In fact, they don't. They all
seek to reduce morality to self-interest, but if you think about it,
genuine morality cannot be brought down to this level. Morality
is not the voice that says, "Be truthful when it benefits you" or
"Be kind to those who are in a position to help you later." Rather,
it operates without regard for such calculations. Far from being
an extension of self-interest, the voice of the impartial spectator is
typically a restriction of self-interest. Think about it: if morality
were simply an extension of selfishness, we wouldn't need it. We
don't need moral prescriptions to tell people to act for their own

benefit; they do that anyway. The whole point of moral prescriptions and injunctions is to get people to subordinate and curb their selfish interests.

There is a second, deeper sense in which evolutionary theories cannot account for human morality. We can see this by considering the various attempts to explain altruism in the animal kingdom. I recently came across an article in the London *Telegraph* titled "Animals Can Tell Right from Wrong."[17] I read with interest, wondering if animals had finally taken up the question of whether it is right to eat smaller animals. After all, the greatest problem with animal rights is getting animals to respect them. Alas, the article was unilluminating on this point. Even so, it provided examples of how wolves, coyotes, elephants, whales, and even rodents occasionally engage in cooperative and altruistic behavior. Perhaps the most dramatic examples of these come from the work of anthropologist Frans de Waal, who has studied gorillas, bonobos, and chimpanzees. According to de Waal, our "closest relatives" the chimpanzees display many of the recognized characteristics of morality, including kin selection and reciprocal altruism.[18]

Yet de Waal recognizes that while chimps may cooperate or help, they have no sense that they ought to help. In other words, chimps have no understanding of the normative basis of morality. And this of course is the essence of morality for humans. Morality isn't merely about what you do; mostly it is about what you should do. Evolutionary theories like kin selection and reciprocal altruism utterly fail to capture this uniquely human sense of morality as duty or obligation. Such theories can help to explain why we act cooperatively or help others, but they cannot explain why it is good or right or obligatory for us to do these things. They commit what philosopher G. E. Moore called the naturalistic fallacy of confusing the "is" and the "ought." In particular, they give an explanation for the way things are and think that they have accounted for the way things ought to be.

But if evolution cannot explain how humans became moral primates, what can? Now it is time to test our presuppositional argument. The premise of the argument is that virtually all conceptions of life after death, especially the religious conceptions, are rooted in the idea of cosmic justice. Consider Hinduism: "You are a greedy and grasping person in this life; very well, we'll be seeing you as a cockroach in the next one." Buddhism, too, has a very similar understanding of reincarnation. Judaism, Islam, and Christianity, by contrast, uphold the notion of a Last Judgment in which the virtuous will be rewarded and the wicked will get their just deserts. The Book of Galatians 6:7 contains the famous quotation, "Whatever a man sows, that he will also reap." And here is a similar passage from the third sura of the Quran: "You shall surely be paid in full your wages on the Day of Resurrection." In all these doctrines, life after death is not a mere continuation of earthly existence, but rather a different kind of existence based on a settling of earthly accounts. These theories hold that even though we don't always find terrestrial justice, there is ultimate justice. In this future accounting, what goes around does come around.

Now let's make the supposition that there is cosmic justice after death and ask, does this help to explain the great mystery of human morality? It seems clear that it does. Humans recognize that there is no ultimate goodness and justice in this world, but they continue to uphold these ideals. In their interior conscience, humans judge themselves not by the standard of the shrewd self-aggrandizer but by that of the impartial spectator. We admire the good man, even when he comes to a bad end, and revile the successful scoundrel who got away with it. Evolutionary theories predict the reverse: if morality were merely a product of crafty and successful calculation, we should cherish crafty schemers and aspire to be like them. But we don't. Rather, we act as if there is a moral law to which we are accountable. We are judged by our consciences as if there is an ultimate tribunal in which our actions will be pronounced "guilty" or "not guilty." There seems to be no reason for us to hold these standards and measure our life against them if the standards aren't legislative in some sense. But if they are legislative, then their jurisdiction must be in another world since it is clearly not in this world. So the presupposition of cosmic justice, in an existence beyond this one, makes sense of human moral standards and moral obligation in a way that evolutionary theories cannot.

Ironically it is the claims of atheists that best illustrate the point I am trying to make. In the last pages of *The Selfish Gene*, a book devoted to showing how we are the mechanical products of our selfish genes, Richard Dawkins writes that "we have the power to turn against our creators. . . . Let us understand what our own selfish genes are up to because we may then at least have the chance to upset their designs."[19] A century ago Thomas Huxley made the same point in regard to the cosmic process of evolutionary survival. "Let us understand, once for all, that the ethical progress of society depends, not on imitating the cosmic process, still less in running away from it, but in combating it."[20] Now these are very strange demands. If we are, as Dawkins began by telling us, robot vehicles of our selfish genes, then how is it possible for us to rebel against them or upset their designs? Can the mechanical car turn against the man with the remote control? Can software revolt against its programmer? Clearly this is absurd.

Why, then, would Dawkins and Huxley propose a course of action that undermines their own argument and runs athwart the whole course of evolution? If we stay within the evolutionary framework, there is no answer to this question. There cannot be, because we are trying to understand why dedicated champions of evolution seek to transcend evolution and, in a sense, subvert their own nature. We don't see anything like this in the animal kingdom: lions don't resolve to stop harassing the deer; foxes don't call upon each other to stop being so sneaky; and parasites show no signs of distress about exploiting their hosts. Even apes and chimpanzees, despite their genetic proximity to humans, don't rebel against their genes or attempt to become something other than nature programmed them to be.

What, then, is up with us humans? What makes even the atheist uphold morality in preference to his cherished evolutionary paradigm? Introduce the presupposition of cosmic justice, and the answer becomes obvious. We humans—atheists no less than religious believers—inhabit two worlds. The first is the evolutionary world; let's call this Realm A. Then there is the next world; let's call this Realm B. The remarkable fact is that we, who live in Realm A, nevertheless have the standards of Realm B built into our natures. This is the voice of morality, which makes us dissatisfied with our selfish natures and continually hopeful that we can rise above them. Our hypothesis also accounts for the peculiar nature of morality. It cannot coerce us because it is the legislative standard of another world; at the same time, it is inescapable and authoritative for us because our actions in this world will be finally and unavoidably adjudicated in the other world. Finally, the hypothesis also helps us understand why people so often violate morality. The reason is that our interests in this world are right in front of us, while the consequences of our actions in the next world seem so remote, so distant, and thus so forgettable.

When Einstein discovered that his theory of relativity could explain something that Newton couldn't—the orbital precession of the planet Mercury—he was thrilled. He knew about the "gap," and he was able to close it not within the old framework, but by supplying a revolutionary new one. Now, within the new paradigm, there was no gap at all. In this chapter we have identified not a gap, but a huge chasm in the evolutionary paradigm. This is the conundrum of human morality, the universal voice within us that urges us to act in ways contrary to our nature as evolutionary primates. There have been supreme efforts, within the evolutionary framework, to plug the gap, but as we have seen, these have proven to be dismal failures. Our rival hypothesis of cosmic justice in a world beyond the world fares vastly better. It provides a way to test our hypothesis of life after death by applying it to human nature and asking whether it helps to illuminate why we are the way we are. In fact, it does. Taken in conjunction with other arguments, this argument provides stunning confirmation that the moral primate is destined for another life whose shape will depend on the character of the life being lived today.

Chapter Eleven

GOOD FOR SOCIETY

The Transcendent Roots of Secular Values

Were mankind's belief in its immortality to be destroyed,
not only love but also any living power to continue the
life of the world would at once dry up.[1]

—Fyodor Dostoevsky, *The Brothers Karamazov*

In my New York debate on "Is Christianity the Problem?" with Christopher Hitchens—a lively affair, against a resourceful opponent—one of the most interesting questions came from a man from the island nation of Tonga. For centuries, the man said, Tonga suffered from terrible vendettas, tribal wars, and even cannibalism. Then the missionaries came with their doctrines of God, universal brotherhood, and the afterlife. Today, the man said, Tonga is a much more peaceful and happy place. Then turning to Hitchens he said, you have given us some interesting theories, but what do you have to offer us? Hitchens was momentarily speechless. What struck him and the audience was the sheer simplicity of the question. The man wasn't debating the fine points of doctrine; he just wanted to know, at the end of it all, which approach made things better for him and his people. This is the practical question, and it is the one we shall be concerned with in the next two chapters.

We have already seen that there is a strong case for life after death. Yet while it is a case supported by a preponderance of the evidence, it is not a case established beyond reasonable doubt. So now what? How do we cross the bridge from probability to conviction? I want to suggest that we do so on the basis of practical considerations. We have to ask whether beliefs in transcendence and life after death are good for our society, and whether they are good for us as individuals. Here I take up the societal impact of these beliefs. Most people in the West have believed in life after death for two thousand years, so it is possible to trace the influence of this idea on Western history. I intend to show that the concept of eternity has been very good for us; it has greatly enhanced the way we live here and now. Even the deepest values that atheists cherish are shaped by these transcendent ideals.

Some may regard this as a startling claim. We are accustomed to hearing Daniel Dennett's insistence that "the belief in a reward in heaven can sometimes motivate acts of monstrous evil" or Richard Dawkins's references to "the devaluing effect that religion has on human life."[2] In the wake of September 11 and the proliferation of terrorist incidents around the world, atheists have raised the specter of Islamic violence that is motivated by the hope of going straight to heaven and enjoying the company of nubile virgins there. Atheists also suggest that these dangers are intrinsic to religion itself. But studies have shown that even radical Muslims don't launch suicide attacks in quest of heaven; typically they are driven by somewhat more mundane motives: they invaded our country, they stole our land, they are corrupting our culture, they raped and killed my sister, and so on.[3] Suicide bombing as a modern phenomenon began with the Japanese, and the kamikazes were not moved by the prospect of paradise but by fanatical loyalty to the emperor. So too the Tamil Tigers launched suicide attacks in a desperate struggle over land and self-determination. If religious beliefs in life after death are the source of terrorism, where are the Buddhist suicide bombers? No one has been able to identify the Christian Bin Laden, the Christian equivalent of al-Qaeda or Hezbollah, the Christian "nation of martyrs" patterned along the lines of post-Khomeini Iran. The vast majority of people in the world believe in life after death, and yet hardly any of them launch suicide strikes in the hope of hastening their journey to heavenly bliss. My own suspicion, for what it is worth, is that the Islamic suicide bombers are not being attended by beautiful virgins in paradise but rather by big hairy guys with tattoos. In any event, the prospect of life after death might marginally increase the propensity of radical Muslims to do what they do, but it hardly poses a danger to global stability or peace.

So the atheist attempt to indict all religion for the crimes of the radical Muslims fails. Beyond it, however, is a larger critique that blames the concept of eternal life for shifting people's allegiance away from this life. Critics allege that belief in the next world detracts from the pressing task of improving this one. "Otherworldliness," writes Walter Kaufmann, "is the child of disenchantment with this world."[4] The afterlife, in this view, is anti-life. This seems to be the impulse behind the harsh subtitle of Hitchens's *God Is Not Great: How Religion Poisons Everything*. Hitchens is far from the first to espouse this view.

Writing in the mid nineteenth century, the philosopher Ludwig Andreas Feuerbach contended that man classifies everything into categories of good and bad. Man then attributes the good things—from immense power to the power to confer immortality to immeasurable virtue and beauty—to God. The bad things—from helplessness to ugliness to moral corruption—man keeps for himself. In this view, God is a human projection and the afterlife a kind of dream image of the way things ought to be; only at some point man forgets his dream and starts thinking of it as reality. Meanwhile, Feuerbach writes, we live short, shivering, and miserable existences on this earth, and we blame ourselves for it. Feuerbach declared his goal to be one of converting "the friends of God into the friends of man, believers into thinkers, worshippers into workers, candidates for the other world into students of this world." For him, rejecting God and immortality is the necessary step for man to restore his own beauty, strength, and greatness. God must decrease in order for man to increase. Moreover, we have to dispose of the next world in order to flourish in this one.[5]

Writing around the same period, Karl Marx presented his own version of this philosophy. While Feuerbach held that beliefs in God and life after death reflect truths about our own psychology, Marx insisted that they reflect truths about our social situation. In an 1844 manuscript, Marx famously wrote, "Religious suffering is at once the expression of real suffering and the protest against real suffering. Religion is the sigh of the oppressed creature, the heart of a heartless world.... It is the opium of the people." Marx is often considered an implacable foe of religious beliefs, but his analysis is much more sympathetic than his reputation might suggest. Marx argues that when people suffer they turn to religion for consolation, and religion does console them, but it also diverts their attention away from the world and its economic evils; thus religion becomes an enemy of social justice. Marx concludes, "The overcoming of religion as the illusory happiness of the people is the demand for their real happiness."[6]

Marx's call to eliminate the next world by establishing a utopia on this one was taken up with a vengeance by Lenin and a host of

Communist leaders who followed him. These despots established atheism as state doctrine in the Soviet Union and other Marxist regimes around the world. In the last hundred years these regimes, led by people like Stalin, Mao, Pol Pot, Nicolae Ceausescu, Enver Hoxha, Fidel Castro, Kim Jong-il, and others, have murdered more than 100 million people. Even Bin Laden, in his wildest dreams, doesn't come close.

Richard Dawkins seeks to minimize the crimes of atheist regimes by arguing that "individual atheists may do evil things but they don't do evil things in the name of atheism."[7] Dawkins is a respected biologist, but this is what sometimes happens when a biologist is permitted to leave the laboratory. Evidently the poor man hardly knows any history. All he has to do is crack open Marx's works to discover that atheism is not incidental to the Communist scheme; it is absolutely central. The whole idea is to create a new man and a new utopia free of the shackles of traditional religion and traditional morality. So if we need to watch out for heaven-seeking Muslims bent on flying planes into buildings, we need to be just as vigilant against atheist fanatics who are willing to murder millions in order to establish their version of heaven on earth.

Let's expand our inquiry to the larger question of whether beliefs in God and the next life are anti-life and somehow "poison everything." Right away we have to ask: did such beliefs poison poets such as Dante, Shakespeare, and Milton? Did they poison painters such as Raphael and Titian? Or artists such as Leonardo and Michelangelo? Did they ruin composers such as Handel and Bach? In his book *Human Accomplishment*, Charles Murray asks what common feature connects the great achievements of the West. He concludes that it is the sense of the transcendental that animates, even if implicitly, our sense of "the true, the beautiful and the good." Murray gives the revealing example of the nameless medieval stone masons who carved gargoyles on the great Gothic cathedrals. Often, he notes, their most detailed carvings were at the very top of the structure, concealed behind cornices and out of public view. Murray writes, "They sculpted these gargoyles as carefully as any of the others, even knowing that once the cathedral was completed and the scaffolding was taken down, their work would remain forever unseen by any human eye. It was said that they carved for the eye of God."[8] The Gothic masons, like many other great artists, did their work *sub specie aeternitatis*, i.e., under the aspect of eternity.

Now I want to show that several of the greatest ideas and institutions of Western civilization were shaped by a similar vision of transcendence. Let's begin with the core idea of Western liberalism, the idea of separating the realms of state and society. We all take for granted the existence of a public sphere which is the domain of government and a private sphere where we make our own decisions. When did this distinction originate? We are so used to equating democracy in classical antiquity with democracy today that we sometimes forget that in ancient Greece, there was no separation between these two realms. The state had the power to regulate all private actions, with nothing to stand in its way. Historian Paul Rahe points out that Sparta, not Athens, was regarded as the model society in classical antiquity, and the Athenians too had no compunction about subordinating private interests to the welfare of the community. In fact, the jurisdiction of the ancient *polis* far exceeded the comprehensive reach of the welfare state or even Islamic law in Muslim countries today.[9]

In the fourth century, the church father Augustine distinguished between the "city of God" and the "city of man." As Augustine envisioned it, the city of God is a heavenly city that will only be fully realized at the end of time. Man cannot by himself create that felicitous city, which is ultimately a product of divine architecture.

Augustine then contrasted this perfect heavenly city with the city of man on earth, a city divided by faction and torn by selfishness and violence. Augustine was aware of the attempts by Plato and other Greek philosophers to provide the intellectual framework for perfect regimes, but he seems to have regarded actual attempts to implement such ideas as futile and dangerous. Historical experience has fully vindicated Augustine on this count.

The main thrust of Augustine's argument, however, was not that man should eschew utopian schemes, but rather that as human beings we have separate allegiances and owe separate duties to the city of God and the city of man. Augustine did not invent this idea. Rather, it was Christ who first issued the injunction to "render unto Caesar what is Caesar's and unto God what is God's." The early Christians, harassed and persecuted by their Roman rulers, easily understood this distinction between the claims of their church and the rival claims of the ruling empire. So Augustine simply developed what the early Christians already believed, drawing out the implications of those ideas. He argued, for example, that the heavenly city provides a transcendent standard of justice that enables citizens to judge and correct the actions of the earthly rulers.[10] He also laid the intellectual groundwork for distinguishing between the realms of church and state. As a consequence, despite their frequent entanglements, church and state developed as separate institutions in Western civilization.

Fast forward now to the eleventh century, when a fierce dispute arose between Pope Gregory VII and the Holy Roman Emperor over which of them had the right to nominate and "invest" bishops and other local church officials. This so-called investiture controversy was the culmination of an ongoing rivalry between ecclesiastical power and secular power. In one of the strangest episodes in the history of the West, Emperor Henry IV knelt in the snow and did penance before Pope Gregory. Later, however,

Henry successfully drove the pope into exile. Although the institutional rivalry continued, over time the dispute laid the foundation for a new kind of Western society. Such a society has limited
government—the government has specific or enumerated powers
and cannot simply do whatever it wants. We also possess civil
society, a kind of protected space in which free citizens operate relatively insulated from state control. Finally we have institutional
pluralism, reflected in such arrangements as separation of powers,
checks and balances, and a free press. These modern institutions
have their roots in a fourth century text and in an old quarrel
between representatives of the city of God and the city of man.

Now let's examine the impact of Christian belief in transcendence and the afterlife on the ideas of human dignity and human
rights. When the American founders sought to establish what they
called a *novus ordo seclorum*, a new order for the ages, they
debated the basis on which they could affirm the radical proposition that "all men are created equal." The formulation eventually
came from Thomas Jefferson. Jefferson was a man of the Enlightenment and a man of science, and he was also, along with Benjamin Franklin, perhaps the least devout among the founders. Yet
despite their departures from Christian orthodoxy, both Jefferson
and Franklin affirmed a belief in God and in life after death. And
when Jefferson finally declared the source for the self-evident
proposition of human equality, it was none other than "the Creator." All rights, according to the American founders, have their
shared source in "the laws of nature and nature's God." The Declaration refers to God as the source of divine providence and also
as the supreme judge of conscience in the hereafter.[11]

Today it may seem odd to hear God and divine providence
invoked as the source of rights, so let's ask: if rights don't derive
from God, where do they derive from? Well, they could come
from evolution. Perhaps natural selection has outfitted us to

respect the dignity of others. The problem, as we have seen, is that even if evolution does this, it has nothing to do with rights. Rights are the moral language of politics. As Alexis de Tocqueville once put it, "The idea of right is simply that of virtue introduced into the political world."[12] Rights don't concern the way we do act; they concern the way we ought to act. So evolution is quite irrelevant here. A second possible source of rights is the idea that we are all equally human and therefore we share the same rights and privileges. But apes are also equal in being apes, and they don't share the same rights and privileges. Sure, apes sometimes enter into their own version of the "social contract," but as anthropologist Frans de Waal points out, these are coalitions of the strong that are organized to dominate and control the rest of the pack.[13] And this is exactly how human communities have been organized for millennia.

So on what basis did the *novus ordo seclorum* assert its new doctrine of human dignity and human rights? Actually, the doctrine was not so new; what was new was the implementation of it. In American and British historical accounts, rights are typically traced to the philosopher John Locke, but Locke himself was a great summarizer and synthesizer of ideas that others had generated before him. In reality the Western ideas of dignity and rights go back to the early sixteenth century. A few decades after the Spanish discovery of the New World, a series of momentous debates erupted in Spain that not only provided the intellectual foundation for rights, but also the first political recognition that such rights should be extended to all human beings. The debate was over whether American Indians had souls.

This is quite a subject for debate. Today, I suppose, atheists would say, "Of course they didn't have souls and neither do we." If you appreciate today the recognition of your dignity and rights, you should be glad that atheists with such a mindset had no influence in the sixteenth century. The reason for the debates in Spain was the clash of views between the conquistadores and the Christian missionaries. Almost immediately following the establishment of colonies in the Americas, the conquistadores and their successors began to enslave the native Indians. The missionaries protested to the Spanish crown and to the church in Rome, asserting that such enslavement was immoral and unjust. The enslavers appealed to the usual arguments: the native Indians are not like us; they are not Christian; they are not even civilized. Juan Gines de Sepulveda, a distinguished scholar of Aristotle, sided with the slave owners. Citing Aristotle's term, he insisted that the Indians were "slaves by nature."

But Francisco de Vitoria, a Dominican theologian at the University of Salamanca, did not agree. He argued that it made no difference if the slaves were not civilized. It didn't even matter if they were not Christian! That's because God has made all human beings, Christians as well as non-Christians, in His image. Since God is immortal, humans have immortal souls that represent our likeness to God. And since we are God's creation, only God, not man, has ultimate claims on us. To enslave the Indians, Vitoria contended, was to reduce immortal souls to tools of material advantage. Whatever the utility of such a practice, whatever the benefit to Spain and the Spanish crown, it should be outlawed because it is an offense against God.

The pope agreed with Vitoria, and in 1536 issued the encyclical *Sublimis Deus* which declared that "Indian and other peoples who may later be discovered by the Christians are by no means to be deprived of their liberty or the possession of their property, even though they be outside the faith of Jesus Christ." A few years later, the Spanish emperor Charles V suspended all further expeditions to the Americas. Never before, writes historian Lewis Hanke, had a powerful empire "ordered its conquests to cease until it was decided if they were just."[14] In 1550, the emperor convened a great debate at a monastery in Valladolid on precisely this subject: the moral legitimacy of the Spanish conquest. Sepulveda argued for the colonial interests. He contended that the Indians were barbarians without souls who should be ruled by the Spanish for their own good. On the other side was a passionate advocate for the Indians, the Spanish friar Bartolome de Las Casas. Las Casas argued that the Indians, as all human beings, have immortal souls that confer on them a special degree of dignity. He also dramatized the abuses that the Indians were subjected to "for their own good." Although the Spanish crown sided with Las Casas, and passed a series of laws seeking to protect Indians' rights, those laws were largely ignored in the Americas, where the great distance from Spain made enforcement almost impossible.

Even so, the Valladolid debates represent an historic landmark. Intellectual and political champions of freedom, such as John Locke in England and the American founders in Philadelphia, drew on these arguments to establish a permanent basis for human dignity and human rights.[15] We learn from the Valladolid debates that it matters whether we regard others as souls with an immortal destiny or not: such beliefs affect how we treat them here and now.

The movement to abolish slavery provides another striking example of the this-worldly consequences of other-worldly convictions. In my previous book *What's So Great about Christianity*, I showed how slavery was a universal practice and the only group to oppose it was the church. Principled opposition to slavery developed entirely as a Christian idea, and that's why the only anti-slavery movements in history were organized by Christians. In addition, the only nations that abolished slavery by their own decision were Christian ones. These nations conferred on the slaves a liberty that they were not in a position to secure for themselves. "Other revo-

lutions have been the insurrection of the oppressed," Ralph Waldo
Emerson wrote. "This was the repentance of the tyrant."[16]

Atheists, of course, dispute the central role of Christianity,
blame the belief in the afterlife for abetting the institution of slavery, and claim that abolition was largely a secular cause. Michael
Shermer, for instance, points out that the Bible raises no objection
to slavery, and in some passages slaves are instructed to obey their
masters. Other atheists claim that this biblical approval of slavery
must have intensified the agony of slavery, especially in America
where most of the slaves were also Christians. Moreover, for centuries Christians took slaves and discouraged revolts by assuring
the slaves of happiness in the life to come. Even in the period leading up to the American Civil War, Christians stood on both sides
of the debate, with Southern Christians vehemently supporting
slavery and Northern Christians denouncing it. Atheists point out
that real opposition to slavery in Europe and America did not
develop until the eighteenth century, precisely corresponding with
the historical epoch known as the Enlightenment. Therefore anti-
slavery is better understood as a secular Enlightenment idea rather
than a Christian idea.

How do we assess this atheist critique? The New Testament call
for slaves to obey masters, and for masters to be kind to slaves,
must be understood in the context of Christians living under the
Roman Empire. So the apostle Paul accepted the institution of
slavery for the same reason that he accepted the Roman tax code
and the rules of Roman military service: because he had no choice
in the matter. In the book of Acts, however, it is clear that Christians should not enslave fellow believers. Now the test of any
social philosophy is how it is interpreted and acted upon by its followers. The Christian leaders, like the church father Gregory of
Nyssa, preached sermons calling on Christians to stop being slave

owners, and as this message spread throughout Europe, the Christians actually did it.

It is widely believed that Christians continued the Greek and Roman practice of slavery until the modern era, but this is not true. Christianity came to power in the fourth century, and slavery was largely abolished in Europe between the fourth and tenth centuries. As historian Rodney Stark points out, by the latter part of the Middle Ages, there were virtually no slaves in Christian Europe. Slavery was replaced by serfdom, not exactly a benign institution, and yet at least one based on reciprocal rights and duties between lords and serfs. Serfs paid rent and kept a portion of what they produced. They could marry whom they wished and make their own decisions about when to work, how to raise their families, and what recreation to pursue. In short, they were not chattels or "human tools."[17] If you are ever forced to choose between being a serf and being a slave, be a serf.

Slavery became widespread in the American South for a simple reason: there was a lot of hard, backbreaking work to be done in the new world, and through the African slave trade there was a large supply of men and women who could be obtained to do it. As the Marxist scholar Eugene Genovese wrote in *Roll, Jordan, Roll*, widely considered the best study of American slavery, the planter class in the South developed a powerful vested interest in slavery. The Southern defense of slavery was entirely motivated by this selfish interest, and while it invoked biblical theology, this was little more than a rationalization for the planter class to extract penniless labor from unwilling Africans. Today it is widely recognized that most of those rationalizations, such as the curse of Ham and so on, are complete nonsense. Nowhere does the Bible even imply that Ham was black! That Southerners who called themselves Christian would nevertheless defend slavery may come as a surprise to some, but it can only be a real surprise to those who do not comprehend the depth of human selfishness.

Genovese began his study expecting to find that Christianity reconciled the slaves to their condition by telling them to wait for their eternal salvation and not to expect freedom in this life. This is precisely what atheists allege. And Genovese did find that the hope of eternal vindication sustained many of the slaves during their dark night of captivity. But Genovese was amazed to discover that such heavenly expectations never taught the slaves to become reconciled or contented with their lot. Rather, the slaves developed a powerful ethos of liberation, one in which the hope of salvation in the next world was inextricably connected with the demand for freedom in this world. Genovese, who later in life converted to Catholicism, shows how the slaves read the Bible to develop this ethos. Consider the lines of the great spiritual: "Go down, Moses, way down to Egypt land and tell old Pharaoh, let my people go." Here, from the Book of Exodus, the slaves drew an analogy between their own condition and that of the Israelites under Egyptian captivity. In this way Moses became a champion not only of the Jews in captivity, but also of the African slaves in America, and many freed slaves later named their children "Moses." Contrary to the atheist critique, the Bible provided the slaves a great message of liberation.[18]

Then, early in the eighteenth century, groups of Quakers and evangelical Christians in America began the first organized campaigns against slavery. They were motivated to do this by a biblical teaching: the simple idea that we are all equal in the eyes of God. Previously this idea was interpreted as a spiritual truth applicable only to the next life. But the Quakers and evangelical Christians insisted that it had profound implications for this life. Thus from the theological proposition of the equality of persons before God, they derived the political lesson that no man has the right to rule another without his consent. This revolutionary idea provided the basis not only for the abolition of slavery, but also for American democracy. The principle of modern representative democracy, after all, is identical; no person has the right to rule another without consent.

So what have we learned here? We have seen that the concepts of transcendence and eternity, far from being hostile to life and civilization as the atheists allege, have in fact shaped some our greatest and most beneficial social and political ideals. These ideals are shared by religious and secular people alike, including the establishment of a private sphere divorced from state control and of a fundamental human equality under God that establishes human rights. Paradoxically it is the world beyond the world that has made the greatest difference in our world. This means that life after death is not merely a rational and even probable belief; it is also a conviction that sustains and strengthens our civilization. Western beliefs in the afterlife have made us what we are, and this means that there is a great practical risk in jettisoning them, because over time we might also lose some of the ideals that we most cherish.

Chapter Twelve

GOOD FOR YOU

The Practical Benefits
of Belief

The object of opening the mind, as of opening the mouth,
is to shut it again on something solid.[1]

—G. K. Chesterton, *Autobiography*

A priest visited Niccolo Machiavelli on his deathbed. The priest urged Machiavelli to repent of his sins and renounce Satan. Machiavelli, eyes closed, said nothing. Again the priest implored, "Repent of your sins and renounce Satan." Still Machiavelli was silent. So the priest raised his voice and demanded, "WILL YOU REPENT OF YOUR SINS AND RENOUNCE SATAN?" And finally Machiavelli opened one eye and whispered, "Father, at a time like this, one tries not to make new enemies." The story is apocryphal. But it is compelling because, in characteristic Machiavellian fashion, it raises the prudential question, which is what this chapter is about. We have seen that a belief in immortality is good for society, at least for those of us in the West. We have also seen that there is a strong probable case for such a belief. Even so, there is a residual uncertainty. So here we continue our exploration of whether it is good for us as individuals to believe. We are going to unabashedly consider the practical consequences of belief and unbelief. Specifically, what's in it for me?

Richard Dawkins asserts that these issues are irrelevant because they sideline the issue of truth and emphasize the issue of utility. To Dawkins, it doesn't really matter whether a belief in God or the afterlife is beneficial or useful or consoling. "How can it be consoling," he says, "to believe in something which is just straight counterfactual? Just simply goes against the facts?" Dawkins mocks those who contend for God and immortality because, without these, life for them "would be empty, pointless, futile, a desert of meaningless and insignificance." Dawkins says, so what? "Maybe life is empty." He gives the analogy of a man who, refusing to come to terms with his wife's death, insists that this cannot be true because it would make his life intolerable, barren, and empty. Dawkins observes, "Life without your wife may very well be intolerable, barren, and empty, but this unfortunately doesn't stop her being dead."[2]

Dawkins's commitment to standing up for the truth even when it is unpalatable seems noble and admirable. Like freedom, truth is one of those core values of our culture, one that makes us automatically want to stand up and cheer. But the philosopher Nietzsche did not join in these accolades. He raised a surprising question: why is truth important? Why this fetishism of reason? Why should we care about veracity without regard to the consequences? To see what Nietzsche is getting at, imagine if the Nazis came and asked you where the Jews were hiding. I hope you would not respond by saying, "I may not want to tell you, but I have to. I am committed to the truth." Or imagine if you took your 15-year-old daughter for a routine medical checkup, after which the doctor informed you privately that she had a terminal illness with only a few years to live. Would you feel obliged, in the name of veracity, to tell your daughter about this death sentence? I'm not sure whether I would do it, but my decision would have nothing to do with some bogus requirement to disclose the truth. Rather, I would decide entirely on the basis of whether or not this information would be good for her life. Truth would take a back seat to practical considerations. The virtues of truth-telling are not, as Dawkins would have us believe, self-evident. Situations exist where it is better to remain silent, or perhaps even to ignore the truth. Nietzsche's argument was even more fundamental. Truth, he stated, is for the enhancement of life. It is not life that must serve truth, but truth that must serve life.

Hume put the point somewhat differently. Perhaps more pene-tratingly than anyone before him, Hume used both speculative and empirical reason to raise powerful questions about how we can claim to know anything. Just because the sun rose yesterday, how can I be sure it is going to rise again tomorrow? Just because A is followed by B, how do I know that A caused B? Although Hume insisted on skepticism as the proper mode of thought, he rejected skepticism as the proper mode of life. Hume recognized how absurd it would be to try to live as if you don't really know whether the sun will come up the next day. In a tellingly candid passage in his *Treatise of Human Nature*, Hume says that he would write philosophy for a while, and then he would put his papers aside and say, in effect, I'm done with that. Then he would go and play backgammon, or have drinks with friends, blithely ignoring the gloomy skepticism of his writings. Hume called his approach "mitigated skepticism" by which he meant skepticism left on the shelf. Basically, Hume would carry on his day as if philosophical theories were one thing, life quite another.[3]

Probably Dawkins's enthusiasm about truth arises largely from his belief in science as the main, if not the only, means of apprehending truth. Actually, as we have seen, science has no capacity to apprehend reality in itself; at best it can discover truths about the world of experience. Here, too, physical science is restricted to the objective domain, and large areas of human experience— all subjective thoughts and feelings, including morality and esthetics and personal and social relationships—lie outside its bounds. Even within its acknowledged jurisdiction, science discovers not final, but only provisional truths, always subject to amendment as new evidence comes in. If we take as truth what science today holds to be true, we would do well to remember that a hundred years ago the advocates of science adopted precisely the same position, and yet virtually every scientific proposition of that era has been radically revised or replaced in the intervening decades. It is quite likely that many scientific truths of today will look quaint, if not ridiculous, a hundred years from now.

The real prestige of science is not based on its claim to truth but on the simple fact that it works so well. Dawkins himself recognizes this. Confronted by an anthropologist who informed him that all cultures are equal and that science is merely a Western way of viewing the world, Dawkins responded, "Show me a cultural relativist at thirty thousand feet, and I'll show you a hypocrite. Airplanes built according to scientific principles work.... Airplanes built to tribal or mythological specifications don't. If you are flying to an international congress of anthropologists, the reason you will probably get there—the reason you don't plummet into a ploughed field—is that a lot of Western scientifically-trained engineers have got their sums right."[4] This is Dawkins at his polemical best, and I have no disagreement with him here. Like most people in the world, I too prefer a society with airplanes, computers, and modern medicine to one with bullock carts, pick-axes, and folk healers. I simply want to note the basis on which Dawkins makes his defense of science. For him, Western science is superior not primarily because it penetrates more deeply into the nature of reality, but because it can send winged machines across the ocean. Ultimately the best case for science is not theoretical but practical.

In one respect, however, Dawkins does have a valid point about truth. Once you stop believing that something is true, you can no longer enjoy the practical benefits of that belief. The philosopher who saw this most clearly was Nietzsche. For Nietzsche, the after-life was bound up with God and the Christian view of the world. In a famous scene, Nietzsche portrays a so-called madman or prophet who comes down from the mountain into the market-place and says he seeks God. "As many of those who do not believe in God were standing around just then," Nietzsche writes, "he provoked much laughter." One asks the madman, did God get lost? Another wonders, did he go on a voyage? A third says, did he emigrate? The madman silences their derisive hoots. "Whither is God?" he cries. "I shall tell you. We have killed him— you and I. All of us are his murderers. But how have we done this? How were we able to drink up the sea? Who gave us the sponge to wipe away the entire horizon?"[5]

The first thing to notice about this passage is that it is not directed at religious believers but at atheists. It is the atheists who mock the God who isn't there, and it is the atheists that Nietzsche's prophet considers to be the real fools. They are fools because they have not come to terms with the meaning of the death of God. They think that they can get rid of God and immortality but hold on to Christian values and Christian morality. Nietzsche's targets here were the Victorian English who affirmed both their disbelief in God and a future life and also their dedication to Christian ethical and social ideals. A classic representative of the Victorian view is the writer George Eliot, who proclaimed God "inconceivable," immortality "unbelievable," but duty "peremptory and absolute."[6] But Nietzsche could just as well have been referring to contemporary atheists who argue that they don't require God or the afterlife in order to be moral. For example, philosopher Daniel Dennett declares, "There is no reason at all why a disbelief in the immateriality or immortality of the soul should make a person less caring, less moral, or less committed to the wellbeing of everybody on earth than someone who believes."[7]

Nietzsche's argument against the Victorians and their modern-day counterparts is that when you destroy the foundation, the building must eventually collapse. For example, consider what happens when a society stops believing in aristocracy and becomes a democracy. For a while the aristocrats think that their way of life can continue despite the extension of the franchise, but then they discover that the ordinary folk won't put up with their superior attitude and their discriminatory practices. Over time even the ruffled shirts and poodles begin to look ridiculous: the democratic way of life stamps out even the last vestiges of aristocracy. Nietzsche's argument follows in the same track. In *Twilight of the Idols*, Nietzsche specifically addresses a section to unbelievers of the George Eliot stripe. "They have got rid of the Christian God, and now feel obliged to cling all the more firmly to Christian morality." What they miss is that God, immortality, and Christian morality are all part of the same package, so that "when one gives up Christian belief one thereby deprives oneself of the right to Christian morality."[8]

Some atheists are happy to go along with Nietzsche here, regarding the prospect of a decline in Christian morality as very

good news. "The worst feature of the Christian religion," philosopher Bertrand Russell wrote in *Why I Am Not a Christian*, "is its
attitude toward sex."[9] Russell anticipates that an erosion of belief
in Christianity will produce a loosening of moral and social
restrictions with regard to sex. As an advocate of public nudity
and free love, Russell naturally found this a very congenial
prospect. He was one of the first apostles of the sexual revolution.
Along the same lines, philosopher Ernest Nagel celebrates the
decline of "moral codes which seek to repress human impulses in
the name of some unrealizable otherworldly ideal."[10] At first the
sexual revolution was confined to bohemian communities of
artists and intellectuals in places in New York's Greenwich Village
and Paris's Left Bank. One does not normally think of economists
as having strong bohemian proclivities, but here is John Maynard
Keynes, commenting on the ethos of the Bloomsbury bohemians.
"We repudiated entirely customary morals, conventions, and traditional wisdom. We were, that is to say, in the strict sense of the
term, immoralists. . . . We recognized no moral obligation on us,
no inner sanction, to conform or to obey. Before heaven we
claimed to be our own judge in our own cause."[11] Since the 1960s,
the bohemian way of life has gone mainstream, so that a kind of
post-Christian morality has now become part of the ethos of the
West. From the point of view of its enthusiasts, sexual liberation
can be counted as one of the practical benefits of a decline in belief
in God and the afterlife.

So far Nietzsche would have agreed. He called himself the "first
immoralist," and he explicitly focused his anti-Christian polemics
on eradicating the traditional concepts of guilt and sin.[12] Thanks
in part to Nietzsche's influence, the West has seen a big reversal.
The prospect of death and the afterlife used to be regarded as a
powerful incentive to morality: we should act well in this life
because there is accountability for our actions in the next one. But

remove the belief in life after death and the whole situation changes. Now death becomes a pretext for immorality, or at least for disregarding the old moral codes. This is the notion of *carpe diem*: life is short and so we are encouraged to "seize the day." In Andrew Marvell's poem "To His Coy Mistress," the narrator says that if life went on forever he wouldn't mind waiting, but since death is around the corner and the body will soon decay, the two of them should jump into bed together and behave as if there were no tomorrow. "The grave's a fine and private place, but none, I think, do there embrace."[13] As Marvell's poem indicates, this kind of thinking predates Nietzsche, but it gained popularity in the late nineteenth and twentieth centuries, as beliefs in God and the after-life declined in the West.

Nietzsche, however, emphatically rejects the idea that we can dispense with Christian moral rules while keeping the remaining infrastructure of Christian morality substantially intact. Get rid of God and life after death, he argues, and you must also give up the ideas of equality, human dignity, democracy, human rights, and even peace and compassion. All of these, he notes, are imports from the age of transcendence, what Nietzsche terms "shadows of God," and none of them can long survive without the assumptions that made them tenable. The only way to go beyond God and the afterlife is to have a revaluation of values and eventually to produce a new type of human being, a kind of "overman" who is, in Nietzsche's terms, "beyond good and evil." But this, Nietzsche recognizes, is a very precarious and hair-raising project. Nietzsche predicts that the death of transcendence will produce a terrible moral crisis, a dissolution of ideals to the point of nihilism. In the twentieth century, he says, "we shall have upheavals . . . and wars the like of which have never yet been seen on earth."[14] Nietzsche's analysis is rendered more plausible by the fact that it has proved so prophetic.

In one respect, however, both Nietzsche and Dawkins are wrong. Both base their analyses on the premise that there is no God and no life after death. For both men, it seems axiomatic that no intelligent person today can uphold theism or the afterlife. At least with regard to the second assumption, we have already seen how dubious this is. But let us not fight one kind of dogmatism with another. The best response to false atheistic certitude is not false certitudes of a rival kind. Rather, let us admit that these questions—especially the issue of what comes after death—cannot be fully and finally resolved on the basis of reason.

This is not because life after death is an unscientific question inhospitable to rational inquiry or empirical verification. On the contrary, the assertion that death is not the end is a factual claim. It can be reasonably assessed, as I have tried to do in this book, and it can be empirically verified in the same manner as other claims about the future. If I say that the stock market will be at least double its value twenty years from now, or that there will be a nuclear war in the second half of the twenty-first century, these are propositions that can be verified. We simply have to wait and see. Theologian John Hick writes that life after death is a claim that is subject to "eschatological verification."[15] If there is life after death, then we will all at some point be in a position to know this. True, if there is no afterlife there will be no one around to congratulate the unbelievers. But either way it will be evident after the fact, perhaps to observers in another galaxy, perhaps only to God, that one side was correct.

Life after death seems to be the ultimate case of Hegel's principle that the owl of Minerva flies only at dusk. Hegel meant that we must live in history, but we can fully recognize its direction only in retrospect, only by looking back. This is certainly true of the afterlife. We must live in the world, and yet until we die we cannot know for sure whether this world is the only one. We can do our best to compute the probabilities, but there is no way on the basis of reason alone to reach certainty. What then should we believe about what comes after death? Even more important, how should we live now?

These questions seem insuperably difficult to answer, but let's remember that most of life's decisions both large and small are made in the face of limited information and uncertain outcomes. Should you try the new Ethiopian restaurant that just opened in town? Is it worth increasing your investments in real estate? Should your son go to law school or become a poet? Is it too late in life for the couple next door to have another child? Should your friend accept a recent proposal of marriage? In every one of these cases we have some data at our disposal but not nearly enough to safely predict what the outcome will be. Here, too, the owl of Minerva flies at dusk. Consequently the agnostic stance is tempting: let's not decide until we have all the facts. But actually this is the most idiotic position of all because it fails to appreciate that we will never have all the facts. If your friend insists on dating until she can be sure what marriage is going to be like for the rest of her life, she will never have that information and therefore she will never get married. To adopt the agnostic stance is to fail to grasp the reality of the situation. The philosopher Soren Kierkegaard once said of life that we have to "live it forward," meaning that we have to make decisions and get on with it. This is not to suggest that one should take actions in resolute ignorance. Rather, we should make our best choice based on what we do know, weighing the risk of saying "yes" against the risk of saying "no." In all of these cases, therefore, practical reason says that we should be prepared to decide and act even in the face of uncertainty. And so it is with life after death.

How then should we decide this issue, given some remaining uncertainty? Toward the end of the nineteenth century, psychologist William James addressed the question of how speculative reason should translate into practical action. James based his analysis on a famous wager proposed almost two centuries earlier by scientist and mathematician Blaise Pascal. Pascal's wager is about the existence of God, but Pascal seems to have adapted his argument from a much earlier one by the medieval Muslim thinker Abu Hamid al-Ghazali. Interestingly al-Ghazali's wager is not about whether God exists, but about whether there is an afterlife. Therefore let us go to the source and begin with al-Ghazali.

In his book *The Alchemy of Happiness*, al-Ghazali describes an encounter between a believer in the afterlife and one who rejects the idea. The unbeliever persists with his doubts, and so the believer changes his approach. The issue, he says, is not what we can know for certain but how we should act in a given situation. The believer says, suppose you are about to eat food, and someone tells you a serpent has spat venom on it. Would you still eat it? The obvious answer is no; it is better to endure the pangs of hunger rather than take the risk and eat, even though the informant may be joking or lying. Or imagine, the believer says, that you are incurably ill and a charm-writer tells you, give me a few coins, and I will write a charm that you can tie around your neck, and you will be cured. In a desperate situation, it's obviously worth a few pennies to give it a try.

But if this is so, the believer says, then consider all the wise men through history who have held that there is life after death. Isn't their testimony worth more than that of charm-writers? When we consider the risks of belief and unbelief, shouldn't we give these sages the benefit of the doubt? Al-Ghazali cites one of the early leaders of Islam, the prophet Muhammad's son-in-law Ali, telling an unbeliever, "If you are right, then neither of us will be any worse in the future, but if we are right, then we shall escape, and you will suffer." So in one scenario there is nothing, but in another there is heaven for the believers and hell for the unbelievers. Given that either scenario could be right, what is the smart way to proceed? Al-Ghazali concludes that when we consider the tremendous issues at stake and the risks involved in belief and unbelief, the practical course of action becomes clear. Even if we are unsure whether there is life after death, reason suggests that we should act as if there is.[16]

Al-Ghazali wrote at a time when life after death was obvious to most people; it was the default position, somewhat complacently held by believers, and the burden of proof was on unbelievers. Taking up the issue a century ago, William James found himself addressing a very different audience. This was the intelligentsia whose default position ranged somewhere between agnosticism and unbelief. This group no less complacently rejected the afterlife, and within its precincts of influence, the burden of proof was very much on believers. James was a pragmatist who spoke in terms of the "cash value" of beliefs. He evaluated beliefs in terms of the actual difference they make in our lives. To understand James, consider an issue that has divided philosophers for centuries: does color reside in objects or in subjects? In other words, is the color green to be found in the drapes or is it located instead in the operations of your eye and your brain? James's answer would be, who cares? This distinction is utterly irrelevant when it comes to decorating your apartment!

Let us follow James as he applies this down-to-earth approach to the issue of life after death. James argued that immortality is a pressing question, somewhat akin to a man who is trapped on a mountain pass and must decide whether to stand still or to venture down one of several paths in front of him. The man can see very little through the snow and mist. The man realizes that if he takes one road, he could very well fall off the mountain. That, James says, is one kind of risk. In the face of the dangers, the man is strongly tempted to stand still and do nothing. But that, James points out, is not an avoidance of risk but taking a different kind of risk. If the man does nothing, he will probably freeze to death.

James's point is that while belief in life after death poses the risk of adopting a position without complete proof, and thus the risk of being wrong, unbelief poses a different kind of risk, the risk of missing out on the blessings of immortality that are promised to believers. The superior rationality of the agnostic position—do not risk being wrong until you are absolutely sure—disappears when we see that there are actually two types of risk. Unlike al Ghazali or for that matter Pascal, James does not say that under the circumstances belief is the only reasonable position. For James, it comes down to what kind of risk a person wants to take: some will go for immortality, recognizing the risk of metaphysical error if they are wrong. Others, who want at all costs to avoid a false belief in life after death, will reject the idea in full awareness that if they are mistaken they may be giving up eternal contentment with God.[17]

In the spirit of James, let's draw up a balance sheet listing the assets and liabilities of belief in the afterlife. As I mentioned in the last chapter, one potential liability of belief in the afterlife is that believers may turn away from this life in the expectation that the only worthwhile life is the next one. The danger, in other words, is one of lassitude and fatalism. This danger has to some extent been realized in Hinduism and Buddhism. Christopher Hitchens contrasts the productive and industrious life of a scientist who spends years collecting and analyzing specimens with that of a Hindu sage or Buddhist monk sitting motionless on a sacred pillar.[18] Like Hitchens, I have a preference for life actively lived in this world, and I have never been attracted to the resigned attitude of Eastern philosophy and religion. Even so, this fatalism does not extend to the Western religions. In fact, the asceticism and industriousness of

modern scientists is a direct legacy of the asceticism and industriousness of medieval monks who were the scholars and scientists of
their day. More broadly, in all the Western religions—Judaism,
Christianity, and Islam—this life is held to be of the highest importance not only because it is a gift from God, but also because our
actions in this life are the ones that decide our eternal fate. Unlike
Hinduism and Buddhism, the Abrahamic religions offer no second
lives and second chances; everything depends on how we live now.
Fatalism, therefore, may be a liability for some views of life after
death, but it doesn't apply to all or even most such views.

On the positive side, I can think of four clear benefits provided
by belief in the afterlife. First, it provides us with hope at the point
of death and with a way to cope with our deaths. Atheists sometimes say they don't fear death, but when they say this they are
having a Pinocchio moment; look for their noses to grow longer.
All evolved creatures fear death because they have a built-in desire
to survive. For the candid atheist, death is a complete disaster
because it turns even the most successful life into a failure at the
end. For the believer in the afterlife, death is also feared and resisted. Believers too have an innate desire to keep on living. But even
though death produces anxiety in believer and unbeliever alike,
for the believer death isn't catastrophic. Indeed, death is viewed
as the gateway to a new life and a better life. With his customary
pragmatism, William James notes that since we are all destined to
die, belief in immortality "makes easy and felicitous what is in any
case necessary," and in doing so it is "performing a function
which no other portion of our nature can so successfully fulfill."[19]

Second, belief infuses life itself with an enhanced sense of meaning and purpose. This is not to say that the unbeliever's life is aim-
less and empty. As many atheists emphasize, there is meaning to
be found in work, in family, and in social relationships. But alas,
these are temporary. When you die, all your projects must be

inevitably abandoned and your relationships irrevocably terminated. This recognition disrupts the smooth flow of life, since humans, uniquely among all creatures, know they are going to die. So we are like creatures seeking happiness on an island, knowing the island itself is slowly sinking into the sea, and whatever we build on the island will soon be completely submerged. As the philosopher Sartre noted, the only honest response to this knowledge is complete despair. Life becomes, in Macbeth's words, "a tale told by an idiot, full of sound and fury, signifying nothing."[20] But not for the believer, who is sustained by the hope and conviction that this life is completed and fulfilled in an eternal life to come.

Third, belief gives us a reason to be moral and a way to transmit morality to our children. Atheists sometimes scorn the mercenary morality of those who perform well in the expectation of being rewarded in the next life. But as philosopher John Locke pointed out, when virtues are rewarded they do not lose their splendor; on the contrary, it offends our sense of justice when this is not the case. So when we believe in life after death, we affirm cosmic justice, and this gives us hope that good will be finally rewarded and evil punished. Morality becomes both easier and more worthwhile in this framework. Now, as we have seen, morality is not entirely a popular notion with unbelievers. One practical motive for atheism is to seek hedonistic escape from the demands of morality. As Victor Stenger writes in *God: The Failed Hypothesis*, "The atheist has the comfort of no fears for an afterlife."[21] But there is always the danger that this security is illusory; you flee through a tunnel only to find the authorities waiting for you at the other end. Locke was himself a hedonist who based his ideas on the principles of pleasure and pain. Precisely for this reason, he accepted life after death, because he recognized the possibility of an omnipotent deity who could hand out superlative rewards and punishments.[22]

Here, of course, we are permitting the idea of life after death to become mixed in with the idea of God and religion, but in practical terms we have to recognize that this is usually the case. Moreover, while the moral sense is part of human nature, religion is the main if not the only way that parents have taught moral behavior to their children across cultures and through the centuries. Some atheists argue, in the manner of psychologist Marc Hauser, that "this marriage between morality and religion is... unnecessary, crying out for a divorce."[23] Atheists would have us replace religious education with secular moral theories advanced by philosophers like Hegel and Heidegger. But we all know people who learned their morality through Hinduism or Christianity; whoever learned his morality from Hegel or Heidegger? As a practical matter, religion is a better transmission belt for moral education of the young than the philosophy seminar.

Finally, there is strong evidence that belief in life after death makes your life better and also makes you a better person. In *Medicine, Religion, and Health*, Harold Koenig summarizes a wide body of data showing that religious people who affirm the afterlife are healthier than nonbelievers. They are less likely to suffer from stress and depression, less likely to attempt suicide, less vulnerable to a host of other ailments, and more likely to live longer. Psychologist Jonathan Haidt cites surveys that show that "religious people are happier, on average, than nonreligious people." Surveys show that religious people even have more fulfilling sex lives than secular people! And sociologist Arthur Brooks concludes his study of philanthropy in America by showing that religious believers are vastly more generous both with their time and money than their secular counterparts. They give more not only to religious causes but also to secular causes.[24] None of this is particularly surprising when you consider the nature of belief: the prospect of an afterlife provides a motive for morality and generosity because it is linked to cosmic justice. These data show that there are immense practical benefits to belief: you are likely to live longer and healthier, be happier in your marriage, and also make a greater contribution to your fellow man.

Some people may respond to this data by saying, wonderful! Let others believe, but not me. This is the position not of belief but of "belief in belief," and it is held by quite a few people who like to think of themselves as sophisticated and above the popular multitude. This position, however, is quite irrational. If others stand to benefit from lives full of hope, purpose, and charity, why not you? Given the weight of the evidence in favor of belief, there is no room for unbelievers to claim that their position enjoys a superior claim to rationality. On the contrary, unbelief is neither intellectually plausible nor practically beneficial.

Chapter Thirteen

LIFE EVERLASTING

Eternity Right Now

O death, where is thy sting?
O grave, where is thy victory?

—Paul, *First Letter to the Corinthians* 15:55

We have reached a surprising pass. We have repelled the atheist case against the believers. In fact, the atheists have hurled every javelin they possess against the idea of life after death, and every throw has fallen short of its mark. But we have accomplished more than a refutation of the other side. We are also equipped with strong positive arguments from several different fields for the afterlife. By examining the arguments for and against life after death, we have concluded that there is a strong intellectual and practical case for belief. Let's review what we have discovered so far.

Near death experiences show that clinical death may not be the end; there may be "something more." The universality and uniformity of near death experiences suggest that consciousness can outlast the breakdown of the body. These experiences cannot be explained away as the product of drugs or dying brains. NDEs don't say much about what life after death might be like, but they do imply the real possibility of some sort of afterlife.

Modern physics shows the existence of matter that is radically different in its attributes from any matter that we are familiar with. Physics also demonstrates the possibility of realms beyond the universe and modes of being unconstrained by the limits of our physical laws. So there is nothing in physics to contradict the idea that we can live beyond death in other realms with bodies that are unlike the bodies we now possess.

Modern biology shows an evolutionary transition from matter to mind that does not seem random or accidental but rather built into the script of nature. This natural teleology from nonliving matter to living things to contemplative minds is a vital clue that as nature progresses from the material to the immaterial, and from the perishable to the imperishable, so too may we. Like nature itself, we may be in a natural transition from living beings made up of matter to minds that are not subject to the limitations of matter.

Neuroscience reveals that the mind cannot be reduced to the brain, and that reductive materialism is a dead end. The whole realm of subjective experience lies outside its domain, and outside the domain of objective science altogether. Two features of the mind—specifically consciousness and free will—define the human soul. These features seem to operate outside the laws of nature and therefore are not subject to the laws governing the mortality of the body. The body dies, but the soul lives on.

Modern philosophy makes a central distinction between experience and reality. Empirical realists seem chronically unable to distinguish between the two, and this is their fatal flaw. Once we abandon empirical realism, mature philosophical reflection in the manner of Kant and Schopenhauer enables us to discover the existence of a noumenal or other world. As humans we inhabit both worlds, and when we die, the unreal world of experience comes to an end for us, but a part of us lives eternally in the real world.

Morality is best understood under the presupposition that there is cosmic justice in a world beyond the world; this would explain why we live even now in two realms: the realm of "the way things are" and the realm of "the way things ought to be." Attempts to explain morality as a Darwinian survival strategy are not only inadequate but miss the point: morality is not about how we do act but about how we should act. This normative aspect of morality only makes sense if we presume that it represents the legislative standard derived from a post-mortem existence. The postulate of an afterlife enables us to make sense of this life.

Finally, practical reason helps us to see that a belief in immortality is good for our society and good for our lives. Such beliefs provided the core foundation for the cherished values of equality and dignity; it remains an open question whether we can preserve these values without their original foundation. As individuals we have little to lose by believing, and everything to lose if we don't. Moreover, belief supplies us an added motive for virtue, a mechanism to teach our children right from wrong, a better way to cope with death, and also a sense of hope and purpose that our lives would not otherwise have.

So far from disproving life after death, reason and scholarship give powerful support to it. On this issue that is central to all the world's religions, knowledge and science have shown themselves to be allies of belief. Reason and revelation don't clash; they reinforce each other. Remarkable though this is, we should have anticipated it. As believers, we expect knowledge and faith to be compatible. This is not the real shocker. The real shocker is the claim, which we will investigate in this chapter, that someone actually died and came back to life. We are not talking about nocturnal apparitions or ghostly visitations, but about bodily resurrection, the resurrection of the whole person. This claim is made exclusively by Christianity about its founder Jesus Christ. No one says of Moses or Muhammad that after their deaths they were encountered again in the flesh. So if the Christian claim is true, it immediately rises above the pack; in fact, it renders every other afterlife theory an "also ran." Here we explore the credibility of this claim, but we also consider the implications of affirming the historicity of the resurrection. An event like this has the power to transform human destiny, to inaugurate a completely new phase of history and a new understanding of reality. I conclude this book by spelling out the astounding Christian view that we can begin to experience eternity not in another life but in this one. In other words, the uniqueness of the Christian message is not life after death but eternal life right now.

Let's begin with Christ's resurrection and treat it as an historical claim no different from any other historical claim. I am not going to give the resurrection privileged treatment on the grounds that it is considered a sacred event; I am also not going to adopt the prejudiced view that it couldn't have happened because such things cannot happen. Very few scholars fall into the first temptation; many succumb to the second. Gerd Lüdemann's *The Resurrection of Jesus* is fairly typical. It applies what it regards as an established scientific principle to the case of Christ: since no one dies and rises again, therefore Christ could not have died and risen again. We find a similar approach in the books of Marcus Borg, John Dominic Crossan, and also in the work of the so-called Jesus Seminar.[1] These scholars are mainly theologians and historians who display little knowledge of science, yet they confidently insist that science has disproved the possibility of life after death. We have seen, of course, how fallacious this claim is. There is a case to be made against the resurrection, but it must be based not on an *a priori* rejection but on an examination of the concrete circumstances.

Here are the four historical facts that have to be accounted for. First, Christ was tried by his enemies, convicted, and crucified to death. Second, shortly after his burial, Christ's tomb was found empty. Third, many of the disciples, but also one or two skeptics, claimed to have seen Christ alive in the flesh, and interacted with him following his death. Fourth, inspired by the belief in Christ's bodily resurrection, the disciples initiated a movement that, despite persecutions and martyrdom, converted millions of people to a new way of life based on Christ's example and his teachings. These facts are affirmed by the mainstream of modern historical scholarship. They are known with the same degree of reliability as other facts that are taken for granted about the ancient world: say the fact that Socrates taught in the marketplace of Athens, or the fact that Caesar crossed the Rubicon, or the fact that Alexander the Great won the battle of Gaugamela.

In history, we take the facts that we do know, and we try to make sense of them. Theologian N. T. Wright, in a mammoth study, argues that while the hypothesis that Christ actually rose from the dead may sound intuitively implausible, it has great explanatory power. In other words, the resurrection is believable because it makes sense of all the other facts listed above. If Christ did rise from the dead, it would help us understand why the tomb was empty, why the disciples thought they saw Christ after his death, and why this realization motivated them to evangelism and strengthened them to face persecutions and martyrdom without renouncing their new convictions. Wright goes much further, though, suggesting that resurrection is not merely a sufficient

hypothesis, but also a necessary one. He means that no alternative hypothesis can explain the given facts with anything
approaching the same degree of plausibility.[2] Since skeptics have
been advancing alternative theories for two thousand years, this
is quite a claim. So let's briefly review some of those alternative
theories.

Perhaps the most popular one, at least since the Enlightenment,
is that the resurrection is a myth; the disciples made it up. "The
myth of the resurrection," writes Corliss Lamont in *The Illusion
of Immortality*, "is just the kind of fable that might be expected
to arise in a primitive, pre-scientific society like that of the ancient
Hebrews."[3] The disciples expected their leader would return, so
they concocted the story that they saw him alive after his death.
While this is the view perhaps most widely held by skeptics today,
it is actually the weakest attempt to make sense of the facts. First,
as Wright shows, the idea that dead people don't come back to life
is not an Enlightenment discovery. The ancient Hebrews knew
that as well as we do. Second, Christ's Jewish followers did not
expect him to return to life. Jews believed in bodily resurrection,
but not until the end of the world. The disciples were utterly
amazed when they saw Christ in the flesh, and some refused at
first to believe it. Third, it is one thing to make up a story and
another thing to be willing to endure persecution unto death for
it. Why would the disciples be ready to die for something they
knew to be a lie?

A second theory is that the disciples stole the body. This theory
is very old; in fact, it was advanced by Christ's Jewish opponents
to account for the empty tomb. Jewish polemics against Christianity for two centuries continued to emphasize this theme. The
theory, however, has several obstacles. Christ's tomb was barred
by a stone and guarded by Roman soldiers. How could the disciples have gotten by the guards? Moreover, if the disciples stole the

body, they would know for a fact that Christ wasn't raised from the dead. We come back to the problem with the previous theory: Why would the disciples' mourning turn to gladness? Why would they embark on a worldwide campaign of conversion? Why would they refuse to recant their beliefs on pain of death? What really requires explanation here is why Christ's opponents would so tenaciously advance such an implausible explanation. The answer seems obvious: they had to account for the fact that the tomb was empty. The empty tomb is significant because we know that Christ's followers were proclaiming his resurrection in Jerusalem almost immediately following his death. If they were simply making this up, there would be an easy way to disprove their claims, by producing Christ's corpse. This didn't happen, and the obvious explanation is that neither the Jews nor the Romans could do this.

A third theory—conveyed in several popular books—holds that Christ didn't really die but was merely in a swoon or trance.[4] In the tomb he revived, made his getaway, and then showed up before the disciples. There are severe problems with this theory. For starters, it presumes that Roman soldiers didn't know how to kill people. Typically crucifixion is death by asphyxiation, and if Roman soldiers weren't sure the victim had perished they would break his legs. Christ's legs were not broken, evidently because the soldiers were convinced he was dead. So the idea of Christ reviving in the tomb is far-fetched. But even if he did, he would have been barely conscious, at the point of death. Imagine a man in this condition rolling back the stone, eluding the guards, and then presenting himself to his followers. Their expected reaction would be, get this man to a doctor! But this is not what happened. The disciples, disconsolate over Christ's death, did not claim to experience a half-dead man in a swoon, they claimed to see a man who had triumphed over death and was fully returned to life and health. Because of its incongruity with the historical evidence, even historian David Strauss, a noted skeptic about the resurrection, rejected the swoon theory.[5]

Finally there is the hypothesis of the hallucinating disciples. This is Gerd Lüdemann's preferred explanation for why we have a resurrection story in the first place. Lüdemann says that even today people claim to have "visions" of the Virgin Mary. In the same manner, the disciples had "visions," and these visions proved contagious and "led to more visions." Eventually just about everyone was reporting Jesus sightings.[6] Lüdemann's hallucination theory has gained credibility in recent years with the emergence of substantial numbers of people who claim to have seen UFOs or Elvis returned to life. But the great problem with the hallucination hypothesis is that hallucinations are almost always private. Except in very rare cases, more than one person does not have the same hallucination. If ten people report seeing something very unlikely, it is not convincing to say they are simply dreaming or imagining things, because you then have to account for why they are all having the same dream or imagining the same thing. Historian Gary Habermas asks us to envision a group of people whose ship has sunk and who are floating in the sea on a raft. Suddenly one man points to the horizon and cries out, "I see a ship." Sure, he may be hallucinating, but then no one else is going to see the same ship. Now if the others on the raft also see it, forget about the hallucination theory, it's time to start yelling for help because there really is a ship out there.[7]

Apply this reasoning to Elvis sightings and it's obvious that if several normal people say they saw Elvis in Las Vegas, they most likely didn't make it up. Probably they saw one of the hundreds of Elvis impersonators who regularly perform in night clubs and casinos. In the same way, when people report witnessing a UFO they are almost certainly not hallucinating; rather, they did see something in the sky but didn't know what it was. The problem in most cases isn't hallucination but misidentification. Now Christ is said to have appeared several times to his disciples. Paul notes that on one occasion he appeared to more than 500 people. Many of them were alive when Paul wrote, and thus they were in a position to dispute the veracity of his account. James, who was a skeptic about Christ's ministry, reportedly became convinced that Christ was the messiah only after seeing his resurrected body; so too, the apostle Thomas, the famous doubter, was convinced of the resurrection only after he touched the wounds of Jesus. Paul himself was by his own account a persecutor of Christians until Christ appeared to him on the road to Damascus. Never in history have so many diverse individuals on different occasions reported the same hallucination. Hallucinations cannot account for the empty tomb, nor for why the Jews and Romans didn't settle the whole controversy by producing Jesus' body.

The remarkable conclusion is that for all their veneer of sophistication, none of the alternative theories provides even a remotely satisfactory account of the historical data before us. On the surface, these theories look deep; but deep down, they are really shallow. The resurrection hypothesis, however fanciful it appears at the outset, turns out upon examination to provide the best available explanation. I'm not trying here to prove the resurrection. One of the most striking discoveries of historical research is how little we definitively know about the past. What I am trying to show is that, based on scholarly standards uniformly applied, the resurrection survives historical scrutiny.

Even more than the historicity of the resurrection, the point I want to emphasize is its significance. I intend to show that the resurrection inaugurates a revolutionary new understanding both of history and of reality. Before I do this, I want to convey Christ's equally transformational teaching on heaven and hell. This should not be confused with some of the tropes and teachings of popular Christianity throughout the centuries. Oddly enough it was the atheist Nietzsche who fully recognized the difference. Nietzsche felt nothing but antipathy towards the institution of Christianity, but nevertheless he treats Christ very gently. At times he is virtually enraptured by Christ, and the harshest accusation he can muster is to call Christ an "idiot." Even here he doesn't mean that Christ is a fool; rather, in the manner of Dostoevsky's novel *The Idiot*, he uses the term to mean a complete innocent. Nietzsche accuses Christ of being a pure, simple soul who is utterly out of place in a rapacious and cynical world.[8] This portrait, we will discover, is very close to the truth.

Christ offers a new teaching about salvation that rejects the concept of meritocracy. This is remarkable because the meritocratic scheme is crucial to every other religion's concept of cosmic justice. In Hinduism and Buddhism, for instance, your fate in the next life is the direct consequence of your conduct in this one. In Judaism and Islam, you must obey the rules to be eligible for heaven; fail often enough, and you should expect to go to hell. But Christ overturns this whole scheme by declaring at the outset that no one is good enough to get to heaven. Some humans may be better than others, but the differences aren't enough to make a difference. Heaven is the pure abode of God, and anyone who gets there must be pure like God.

Christ also redefines virtue so that it is not merely about what we should do, but also how we should be. For Christ, genuine virtue means purity of heart. This is the meaning of Christ's mysterious injunction that we must become like little children to enter heaven. He doesn't mean we should become intellectually naïve but rather morally innocent. This explains Christ's insistence that if we have contemplated the sin we have, in effect, committed it. What we require is inner reformation, a kind of internal cleansing. This is a radical raising of the moral bar. Now we can see why, by this elevated standard, we all are sinners, unworthy to enter heaven.

Before we despair, however, Christ offers a solution. In contrast with the difficulty of our situation, the solution is breathtakingly simple. It turns out that we don't have to scale the high moral bar. We are not being asked to do the impossible. Rather, Christ wants us to acknowledge that we are sinners and to accept God's grace by way of his sacrifice on the cross. There is a penalty for sin, we are told, but Christ has already paid it. In other words, the one who came back from the dead has cleared the way for the rest of us to enjoy eternal happiness. Therefore our job is almost embarrassingly easy: a guilty plea is all that is required for us to obtain an acquittal. Is this an excuse to avoid moral responsibility? Not at all. In accepting Christ's sacrifice we repent of our misdeeds and seek to emulate his example in seeking purity of heart. We may never fully achieve this goal in the present life, but it at least supplies a standard to aspire to now, and one that will be realized in the life to come.

Who can say no to such an offer? Alas, there are some who will. This is not because they seek eternal misery. Rather, they refuse to go Christ's way because they insist on going their own way. Their motto is that of Milton's Satan, "Better to reign in hell than to serve in heaven."[9] Their destiny is determined by their own decision. They choose to reject heaven, and God acquiesces in their choice. As C. S. Lewis writes in *The Great Divorce*, there are two kinds of people in the end, those who willingly say to God, "Thy will be done," and the kind to whom God reluctantly says, "Thy will be done."[10]

The atheist Christopher Hitchens has said in our debates that he does not want to go to heaven. Hitchens rejects heaven because, he says, he doesn't want to spend eternity living under a celestial dictatorship. In Hitchens's view, heaven is a monotonous, regimented place where everyone is forced to stand around, sing hymns, and hand out garlands. Hitchens reminds me of some of my college friends who liked to say, "Yeah, man, I want to be in hell. All my friends are going to be there. We are going to party." Some Christians will be horrified at these descriptions, but, to some degree, popular Christian depictions of heaven and hell are to blame. When most of the portraits of heaven feature celestial cherubs and heavenly choirs, it is easy to get the idea that all people do there is serve in the harp section. In Milton's *Paradise Lost*, the most interesting character by far is Satan, who is portrayed as a wily and scheming explorer. Somehow in popular Christian depictions of life after death, vice appears glamorous and virtue loses all her loveliness.

But this is not the way things ought to be, and, according to Christ, it is not the way they will be. It is important to note what Christ has to say about hell, because there are some who think of Christ as a gentle, loving person who would never send anyone to hell. Christ is indeed gentle and loving, but he certainly believes in the existence of hell, and he never talks as though the place is empty. Indeed, Christ speaks in Matthew 7:13–14 of the wide gate and the narrow gate and emphasizes that many more people are headed down the broad road to hell. Perhaps to avert this, Christ speaks at great length about hell and constantly emphasizes how terrible it is and how we can avoid going there.

Why is hell so terrible? Because it is the place where God is not. And since Christ emphasizes that all good things come from God, it follows that there is nothing good to be found in the realm of God's absence. Hell in Christ's depiction is not a place of horned demons and pitchforks. Hell is where you get exactly what you want, and if what you want is something other than God, that something will describe hell for you. In Dante's *Inferno* the sinners in the circle of lust are buffeted helplessly this way and that; they wanted to subordinate reason to desire, they wanted to be "out of control," and this is precisely what they get. Interestingly Dante uses fire quite sparingly in hell; in the deepest circle, Satan and his closest followers are encrusted in a lake of ice. In Dante's poetic imagination, hell is an icy blast of isolation from the warmth of God's love.

One way to think about hell is to envision the worst things that have happened to you, and then imagine them as a kind of permanent condition. That would be hell, and perhaps hell is a lot like that. I don't take all the metaphors about cauldrons of fire literally, but I do take them seriously. If we believe Christ, hell is a place we would do well to avoid. I doubt there are parties in hell. Nor is the company likely to be interesting. As C. S. Lewis envisioned it, hell is painted in colors of grey. It displays the full banality of evil. I hope to convince Hitchens that hell is eternally boring. I want him to picture a graduate student who won't go away eternally pestering him, "Christopher, let me show you my 50,000-page thesis disproving the Trinity." I want Hitchens to envision the tedium of constantly yelling back, "For heaven's sake, shut up!"

Heaven, too, is not what our naïve expectations and popular images make it out to be. We shouldn't adopt the attitude of the ancient Greenlanders. They told the missionaries that they wanted nothing to do with heaven as soon as they heard there wouldn't be any seals there. Notwithstanding two thousand years of Christian art, we have to get over the whole cherub and harp thing. We also have to reject the idea of disembodied souls taking part in a kind of eternal church service. Actually, there is no reason to expect churches in heaven. Why should there be, when we can experience directly the resplendence of God? What was denied to Moses—the chance of seeing God face-to-face—is promised to the believer. The beatific vision is surely the best part of heaven, and it is virtually indescribable. Here we require the resources not of the intellect but of art. Dante perhaps comes closest in the final cantos of his *Paradiso*, when he describes the radiance of God reducing him to babbling and baby talk. And glancing back at earth from heaven's highest empyrean, Dante says he had to smile because earth seemed to him so distant and so paltry, "this puny threshing ground of ours."[11] This is no attempt to diminish earth or devalue life; rather, Dante is invoking here a God's-eye view that puts everything in proper perspective. And Dante implies that this is one of heaven's gifts: for those who hunger to know, heaven promises full disclosure of the true nature of things.

In his recent book, *Heaven*, Randy Alcorn argues that we cannot underestimate the delights of heaven because we have no idea what the resources of omnipotence can deliver. Even so, Alcorn wants to make heaven accessible to our understanding, and so he insists that supernatural happiness is continuous with natural happiness. It differs in magnitude but not in kind. Our experience of the beautiful and the sublime on earth is a preview of heaven; if we think of the best things we have experienced on earth and envision them continuing, magnified and without interruption, that's heaven. Yes, Alcorn thinks there will be soccer matches and fine dinners in heaven.[12]

Extrapolating based on Christ's teachings and those of Scripture, Alcorn addresses such fascinating questions as whether families reunite in heaven, whether animals make it there, and so on. Since mine is a different kind of book, I cannot follow him much further here. My own approach to such questions is that of Aquinas. Asked whether there is a gold-gilded book in heaven in which the names of the saved are listed alphabetically, Aquinas replied that as far as he knew this was not the case, but there was no harm in believing it. This is what I tell people who ask me if their pet parrot—"A holy bird! Doesn't even swear!"—is going to enjoy eternal happiness: I don't really know, but there's no harm in believing it.

It seems irresistible for us as Christians to anticipate what is going to happen in "the next life" or "the next world." But this way of thinking misses both the significance of Christ's resurrection and the force of Christ's revolutionary teaching. We can see this by considering an episode in Luke's gospel in which Christ is asked by the Pharisees, "When is the kingdom of God coming?" Christ replies in Luke 17:20–21 that "the kingdom of God is in the midst of you." What does Christ mean by this? Throughout the New Testament, the gospel writers use the terms "kingdom of heaven" and "kingdom of God" interchangeably. In view of this, Christ's words mean that in some sense the kingdom of heaven is *already here*. What a strange, outrageous, ravishing idea!

We can understand it better with the aid of Augustine's rival images of the "city of God" and the "city of man." We think of these as distinct, one referring to the heavenly city of the future, the other referring to the earthly city of the present. But if they are distinct, then eternal life becomes a matter of wait, wait, wait. And this is precisely what's going on in other religions—everyone is waiting. Indeed, life itself becomes one long wait, a frustrating human predicament symbolized in Samuel Beckett's play *Waiting for Godot*. In this scheme, what we build on earth seems futile since one day the world is going to be destroyed, and we are going to have to relocate to another world. God's plan, in this view, requires the abolition of His original work of creation so that He can build afresh somewhere else. But this does not seem to be the biblical view of eternity. Augustine himself rejects the total separation of the two cities; he emphasizes that the heavenly city supplies the standard or guideline for the operations of the earthly city. The earthly city should be patterned on the heavenly city, even if the heavenly city cannot be realized on earth. Augustine also stresses that when we become Christians, we immediately become citizens of the heavenly city. We don't have to wait for the next life to get our membership cards; we get them right here and now. Philosopher Dallas Willard writes that when it comes to eternity there is no waiting period; rather, "Eternity is now in process."[13]

The event that makes this possible is Christ's resurrection, which was not merely a promise of things to come; it also brought about a transformation in the present. The resurrection represents Christ's victory over death. This is not to say that death ceases to be an enemy; only now it is a vanquished enemy. As the poet John Donne concludes his beautiful poem, "Death Be Not Proud": "And death shall be no more. Death, thou shalt die."[14] Christ's victory over death is achieved not at the end of history but in the course of history. History begins anew after that, as our calendars suggest by separating time into the eras before and after Christ. The resurrected Christ in a sense brought the heavenly city down to earth, not as an actual city, but as a spiritual community of like-minded Christians. The dividing line is no longer the one between life and the afterlife, but between life before becoming a Christian and the eternal life beyond that point. Consequently Christians are, even here on earth, residents of a heavenly kingdom, and since this kingdom is eternal, the astounding conclusion is that we can have eternal life in the present.

Consider the profound implications of the idea of eternity right now. It means that we should treat other people as immortal souls and not as perishable bodies. It means that what good we build here on earth becomes part of God's eternal kingdom. It means that heaven is now a dimension of everyday existence, and we can enjoy even in this life a foretaste of the life to come. In other words, heaven can be experienced at least in some measure even

before we "go to heaven." Moreover, we may not be going anywhere. The book of Revelation 21:1 speaks of a "new heaven and
a new earth," and while the meaning of these terms is not entirely
clear, one plausible reading is that heaven may be instituted here
through a radical transformation of the earth. If this happens it
would be a final answer to the Lord's Prayer: "Thy kingdom
come, thy will be done, on earth as it is in heaven." How astounding it would be if these words prove to be literally true, these long-
recited hopes and petitions concretely realized.

I think you know where I come out on all this, but as I conclude
this book I cannot help but wonder, what about you? Throughout this book I have envisioned you sitting in the jury box. You
have heard the evidence, and when you have deliberated over it,
you must act. In this case, as so often in life, you cannot permanently wait and waffle; you have to go one way or the other. And
here is the supreme irony: ordinarily a juror is given the task of
deciding the fate of another. But in this case the fate you are deciding is your own. In my opening chapter I introduced you to the
San Francisco entrepreneur who said that he didn't care if there
was life after death or not; it made no difference to him. But on
this he couldn't be more wrong: it makes all the difference in the
world! Therefore, choose as if everything depends on your decision, because it does.

ACKNOWLEDGMENTS

First I want to thank my lovely wife Dixie, who brightens every day and is my confidante in everything I do. I also want to acknowledge my daughter Danielle; I wish I had been as poised and graceful as she is in my teenage years. How much richer my life is with these two! Pete Marsh is trying to multiply my work through the Peter Marsh Foundation; much more than a supporter, he is also a guide and an inspiration. Bruce Schooley has been involved in every aspect of this book; he has helped me to formulate my ideas and answer objections. I am grateful to my friend Ed McVaney for his support, encouragement and advice; he too read the manuscript and made helpful suggestions. I'd like to thank John and Carol Saeman for their friendship and for helping to sponsor some of my debates. My research assistants Michael Hirshman and Josh House performed valuable tasks of criticism, brainstorming, and fact checking. Working at breakneck pace, Stan Guthrie helped me shape and improve the manuscript. Philosopher Daniel Robinson and physicist Stephen Barr read the book in draft form, and their suggestions have made it much better. I also want to thank Andrew Accardy, Clark Van Deventer, Michael Hirshman, Ed and Caroline Hoffman, B. J. Marsh, Spencer Masloff, Carole McVaney, Harvey Popell, Sam Reeves, Valerie Schooley, Larry Taunton, Suzanne Thompson, and Byron Van Kley. Pastors Ray Bentley, Bob Botsford, Ed Cornwell, Joe Fuiten, and Dave Menard are always there if I need advice and counsel. Finally I wish to thank Harry Crocker, longtime friend and the editor of this book, and his assistant Mary Beth Baker who worked patiently on the little details.

NOTES

Chapter One

1. Andrew Marvell, "To His Coy Mistress," in M. H. Abrams, ed.
   The Norton Anthology of English Literature (New York: W.W.
   Norton, 1986), 1388.
2. Arthur Schopenhauer, *Essays and Aphorisms* (New York: Penguin
   Books, 1970), 72.
3. George Eliot, "O May I Join the Choir Invisible," in *O May I
   Join the Choir Invisible* (Boston: D. Lothrop Company, 1884), 1;
   and Woody Allen, cited in *The Observer*, London, May 27, 2001,
   p. 30.

4. Cited by Barry Morrow, *Heaven Observed* (Colorado Springs, CO: NavPress, 2001), 89.

5. Philippe Aries, *The Hour of Our Death* (New York: Vintage Books, 1981), 559–601.

6. The Harris Poll, "The Religious and Other Beliefs of Americans," February 26, 2003, harrisinteractive.com; Gallup News Service, "Americans More Likely to Believe in God Than the Devil, Heaven More Than Hell," June 13, 2007, gallup.com.; Erlendur Haraldsson, "Popular Psychology, Belief in Life After Death and Reincarnation in the Nordic Countries, Western and Eastern Europe," *Nordic Psychology* 58: 171–80 (2006); and World Values Survey, "Belief in Life After Death, 1981-2004," jdsurvey.net.

7. Owen Flanagan, *The Problem of the Soul* (New York: Basic Books, 2002), 12.

8. Peter Atkins, *The Creation* (San Francisco: W.H. Freeman, 1981), 39.

9. Victor Stenger, *Has Science Found God?* (Amherst, NY: Prometheus Books, 2003), 19.

10. Richard Dawkins, "Religion's Misguided Missiles," *The Guardian*, September 15, 2001.

11. Sam Harris, *The End of Faith* (New York: W.W. Norton, 2005), 39.

12. The Barna group, "A New Generation Expresses Its Skepticism and Frustration with Christianity," September 24, 2007, barna.org; see also: David Kinnaman and Gabe Lyons, *Unchristian* (Grand Rapids, MI: Baker Books, 2007).

Chapter Two

1. William Shakespeare, *Hamlet*, in *The Complete Works of William Shakespeare* (New York: Barnes and Noble, 1994), 688.

2. James Boswell, "David Hume, Just A-Dying," *The Journals of James Boswell* (New Haven: Yale University Press, 1991), 247; and Adam Smith, letter to William Strahan, November 9, 1776,

reprinted in D. J. Enright, ed. *The Oxford Book of Death* (New York: Oxford University Press, 2008), 60.

3. Daniel Dennett, "Thank Goodness!" in Louise Antony, ed. *Philosophers without Gods: Meditations on Atheism and the Secular Life* (New York: Oxford University Press, 2007), 113–17.

4. Sam Harris, *The End of Faith*, 19, 72.

5. Michael Shermer, "Hope Springs Eternal," The Great Afterlife Debate, skeptic.com.

6. Sam Harris, *The End of Faith*, 35.

7. Richard Dawkins, *The God Delusion* (Boston: Houghton Mifflin, 2006), 282.

8. Victor Stenger, *God: The Failed Hypothesis* (Amherst, New York: Prometheus Books, 2007), 103.

9. Francis Crick, *The Astonishing Hypothesis* (New York: Touchstone Books, 1994), 258.

10. W. K. Clifford, "The Ethics of Belief," in Gerald McCarthy, ed. *The Ethics of Belief Debate* (Atlanta: Scholars Press, 1986).

11. Richard Dawkins, *The God Delusion*, 52–53. The relevant passage from Russell is cited by Dawkins.

12. David Hume, *An Enquiry Concerning Human Understanding* (New York: Barnes and Noble, 2004), 128.

13. Karl Popper, *Objective Knowledge* (Oxford: Clarendon Press, 1979).

14. David Hume, *A Treatise of Human Nature* (New York: Penguin Books, 1983), 138.

15. Joel Primack and Nancy Ellen Abrams, *The View From the Center of the Universe* (New York: Riverhead Books, 2006), 134–37.

16. Richard Rorty, *Achieving Our Country* (Cambridge: Harvard University Press, 1998), 18; and Richard Dawkins, *The God Delusion*, 190, 206.

17. Sigmund Freud, *The Future of an Illusion* (New York: W.W. Norton, 1989), 39–40, 55.

18. Pascal Boyer, *Religion Explained* (New York: Basic Books, 2001), 20, 207; and Mary Lefkowitz, *Greek Gods, Human Lives* (New Haven, CT: Yale University Press, 2003), 236.

19. Lewis Wolpert, *Six Impossible Things Before Breakfast* (New York: W.W. Norton), 27.

20. Steven Pinker, *How the Mind Works* (New York: W.W. Norton, 1997), 555.

Chapter Three

1. Peter Berger, *The Desecularization of the World: Resurgent Religion and World Politics* (Grand Rapids, MI: Eerdmans, 1999), 13.

2. Kai Nielsen, "An Atheist's Rebuttal," in J. P. Moreland and Kai Nielsen, *Does God Exist* (Amherst, New York: Prometheus Books, 1993), 67.

3. Bertrand Russell, *Why I Am Not a Christian* (New York: Simon & Schuster, 1957), v.

4. Cited by Peter Kreeft, *Fundamentals of the Faith: Essays in Christian Apologetics* (San Francisco: Ignatius Press, 1988), 74.

5. Alan Segal, *Life after Death: A History of the Afterlife in Western Religion* (New York: Doubleday, 1989).

6. John Hick, *Death and Eternal Life* (Louisville, KY: Westminster Press, 1994), 62.

7. Pascal Boyer, *Religion Explained*, 196.

8. Rudolf Otto, *The Idea of the Holy* (New York: Oxford University Press, 1958).

9. Leo Strauss, *Natural Right and History* (Chicago: University of Chicago Press, 1953), 15.

10. Jacob Neusner, "Judaism," in Jacob Neusner, ed. *Death and the Afterlife* (Cleveland, OH: The Pilgrim Press, 2000), 43; and Abraham Neuman, "A Jewish Viewpoint," in *In Search of God and Immortality* (Boston: Beacon Press, 1961), 5.

11. Thomas Huxley, *Evolution and Ethics* (New York: Barnes and Noble, 2006), 40.

12. Confucius, *The Analects* (New York: Penguin Books, 1986), 107.

13. Confucius, *The Analects*, 89; Tu Wei-Ming, "Confucianism," in Arvind Sharma, *Our Religions* (New York: HarperOne, 1993), 145.

14. Burton Watson, *The Lotus Sutra* (New York: Columbia University Press, 1993); and Rodney Stark, *Discovering God: The Origins of the Great Religions and the Evolution of Belief.* (New York: HarperOne, 2007), 242.

15. Carl Becker, *Breaking the Circle: Death and the Afterlife in Buddhism* (Carbondale, IL: Southern Illinois University Press, 1993), 46–55.

16. Liu Xiaogan, "Taoism," in Arvind Sharma, *Our Religions*, 239.

Chapter Four

1. A. J. Ayer, "What I Saw When I Was Dead," *Sunday Telegraph*, August 28, 1998.

2. The Harris Poll, "The Religious and Other Beliefs of Americans," February 26, 2003; Gallup News Service, "Three in Four Americans Believe in Paranormal," June 16, 2005; and Erlendur Haraldsson, "Popular Psychology, Belief in Life after Death and Reincarnation in the Nordic Countries, Western and Eastern Europe," *Nordic Psychology* 58: 171–80 (2006).

3. David Hume, "Of the Immortality of the Soul," reprinted in Paul Edwards, ed. *Immortality* (Amherst, NY: Prometheus Books, 1997), 134–40.

4. Paul Edwards, "Introduction," in Ibid., 8–9.

5. C. J. Ducasse, *A Critical Examination of the Belief in a Life after Death* (Springfield, IL: Charles Thomas, 1961), 224.

6. Paul Edwards, *Reincarnation: A Critical Examination* (Amherst, NY: Prometheus Books, 2002), 226.

7. Deepak Chopra, *Life After Death: The Burden of Proof* (New York: Three Rivers Press, 2006), 174–76.

8. Ian Stevenson, *Twenty Cases Suggestive of Reincarnation* (Charlottesville, VA: University of Virginia Press, 1974), 20–32; Ian Stevenson, *Children Who Remember Previous Lives* (Char-

lottesville, VA: University Press of Virginia, 1987); and *Where Reincarnation and Biology Intersect* (Westport, CT: Praeger Press, 2003).

9. Leonard Angel, "Reincarnation All Over Again," *Skeptic*, Fall 2002; and John Beloff, "Is There Anything Beyond Death?" in Paul Edwards, ed. *Immortality*, 262–63.

10. Raymond Moody, *Life after Life: The Investigation of a Phenomenon—Survival of Bodily Death* (New York: HarperOne, 2001), 10–12.

11. Plato, *The Republic* (New York: Penguin Books, 1984), 448–55; and Bede, *A History of the English Church and People* (New York: Penguin Books, 1968), 420–21.

12. Frederick Hoffman, "The Secret Wound," in Jay Gellens, ed. *Twentieth Century Interpretations of A Farewell to Arms* (Englewood Cliffs, NJ: Prentice Hall, 1970), 108–11; Carl Jung, "Visions: Life After Death," in Lee Bailey and Jenny Yates, eds. *The Near-Death Experience* (New York: Routledge, 1996), 105–6; and A. J. Ayer, "What I Saw When I Was Dead."

13. Kenneth Ring, *Life at Death: A Scientific Investigation of the Near-Death Experience* (New York: William Morrow, 1982); Melvin Morse with Paul Perry, *Closer to the Light: Learning from the Near-Death Experiences of Children* (New York: Ballantine Books, 1990), 26–30; and Michael Sabom, *Light & Death: One Doctor's Fascinating Account of Near-Death Experiences* (Grand Rapids, MI: Zondervan, 1998), 13.

14. Kimberly Clark, "Clinical Interventions with NDEs," in Bruce Greyson and C. P. Flynn, eds. *The Near- Death Experience* (Springfield, IL: Charles Thomas Publisher, 1984), 242–55.

15. Kenneth Ring and Sharon Cooper, *Mindsight: Near-Death and Out-of-Body Experiences in the Blind* (Bloomington, IN: iUniverse Press, 2008); Kenneth Ring and Sharon Cooper, "Near Death and Out of Body Experiences in the Blind," in *Journal of Near-Death Studies* 16 (1997): 215–44; and Elisabeth Kübler-Ross, *On Life after Death* (Berkeley, CA: Celestial Publishers, 2008), 7.

16. George Gallup Jr. with William Proctor, *Adventures in Immortality* (New York: McGraw Hill, 1982); and "Most Doctors Believe in God, Afterlife," Associated Press, June 23, 2005.

17. Billy Graham, *Death and the Life After* (Nashville: Thomas Nelson, 1987), 20; and John Ankerberg and John Weldon, *The Facts on Life after Death* (Eugene, OR: Harvest House Publishers, 1992), 9, 27.

18. Maurice Rawlings, *Beyond Death's Door* (Nashville: Thomas Nelson, 1978); Bruce Greyson and Nancy Evans Bush, "Distressing Near-Death Experiences," in Lee Bailey and Jenny Yates, eds. *The Near-Death Experience*, 209–30; Margot Grey, *Return from Death* (London: Arkana, 1985); and Michael Sabom, *Light & Death*, 16.

19. Pim van Lommel, Ruud van Wees, Vincent Myers, and Ingrid Elfferich, "Near-Death Experience in Survivors of Cardiac Arrest," *The Lancet* 358, Issue 9298 (2001): 2039–45.

20. Carl Sagan, *Broca's Brain: Reflections on the Romance of Science* (New York: Random House, 1979), 143; and Carl Becker, "The Failure of Saganomics," *Anabiosis* 5 (1982): 39–47.

21. Carol Zaleski, *Otherworld Journeys: Accounts of Near-Death Experience in Medieval and Modern Times* (New York: Oxford University Press, 1987); Allan Kellehear, *Experiences Near Death: Beyond Medicine and Religion* (New York: Oxford University Press, 1996); and Susan Blackmore, *Dying to Live: Near Death Experiences* (Amherst, New York: Prometheus, 1993), 19.

22. Melvin Morse with Paul Perry, *Closer to the Light*, 21–23.

23. Karl Jansen, "Neuroscience, Ketamine, and the Near-Death Experience," in Lee Bailey and Jenny Yates, eds. *The Near-Death Experience*, 265–82.

24. Michael Shermer, "Hope Springs Eternal," *Scientific American*, July 2005.

25. Susan Blackmore, *Dying to Live*, 6, 75, 81, 93, 261.

Chapter Five

1. Brian Greene, *The Fabric of the Cosmos: Space, Time, and the Texture of Reality* (New York: Alfred Knopf, 2004), 5.
2. Bertrand Russell, *Why I Am Not a Christian*, 97.
3. Brian Greene, *The Fabric of the Cosmos*, 80, 112–22.
4. Ibid., 18.
5. Lisa Randall, "Toward the Invisible," in Lynn Margulis and Eduardo Punset, eds. *Mind, Life and Universe: Conversations with Great Scientists of Our Time* (White River Junction, VT: Chelsea Green Publishers, 2007), 301.
6. Paul Steinhardt and Neil Turok, *Endless Universe: Introduction to the Cyclic Universe* (New York: Broadway Books, 2007), 39; and Neil deGrasse Tyson and Donald Goldsmith, *Origins: Fourteen Billion Years of Cosmic Evolution* (New York: W.W. Norton, 2004), 69–71.
7. John Barrow, *The Origin of the Universe* (New York: Basic Books, 1994), 37.
8. Steven Weinberg, *Facing Up: Science and its Cultural Adversaries* (Cambridge: Harvard University Press, 2001), 54.
9. Stephen Hawking, *A Brief History of Time* (New York: Bantam Books, 1996), 144, 190.
10. Ibid., 126; Steven Weinberg, *Facing Up*, 80–81; Martin Rees, *Just Six Numbers: The Deep Sources That Shape the Universe* (New York: Basic Books, 2000), 25; and John Barrow and Frank Tipler, *The Anthropic Cosmological Principle* (New York: Oxford University Press, 1996).
11. Richard Dawkins, *The Ancestor's Tale: A Pilgrimage to the Dawn of Evolution* (Boston: Houghton Mifflin, 2004), 2; and John Leslie, *Immortality Defended* (Oxford: Blackwell Publishing, 2007), 72.
12. Leonard Susskind, *The Cosmic Landscape* (New York: Back Bay Books, 2006), x, xi, 21.
13. Fred Hoyle, *The Intelligent Universe* (London: Michael Joseph Publications, 1983), 218.

14. Alex Vilenkin, *Many Worlds in One* (New York: Hill and Wang, 2006); Lee Smolin, *The Life of the Cosmos* (New York: Oxford University Press, 1997); and Max Tegmark, "Parallel Universes," Special Report, *Scientific American*, 2007, sciam.com

15. Cited by Tim Folger, "Science's Alternative to an Intelligent Creator," *Discover*, December 2008, discovermagazine.com.

16. Stephen Barr, *Modern Physics and Ancient Faith* (Notre Dame, IN:. University of Notre Dame Press, 2003), 155–56.

17. Carl Sagan, *Billions and Billions: Thoughts on Life and Death at the Brink of the Millennium* (New York: Random House, 1997), 56.

18. Owen Gingerich, "God's Goof," in Paul Kurtz, ed. *Science and Religion: Are They Compatible?* (Amherst, NY: Prometheus Books, 2003), 57, 63.

Chapter Six

1. Paul Davies, *The Fifth Miracle: The Search for the Origin and Meaning of Life* (New York: Simon & Schuster, 1999), 271.

2. Jacques Monod, *Chance and Necessity* (New York: Vintage Books, 1971), 112; Stephen Jay Gould, *Full House: The Spread of Excellence from Plato to Darwin* (New York: Three Rivers Press, 1996), 175, 214; and William Provine, "Evolution and the Foundation of Ethics," 1988 paper, cited by Kenneth Miller in *Finding Darwin's God: A Scientist's Search for Common Ground between God and Evolution* (New York: Harper Perennial, 1999), 171.

3. Charles Darwin, letter to Asa Gray, June 5, 1874, in Charles Darwin, *Life and Letters* (London: John Murray, 1888), Vol. 3, 189; and Charles Darwin, *The Descent of Man* (Princeton, NJ: Princeton University Press, 1981), 201.

4. Stuart Ross Taylor, *Destiny or Chance: Our Solar System and Its Place in the Cosmos* (Cambridge: Cambridge University Press, 1998), 71

5. Michael Denton, *Nature's Destiny: How the Laws of Biology Reveal Purpose in the Universe* (New York: Free Press, 1998), 28–45, 184–86.

6. Franklin Harold, *The Way of the Cell: Molecules, Organisms, and the Order of Life* (New York: Oxford University Press, 2003), 10, 35, 56, 101, 245.

7. Michael Shermer, *Why Darwin Matters: The Case Against Intelligent Design* (New York: Times Books, 2006), xvi.

8. Richard Dawkins, *The Blind Watchmaker: Why the Evidence of Evolution Reveals a Universe without Design* (New York: W.W. Norton, 1996), 165.

9. Peter Atkins, *The Creation*, 31.

10. Francis Crick, *Life Itself: Its Origin and Nature* (New York: Simon & Schuster, 1981), 88.

11. Stuart Kauffman, *Reinventing the Sacred: A New View of Science, Reason, and Religion* (New York: Basic Books, 2008), xi, 231.

12. Paul Davies, *Cosmic Jackpot: Why Our Universe is Just Right for Life* (Boston: Houghton Mifflin, 2007), 4.

13. Freeman Dyson, *A Many-Colored Glass: Reflections on the Place of Life in the Universe* (Charlottesville, VA: University of Virginia Press, 2007), 76.

14. Stephen Jay Gould, *Full House*, 10, 14, 145, 176, 178.

15. Simon Conway Morris, "Introduction," in Simon Conway Morris, ed. *The Deep Structure of Biology* (West Conshohocken, PA: Templeton Foundation Press, 2008), viii.

16. Simon Conway Morris, *Life's Solution* (Cambridge: Cambridge University Press, 2003), 307.

17. Christian de Duve, *Vital Dust: The Origin and Evolution of Life on Earth* (New York: Basic Books, 1995), xv, xvii, 9, 299; and *Life Evolving: Molecules, Mind, and Meaning* (New York: Oxford University Press, 2002), 171, 182.

Chapter Seven

1. Francis Crick, *The Astonishing Hypothesis*, 3.
2. V. S. Ramachandran, *A Brief Tour of Human Consciousness: From Imposter Poodles to Purple Numbers* (New York: Pi Press, 2004), 3.
3   Owen Flanagan, *The Problem of the Soul* (New York: Basic Books, 2002), 6, 10;. Paul Churchland, *Matter and Consciousness* (Cambridge: MIT Press, 1988), 167; Carl Sagan, *The Demon-Haunted World* (New York: Ballantine Books, 1996), 13.
4. Antonio Damasio, *Descartes' Error: Emotion, Reason, and the Human Brain* (New York: Penguin Books, 2005); and V. S. Ramachandran, *A Brief Tour of Human Consciousness*.
5. William James, "Human Immortality," in William James, *The Will to Believe* (New York: Barnes and Noble Books, 2005), 265–84.
6. Paul Churchland, "Folk Psychology," in Samuel Guttenplan, ed. *A Companion to the Philosophy of Mind* (Oxford: Blackwell Publishers, 1994); see also Paul Churchland, *Matter and Consciousness: A Contemporary Introduction to the Philosophy of Mind* (MIT Press, Cambridge, 1988), 43–49.
7. James Boswell, *Life of Johnson* (New York: Oxford University Press, 1934) Vol. 2, p. 82.
8. Daniel Dennett, *Breaking the Spell* (New York: Viking, 2006), 107.
9. Thomas Nagel, "What Is It Like to Be a Bat?" in Thomas Nagel, *Mortal Questions* (Cambridge: Cambridge University Press, 1979), 165–80.
10. Frank Jackson, "What Mary Didn't Know," *Journal of Philosophy* 83: 291–95 (1986).
11. Daniel Dennett, *Consciousness Explained* (Boston: Little Brown, 1991), 398–401; and *Sweet Dreams: Philosophical Obstacles to a Science of Consciousness* (Cambridge: MIT Press, 2006), 103–29.
12. Steven Pinker, *How the Mind Works*, 21.

13. Alan Turing, "Computing Machinery and Intelligence," *Mind*, Vol. LIX, No. 236 (1950).

14. John Searle, "Minds, Brains and Programs," *The Behavioral and Brain Sciences*, Vol. 3 (1980); see also John Searle, *Minds, Brains and Science* (Cambridge: Harvard University Press, 1984).

15. Jacques Monod, *Chance and Necessity*, 21.

Chapter Eight

1. Michael Gazzaniga, *The Ethical Brain: The Science of Our Moral Dilemmas* (New York: HarperPerennial, 2005), 99.

2. Jeffrey Schwartz and Sharon Begley, *The Mind and the Brain: Neuroplasicity and the Power of Mental Force* (New York: HarperPerennial, 2002); and Sharon Begley, *Train Your Mind, Change Your Brain* (New York: Ballantine Books, 2008).

3. Mario Beauregard and Denyse O'Leary, *The Spiritual Brain: A Neuroscientist's Case for the Existence of the Soul* (New York: HarperOne, 2007), 140–49.

4. Norman Doidge, *The Brain That Changes Itself* (New York: Penguin Books, 2007), 173, 259.

5. Paul Davies and John Gribbin, *The Matter Myth: Discoveries That Challenge Our Understanding of Physical Reality* (New York: Simon & Schuster, 2007), 215.

6. Jeffrey Schwartz and Sharon Begley, *The Mind and the Brain: Neuroplasicity and the Power of Mental Force*, 16–18, 255–89, 325–64.

7. Steven Pinker, *How the Mind Works*, 148; and David Chalmers, *The Conscious Mind: In Search of a Fundamental Theory* (New York: Oxford University Press, 1996), 3.

8. John Locke, *An Essay Concerning Human Understanding* (Oxford: Clarendon Press, 1975), 460.

9. Nicholas Humphrey, *Conscious Regained: Chapters in the Development of the Mind* (New York: Oxford University Press, 1984), 35–37.

10. Daniel Dennett, *Consciousness Explained*; and the exchange between John Searle and Daniel Dennett in John Searle, *The Mystery of Consciousness* (New York: New York Review Press, 1997), 97–131

11 David J. Chalmers, *The Conscious Mind*, 125.

12. Owen Flanagan, *The Problem of the Soul*, 114; Daniel Wegner, *The Illusion of Conscious Will* (Cambridge: MIT Press, 2002), 14, 27, 325; and E. O. Wilson, *Consilience: The Unity of Knowledge* (New York: Alfred Knopf, 1998), 119.

13. Benjamin Libet, "Unconscious Cerebral Initiative and the Role of Conscious Will in Voluntary Action," *Behavioral and Brain Sciences* 8, (1985): 529–66.

14. Daniel Dennett, *Elbow Room* (Cambridge: MIT Press, 1999), 169.

15. Stephen Barr, *Modern Physics and Ancient Faith*, 179.

16. J. B. S. Haldane, *Possible Worlds* (New York: Harper & Row, 1928), 220.

17. E. O. Wilson, *The Creation: An Appeal to Save Life on Earth* (New York: W.W. Norton, 2006), 13, 35, 99, 123, 142.

18. Immanuel Kant, *Religion Within the Limits of Reason Alone* (New York: Harper & Row, 1960), 55.

Chapter Nine

1. Ludwig Wittgenstein, *Tractatus Logico-Philosophicus* (New York: Routledge Press, 1974), 86.

2. Bryan Magee, *The Philosophy of Schopenhauer* (Oxford: Clarendon Press, 1997), 3, 19, 274–75.

3. Ibid., 19.

4. Francis Crick, *The Astonishing Hypothesis*, 12; Steven Weinberg, *Facing Up*, 91; and E. O. Wilson, *Consilience*, 61, 258.

5. George Berkeley, *Principles of Human Knowledge* (New York: Penguin Books, 1988).

6. Karl Popper, "Metaphysics," in David Miller, *Popper Selections* (Princeton, NJ: Princeton University Press, 1985), 224–25.

7. Steven Pinker, *How the Mind Works*, 115.

8. George Berkeley, *Principles of Human Knowledge*, 55

9. David Hume, *A Treatise of Human Nature*, 205–23, 300.

10. Arthur Schopenhauer, *Parerga and Paralipomena* (Oxford: Clarendon Press, 1974), Vol. I, p. 170; and *On the Basis of Morality* (Indianapolis, IN: Hackett Publishing, 1995), 206.

11. Cited by Shimon Malin, *Nature Loves to Hide* (New York: Oxford University Press, 2003), 23; see also Tim Folger, "Time May Not Exist," *Discover*, June 12, 2007, discovermagazine.com..

12. Immanuel Kant, *Critique of Pure Reason* (New York: St. Martin's Press, 1965), 27–29, 56, 67–90, 163, 172–73, 265–75, 385, 467–78, 511.

13. Arthur Schopenhauer, *The World As Will and Idea*, (New York: Everyman Press, 2004), 59.

14. Ibid., 3, 18–20.

15. Arthur Schopenhauer, *On the Basis of Morality*, 212–13.

16. Bryan Magee, *The Philosophy of Schopenhauer*, 15.

17. Arthur Schopenhauer, *Suffering, Suicide and Immortality* (Mineola, NY: Dover Publications, 2006), 34–35; *The World as Will and Idea*, 185; and *On the Basis of Morality*, 213.

Chapter Ten

1. Adam Smith, *The Theory of Moral Sentiments* (Indianapolis, IN: Liberty Fund, 1982), 25.

2. Carl Sagan, *The Varieties of Scientific Experience: A Personal View of the Search for God* (New York: Penguin Books, 2006), 64.

3. This point is made in Robert Clark, *The Universe: Plan or Accident? The Religious Implications of Modern Science* (Grand Rapids, MI: Zondervan Publishing, 1972), 7–10.

4. Thomas Kuhn, *The Copernican Revolution* (Cambridge: Harvard University Press, 1985), 76.

5. Walter Isaacson, *Einstein: His Life and Universe* (New York: Simon & Schuster, 2007), 107–35, 218.

6. Adam Smith, *The Theory of Moral Sentiments*, 215.

7. Charles Darwin, *The Descent of Man*, 500.
8. Matt Ridley, *The Origins of Virtue* (New York: Penguin Books, 1996), 56; see also Robert Wright, *The Moral Animal* (New York: Pantheon Books), 186–87.
9. Richard Dawkins, *The Selfish Gene* (New York: Oxford University Press, 1989), v.
10. E. O. Wilson, *Sociobiology: The New Synthesis* (Cambridge: Harvard University Press, 1975), 3.
11. William Hamilton, "The Genetical Evolution of Social Behavior," *Journal of Theoretical Biology* 7: 1–52 (1964).
12. Robert Trivers, "The Evolution of Reciprocal Altruism," *Quarterly Review of Biology* 46: 35–57 (1971).
13. Ernst Mayr, *What Evolution Is* (New York: Basic Books, 2001), 259.
14. Michael Shermer, *Why Darwin Matters*, 136; and David Barash, "How Did Honor Evolve?" *The Chronicle Review*, May 23, 2008, p. B-12.
15. Niccolo Machiavelli, *The Prince* (New York: Penguin Books, 1986), 91–94, 100–1.
16. Dante Alighieri, "Inferno," in *the Divine Comedy* (New York: Penguin Books, 2003), Vol. 1, pp. 315–19.
17. Richard Gray, "Animals Can Tell Right From Wrong," *The Telegraph*, London, May 23, 2009.
18. Frans de Waal, *Peacemaking Among Primates* (Cambridge: Harvard University Press, 2002), 37; and *Good Natured* (Cambridge: Harvard University Press, 1996).
19. Richard Dawkins, *The Selfish Gene*, 3, 201.
20. Thomas Huxley, *Evolution and Ethics*, 49.

Chapter Eleven

1. Fyodor Dostoevsky, *The Brothers Karamazov* (New York: Vintage Books, 1991), 69.

2. Daniel Dennett, *Breaking the Spell*, 280; and Richard Dawkins, "Religion's Misguided Missiles," *The Guardian*, London, September 15, 2001.

3. Robert Pape, *Dying to Win* (New York: Random House, 2006); see also Dinesh D'Souza, *The Enemy at Home* (New York: Doubleday, 2007).

4. Walter Kaufmann, *Critique of Religion and Philosophy* (Princeton, NJ: Princeton University Press, 1958), 359.

5. Ludwig Feuerbach, *The Essence of Christianity* (New York: Harper and Row, 1957), xi.

6. Karl Marx, "Contribution to the Critique of Hegel's Philosophy of Right," in *The Portable Karl Marx* (New York: Penguin Books, 1985), 115.

7. Richard Dawkins, *The God Delusion*, 278.

8. Charles Murray, *Human Accomplishment* (New York: HarperPerennial, 2003), 458.

9. Paul Rahe, *Republics Ancient & Modern* (Chapel Hill, NC: University of North Carolina Press, 1994), Vol. I.

10. Augustine, *City of God* (New York: Penguin Books, 1984).

11. James Reichley, *Religion in American Public Life* (Washington, D.C.: Brookings Institution Press, 1985), 94, 101–6.

12. Alexis de Tocqueville, *Democracy in America* (New York: Vintage Books, 1990), Vol. I, p. 244.

13. Frans de Waal, *Chimpanzee Politics* (Baltimore: Johns Hopkins University Press, 1998).

14. Lewis Hanke, *Aristotle and the American Indians* (Chicago: Henry Regnery, 1959), 37.

15. Bartolome de Las Casas, *A Short Account of the Destruction of the Indies* (New York: Penguin, 1999).

16. Cited by David Brion Davis, *The Problem of Slavery in Western Culture* (New York: Oxford University Press, 1988), 26.

17. Rodney Stark, *The Victory of Reason* (New York: Random House, 2005), 27–28.

18. Eugene Genovese, *Roll, Jordan, Roll* (New York: Vintage Books, 1972), 248–53.

Chapter Twelve

1. G. K. Chesterton, *Autobiography* (London: Hutchinson Press, 1937), 223–24.
2. Richard Dawkins, *The God Delusion*, 360; and Bill Moyers, "Interview with Richard Dawkins," PBS, December 3, 2004, www.pbs.org.
3. David Hume, *A Treatise of Human Nature*, 316–19.
4. Richard Dawkins, *River Out of Eden* (New York: Basic Books, 1995), 31–32.
5. Friedrich Nietzsche, excerpts from "The Gay Science," in Walter Kaufmann, ed. *The Portable Nietzsche* (New York: Penguin Books, 1976), 96.
6. Cited by Gertrude Himmelfarb, *Marriage and Morals Among the Victorians* (New York: Alfred Knopf, 1986), 21.
7. Daniel Dennett, *Breaking the Spell* (New York: Viking, 2006), 305.
8. Friedrich Nietzsche, *Twilight of the Idols* (New York: Penguin Books, 1990), 80–81.
9. Bertrand Russell, *Why I Am Not a Christian*, 26.
10. Ernest Nagel, "Philosophical Concepts of Atheism," in Peter Angeles, ed. *Critiques of God* (Amherst, NY: Prometheus Books, 1997), 17.
11. Cited by Gertrude Himmelfarb, *Marriage and Morals Among the Victorians*, 43.
12. Friedrich Nietzsche, *Ecce Homo* (New York: Vintage Books, 1989), 280; and *Twilight of the Idols*, 64.
13. Andrew Marvell, "To His Coy Mistress," in M. H. Abrams, ed. *The Norton Anthology of English Literature* (New York: W.W. Norton, 1986), 1388.
14. Friedrich Nietzsche, *Ecce Homo*, 327; and *On the Genealogy of Morals* (New York: Vintage Books, 1989), 161.

15. John Hick, *Philosophy of Religion* (Englewood Cliffs, NJ: Prentice-Hall,1983), 100–1.
16. Abu Hamid al-Ghazali, *The Alchemy of Happiness*. (Amonk, NY: M.E. Sharpe Publishers, 1991), 42–43.
17. William James, *The Will To Believe* (New York: Barnes and Noble, 2005), 3–26.
18. Christopher Hitchens, *God Is Not Great* (New York: Twelve Publishing, 2007), 94.
19. William James, *The Varieties of Religious Experience* (New York: Penguin Books, 1982), 51–52.
20. Jean Paul Sartre, *Being and Nothingness* (New York: Philosophical Library, 1956); and William Shakespeare, *Macbeth*, in *The Complete Works of William Shakespeare*, 882.
21. Victor Stenger, *God: The Failed Hypothesis*, 257.
22. John Locke, *The Reasonableness of Christianity* (Stanford: Stanford University Press, 1958), 70.
23. Marc Hauser, *Moral Minds* (New York: HarperPerennial, 2006), xx.
24. Harold Koenig, *Medicine, Religion and Health* (West Conshohocken, PA: Templeton Foundation Press, 2008); Jonathan Haidt, *The Happiness Hypothesis* (New York: Basic Books, 2006), 88; Arthur Brooks. *Who Really Cares?* (New York: Basic Books, 2006); and D. G. Myers, "The Funds, Friends and Faith of Happy People," *American Psychologist* 55 (2000): 56–67.

Chapter Thirteen

1. Gerd Ludemann, *The Resurrection of Jesus: History, Experience, Theology* (London: SCM Press, 1994); John Dominic Crossan, *The Historical Jesus: The Life of a Mediterranean Jewish Peasant* (San Francisco: HarperSanFrancisco, 1991); and Marcus Borg, *Jesus: A New Vision* (San Fransisco: HarperSanFrancisco, 1994).
2. N. T. Wright, *The Resurrection of the Son of God* (Minneapolis: Fortress Press, 2003), 717.

3. Corliss Lamont, *The Illusion of Immortality* (New York: Continuum Press, 1990), 121.

4. Hugh Schonfield, *The Passover Plot* (New York: Bantam Books, 1965); and Donovan Joyce *The Jesus Scroll* (New York: New American Library, 1972).

5. David Strauss, *A New Life of Jesus* (Edinburgh: Williams and Norgate, 1879), Vol. I, pp. 408–14.

6. Gerd Ludemann, "Opening Statement," in *Jesus' Resurrection: A Debate Between William Lane Craig and Gerd Ludemann* (Downers Grove, IL: InterVarsity Press, 2000), 45.

7. Gary Habermas and Michael Licona, *The Case for the Resurrection of Jesus* (Grand Rapids, MI: Kregel Publications, 2004), 106.

8. Friedrich Nietzsche, *The Antichrist* (New York: Penguin Books, 1990), 151–64, 187, 199.

9. John Milton, *Paradise Lost* (New York: W.W. Norton, 1975), 13.

10. C. S. Lewis, *The Great Divorce* (San Francisco: HarperSanFrancisco, 1973), 75.

11. Dante Alighieri, "Paradise" in *The Divine Comedy*, Vol. 3, pp. 262, 390–94.

12. Randy Alcorn, *Heaven* (Carol Stream, IL: Tyndale House, 2004), 28, 45–49, 135–37, 265.

13. Dallas Willard, *Knowing Christ Today: Why We Can Trust Spiritual Knowledge* (New York: HarperOne, 2009), 139.

14. John Donne, "Death, Be Not Proud," in Helen Gardner, ed. *The New Oxford Book of English Verse* (New York: Oxford University Press, 1972), 197.

INDEX

Still the Greatest Country on Earth

America is under attack as never before. Not only from foreign terrorists, but also from within.

Islamic terrorists declare America the "Great Satan." Many Europeans complain about America spreading its cultural wasteland. And perhaps worst of all, here in our own country, there are those on the political Left who still blame America for every ill in the world. Left-wing multiculturalism—dominant in our own schools and universities—teaches students that Western and American culture is no better than, and probably worse than, Third World cultures.

Does this imply the death of the West? Quite the opposite, says best-selling author Dinesh D'Souza. In *What's So Great About America*, D'Souza claims that the flood of immigrants coming to America *proves* that our values, our system, our freedoms, and our culture are irresistible and superior. The problem, he asserts, is our own inability or refusal to celebrate what makes America great.

What's So Great About America offers a powerful defense for America and exposes the truth about who our enemies really are.

Since 1947
REGNERY PUBLISHING, INC.
An Eagle Publishing Company • Washington, DC

IS CHRISTIANITY OBSOLETE?

Can an intelligent, educated person really believe the Bible? Or are atheists correct?

Does science disprove Christianity, debunk it as a force for good, and discredit it as a guide to morality?

IN HIS GROUNDBREAKING *New York Times* bestseller, *What's So Great About Christianity*, author Dinesh D'Souza raises the culture war debate to a whole new level by challenging atheists on their own secular turf. Using compelling evidence, scientific and otherwise, D'Souza disproves the atheists' arguments and shows why a resurgent Christianity is the real wave of the future—and atheism a trend of the past.

Perfect for the skeptic, seeker, and true believer!

Go to WhatsSoGreatAboutChristianity.com to receive your FREE chapter and to order your copy today!

Since 1947
REGNERY PUBLISHING, INC.
An Eagle Publishing Company • Washington, DC
www.regnery.com